DYNAMICS OF ORGANIZATIONAL POPULATIONS

Dynamics of Organizational Populations

Density, Legitimation, and Competition

MICHAEL T. HANNAN

GLENN R. CARROLL

New York Oxford
OXFORD UNIVERSITY PRESS
1992

Oxford University Press

Oxford   New York   Toronto
Delhi   Bombay   Calcutta   Madras   Karachi
Petaling Jaya   Singapore   Hong Kong   Tokyo
Nairobi   Dar es Salaam   Cape Town
Melbourne   Auckland

and associated companies in
Berlin   Ibadan

Library of Congress Cataloging-in-Publication Data
Hannan, Michael T.
Dynamics of Organizational populations / Michael T. Hannan,
Glenn R. Carroll.
p.   cm.   Includes bibliographical references and index.
ISBN 0-19-507191-3
1. Organizational sociology–Methodology.
2. Organizational change. I. Carroll, Glenn. II. Title.
HM131.H238   1992
302.3'5–dc20   91–23910

9 8 7 6 5 4 3 2 1

Printed in the United States of America
on acid-free paper

To Amos H. Hawley

Preface

With increasing frequency, social scientists and other observers of modern society are emphasizing the importance of formal organizations in all realms of social and economic life. Yet, the dynamics of organizational change remain poorly understood. There is little systematic evidence regarding the processes by which forms of organization arise and develop over time.

In an attempt to redress the paucity of empirical knowledge about organizational evolution, this book refines and tests a theory of long-term change in populations of organizations. The theory addresses an empirical commonality observed for populations of many different kinds of business firms, voluntary associations, and social movement organizations. To wit, the numbers of organizations grow slowly during the early history of populations, surge at some point, reach a peak, and then decline modestly and fluctuate in a fairly narrow range for protracted periods. Because the pattern is a common one, it begs a general explanation, one that abstracts from the details of the kinds of organizations in the populations and the specific features of the social environments they occupy.

The theory we propose in this book explains the historical pattern in organizational evolution as a consequence of the opposing force of two sociological processes: legitimation and competition. *Legitimation* of an organizational population means that its organizational form acquires the status of a "taken-for-granted" solution to given problems of collective action. *Competition* refers to constraints arising from the joint dependence of multiple organizations on the same set of finite resources for building and sustaining organizations. One core idea of the theory is that the vital rates of organizational populations—rates of founding and mortality—vary as functions of legitimation and competition. That is, founding rates rise and mortality rates fall as the legitimation of a population increases. Conversely, founding rates fall and mortality rates rise as competition within and among populations intensifies.

The second core idea of the theory is that both legitimation and competition are affected by *density*, defined as the number of organizations in the population. We argue that increasing density conveys legitimation in the sense of taken-for-grantedness but that there is a ceiling on the process which means that the effect diminishes as density grows large. Competition also grows with density, we argue, but at an increasing rate.

Combining the two main ideas yields a qualitative theory of density dependence in vital rates of organizational populations. We concentrate on three testable implications of this theory regarding the form of organizational density dependence. First, the relationship between contemporaneous density and founding rates is nonmonotonic with the form of an inverted U. Second, the relationship between contemporaneous density and mortality rates is nonmonotonic with a U shape. Third, density has a delayed effect on mortality rates, namely, that high density at the time of an organization's founding produces a permanent increase in mortality rates.

Our strategy of model building and empirical research centers on density dependence in vital rates. This means that we take an indirect approach to analyzing legitimation and competition. In our scheme, legitimation and competition are *processes* that relate density to vital rates in particular ways, rather than variables to be measured and used in empirical analyses. We take this approach because it is extremely difficult to reconstruct the detailed histories of changes in legitimation and competition over complete lifetimes of real organizational populations. Moreover, our use of legitimation and competition as processes facilitates comparisons of results across many diverse kinds of populations of organizations, as we show in this book.

In testing the theory, we rely on parametric models of density dependence that agree with the qualitative theory. We estimate their parameters by analyzing data on the life histories of all organizations in seven populations. These are national labor unions in the United States (1836–1985), newspapers in Argentina (1800–1900) and Ireland (1800–1975), newspaper publishing organizations in the San Francisco Bay area (1840–1975), American brewing firms (1633–1988), banks in Manhattan (1791–1980), and American life insurance firms (1759–1937).

In the five years since Hannan (1986a) proposed the initial version of the theory, there has been a rapid proliferation of research to test its implications. Most of the "first-generation" studies yielded results that support the theory. However, there are some important differences among the studies—especially in research designs, choice of parametric models, and methods of estimation—that complicate the task of comparison. We think it important to conduct a more systematic comparative test of the theory, using the same research design, models, and estimators.

One of the main tasks of the book is to extend and refine the basic theory. This involves clarifying the conditions under which the theory holds, providing a unified treatment of contemporaneous and delayed density dependence, and presenting an axiomatic formulation of the complete "second-generation" theory. In addition, we devote considerable attention to complicating the representation of legitimation processes in ways that make the theory more realistic.

We also present a detailed analysis of the several parametric models that have been used to represent density dependence in vital rates of organizational populations. We show that the two most common models (the so-called generalized-Yule and log-quadratic models) imply different behavior in small populations and correspond to two different kinds of legitimation processes.

Because the methods used in the early studies of density dependence in founding rates were relatively crude, we also devote considerable attention to devising and applying more appropriate methods. Our explorations show that annual time series of counts of foundings (the focus of most analyses) pose two methodological problems: overdispersion and autocorrelation. The results reported in this book deal with these problems for the first time. There are also methodological challenges to prior research that need to be addressed. We pay particular attention to three issues: effects of unobserved heterogeneity, proper specification of units of analysis, and implications of designs that ignore observations from the early histories of populations.

The heart of the book consists of our reports of estimates of models of density dependence for the seven populations as well as for subpopulations in four of them. The results strongly support the theory. In almost all cases, the estimated effects agree with the theory and also imply that density had powerful effects in shaping the growth of these populations (and subpopulations).

Finally, we go well beyond the previous research by putting the various pieces of the model together in order to learn about the implications of our findings for dynamics of organizational populations. We do so with simulations of the effect of density dependence on rates of founding and mortality (as estimated) on the growth and decline of population density. These simulations suggest that the theory and models we use can do a very credible job of explaining the common historical pattern of long-term growth.

Because it is unusual in the sociology of organizations, we comment briefly on our reasons for pursuing ideas about density dependence so single-mindedly. Social scientists agree widely that programmatic research guided by theory is desirable in principle as a means of producing reliable knowledge. But the premium placed on novelty in theoretical formulations and empirical applications discourages many from investing in theoretical research programs. In our opinion, it is critical to any science—especially to modern social science—to develop and scrutinize sets of fundamental empirical results. Our goal here has been to make progress in establishing such findings about large-scale organizational change.

We incurred many debts in the course of performing the research reported in this book. The most important are to our graduate student collaborators. David N. Barron helped us upgrade our methods of analyzing founding rates and of simulating population histories in addition to assisting in much of the empirical analysis reported. Jane Banaszak-Holl and James Ranger-Moore collaborated in collecting and analyzing data on life insurance companies and banks. Anand Swaminathan collaborated in the collection and analysis of the data on brewing firms and assisted with the analysis of newspapers. Albert Teo and James Wade also collaborated in various phases of the study of brewing firms, and Heather Haveman assisted with the early stages of the analysis of newspapers.

Several colleagues generously provided comments on earlier versions of the manuscript. These include William Barnett, John Freeman, Daniel Levinthal, Susan Olzak, and our graduate students (mentioned above).

Financial support for the research was provided by the National Science Foundation (grants SES–8809006 and SES–9008493), the University of California at Berkeley's Institute of Industrial Relations and the Center for Research on Management. Hannan's work on the early stages of this project was supported by a fellowship from the John Simon Guggenheim Foundation and a year's stay at the Max-Planck-Institut für Bildungsforschung (Berlin) with Karl Ulrich Mayer's research team. Carroll's work on this project was supported during stays at the Center for Advanced Study in the Behavioral Sciences (Palo Alto) and the Netherlands Institute of Advanced Study (Wassenaar).

Stanford   M.T.H.

Berkeley   G.R.C.

August 1991

Contents

DYNAMICS OF ORGANIZATIONAL POPULATIONS

1

Introduction

Sociological and economic analyses of modern societies grant special significance to the corporate actors we call organizations. Modern economies, polities, and social structures are composed largely of organizations, such as business firms, government agencies, labor unions, political parties, and the networks of relations that connect them. Alterations in the structures of organizations and of their networks have far reaching consequences for the larger systems. Thus knowledge about the causes and consequences of organizational change is central to understanding the dynamics of modern economies, states, and societies.

Centrality notwithstanding, dynamics of the world of organizations have received surprisingly little attention in the social sciences. Far greater heed has been paid to the structures of organizations in equilibrium and to the responses of organizations to small departures from equilibrium. Moreover, the study of organizational change has been conducted mainly at the microlevel and has envisioned only a single mechanism of change.

In particular, most efforts to explain organizational change have focused narrowly on individual organizations and their adaptive capacities. So, for instance, economic theories of the firm, though sometimes based loosely on an evolutionary analogy (Friedman 1953; Koopmans 1957), typically characterize firms as rational optimizers of changing market conditions. In a similar vein, theories of political organization emphasize the adaptive responses of political parties and other kinds of political organizations to changing electoral demographics, environmental shocks, and so forth. Sociological theories of organizations have broadly similar orientations in that they attend to processes by which formal structures adjust to fit internal and external contingencies such as technology.

The dual focus on equilibrium and processes of adaptation that preserve equilibrium misses much of action. Among other things, it overlooks important connections between organizational change and broader social changes. For instance, structural change in an economy almost always entails turnover in its firms in addition to modifications in the behavior of individual firms. Likewise, political revolution usually means the wholesale replacement of one set of political and bureaucratic organizations with another. And social structural change typically implies modifications in the strategies of key organizations and also alterations in the rosters of collective actors and the networks of relations that connect them.

Organizational worlds transform over time in two sharply different ways. Some individual organizations adjust their routines and behavior in response to changed environmental conditions, as the conventional theories emphasize. But another key mechanism operates as well—populations of organizations evolve because some existing organizations perish and other (sometimes novel) organizations emerge. In other words, economic, political, and social transformations entail both *adaptation* by individual organizations and *selection* at the level of populations of organizations.

Few organizations succeed in solving their adaptive problems for very long in a turbulent world. Hence, few of them achieve either great longevity or great social power. There is an indisputable, though often overlooked, danger in generalizing from a few well-known success stories to broad classes of organizations. In order to avoid the selection bias entailed in analyzing only successful organizations, some social scientists now analyze processes of change in populations of organizations. These analysts focus on the changing makeup of populations rather than on changes in the behavior of individual organizations. In terms of research, they study the processes and environmental conditions that govern rates of organizational founding and mortality. This shift in focus—from the individual organization to the organizational population and from adaptation to selection—raises many interesting new questions.

In originally proposing a population ecology of organizations, Hannan and Freeman (1977) posed a seemingly simple question:

Why are there so many different kinds of organizations? The answers subsequently put forth emphasize such diverse causal factors as variability in the abundance of essential resources (Freeman and Hannan 1983), uncertain and discontinuous changes in technology (Anderson 1988; Barnett 1990; Freeman and Hannan 1990), cultural norms constraining the variability of organizational forms (DiMaggio and Powell 1983; Meyer and Scott 1983), and features of the state (Carroll, Delacroix, and Goodstein 1988).[1]

Our efforts in this book explore a different facet of the ecology and demography of organizations. In particular, we concentrate on the dynamics of *organizational density*. We define the density of an organizational population as the number of organizations it contains. In common language, density usually refers to a count for some geographic area such as the number of buildings per square mile. Our use of the term *density,* which conforms with its usage in mathematical demography and ecology, refers to a count of the number of organizations within a specified population, defined in terms of specified spatial and temporal boundaries.[2]

We also address the general question, What processes control the growth and decline in density in organizational populations? Although this question appears more narrow than Hannan and Freeman's original query, it has a sharper empirical focus. The question is also prompted by recurring empirical features of organizational populations. To wit, comparisons of growth in density reveal a common rough pattern for populations of very different types of organizations. Organizational populations initially grow slowly from zero, increase very rapidly over a brief period, reach a peak, and then often decline moderately before stabilizing for some, usually extended, period. Patterns of growth and takeoff are more regular than patterns of decline, which are sometimes rapid and sometimes gradual. This rough regularity serves as a point of departure for our theory building and research efforts.

---

[1] Reviews of recent theory and research on organizational ecology include those by Aldrich and Marsden (1988), Freeman and Hannan (1989), and Singh and Lumsden (1990).

[2] We discuss this issue in greater detail in Appendix A.

Organizational Populations Studied

What do historical trajectories of organizational density actually look like? We begin our analysis by briefly describing the seven organizational populations that we shall study and presenting plots of density over their histories. Because this section also introduces the empirical materials we analyze, we explain briefly each organizational form and the data we use.[3]

National Labor Unions

Among the types of organizations we examine, labor unions fall on one extreme of the dimension of "profit orientation." These organizations arose when collective action by workers to affect conditions of work became embodied in permanent formal organization. From a historical perspective, American labor unions emerged as social movement organizations. Unlike most business firms, they encountered strenuous efforts at repression by employers and the state over much of the history of the population. Consequently, an analysis of labor unions provides an opportunity to establish that theoretical arguments concerning density processes are sufficiently general to apply to social movement organizations operating in a highly conflictual political environment.

Figure 1.1 displays the historical fluctuations in the number of national labor unions in the United States over the population's full history. The first such organizations appeared in 1836, and the number of unions remained near zero until the Civil War era. The number of unions thereafter rose modestly until about 1885 before growing explosively until 1905. The number of national unions then grew more slowly and erratically to its peak level of 211 in 1954. At that point it began a modest but consistent contraction to 144 at the beginning of 1985.

Newspaper Publishing

The second type of organization—newspaper publishing—provides an opportunity to examine density processes cross nationally, as comparable data are available for several countries. Newspaper publishing is not only a significant economic activity; it also has important

[3] Detailed descriptions of populations and the sources of data can be found in Appendix A.

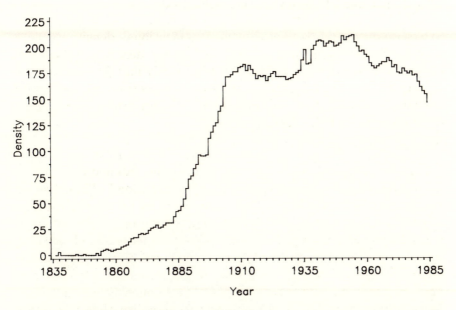

Figure 1.1.   Historical evolution of the density of American national labor unions

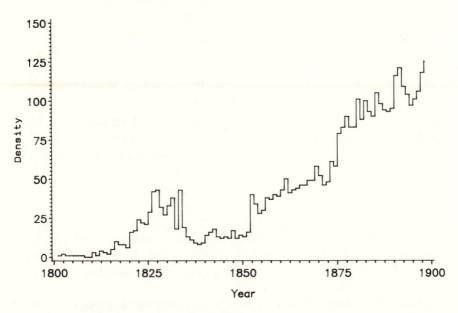

Figure 1.2.   Historical evolution of the density of Argentine newspapers

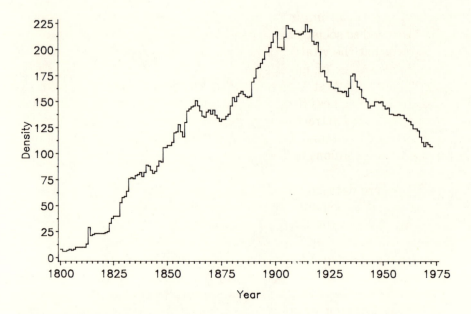

Figure 1.3. Historical evolution of the density of Irish newspapers

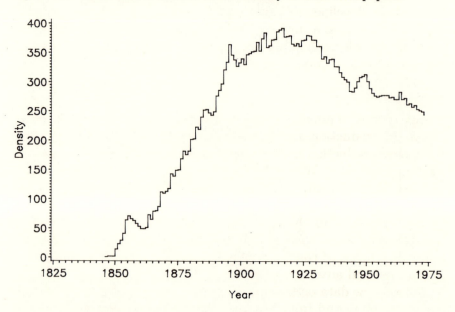

Figure 1.4. Historical evolution of the density of San Francisco Bay Area newspaper publishers

political and social implications. Indeed, newspapers have historically been tied to social and political movements, and recent research
has shown that the vital rates of newspaper populations are strongly
affected by surges of unruly political action (Carroll 1987; Olzak
1992; Olzak and West 1991). The combination of economic form of
organization (business firm) and sociopolitical centrality makes the
newspaper a very attractive candidate for ecological analysis. In our
view, newspapers stand between the pure social movement organizations of labor unions and the pure business organizations of banks
and breweries.

We analyze data on populations of newspapers in Argentina and
Ireland and of newspaper publishing organizations in the San Francisco Bay Area in the United States. Figures 1.2, 1.3, and 1.4 show
fluctuations in the number of newspapers from 1800 to 1900 for
Argentina and from 1800 to 1975 for Ireland and San Francisco.
The Irish and San Francisco populations exhibit a similar pattern of
growth and decline. The Irish population grows to a peak level of
224 before declining by roughly half by 1975. In the San Francisco
area, the number of newspaper publishers grows to a peak level of
395 and then declines by about 40% by 1975. The data for the population in Argentina are censored at what would appear to be its
approximate peak (the observed maximum is 125), assuming that it
follows the pattern observed for Ireland and San Francisco.

Brewing Firms

The third kind of population consists of business firms in a particular
consumer production market—beer brewing. Although this may be
the oldest production industry, it remains an important activity in
modern economies. We study the American brewing industry, which
has experienced many transformations over its long history. The
best known of these are the long-term decline in the number of firms
in the industry and the attendant increase in the average size of
the surviving firms. Today the American brewing industry shows
fairly high levels of concentration with strong economies of scale in
production and advertising favoring the largest firms.

We analyze data on the foundings and closures of beer producers
spanning the period from 1633 to 1988, an unprecedented length of
observation for organizational studies. Figure 1.5 shows the number
of firms in the American brewing industry by year from 1633 to 1988.

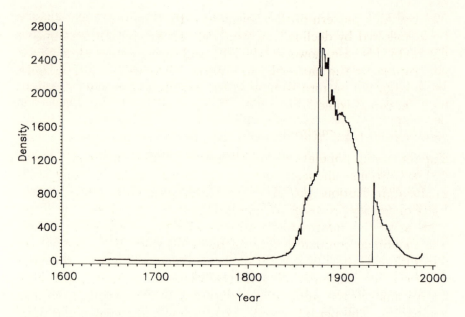

Figure 1.5. Historical evolution of the density of American brewing firms

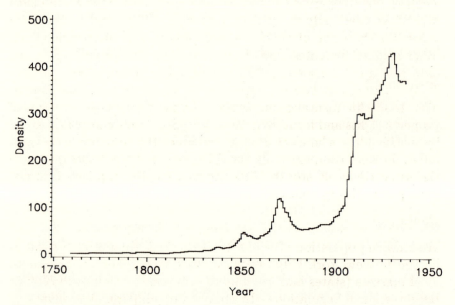

Figure 1.6. Historical evolution of the density of American life insurance companies

The common pattern of slow initial growth, then rapid growth to a peak, followed by decline to a seemingly stable equilibrium appears again. In this case, however, the long and severe period of decline is interrupted by the national Prohibition (1920–1933). Remarkably, the population pattern resumes after Prohibition in what seems to be a "natural" trend.

Life Insurance Companies

The remaining populations are composed of different types of financial institutions—life insurance companies and banks. An analysis of financial institutions provides useful information about the applicability of density processes to populations of core "business" organizations as well as informative contrasts with previous studies. Banks and insurance companies rely on different kinds of resources and face different kinds of institutional constraints (mainly in the form of governmental regulation) than the other organizational forms do.

We analyze the *national* population of American life insurance companies. The periods studied differ for founding rates and mortality rates. Information on foundings of life insurance companies are available for the period from 1759 through 1937, but information on mortality covers only the period between 1759 and 1900. Figure 1.6 shows the evolution of density in this population. Information from other sources indicates that density had not yet peaked when the data were right censored in 1937 (see Ranger-Moore 1990).

We distinguish two subpopulations: stock and mutual companies. In the life insurance industry, these two forms differ in terms of property rights and forms of governance. Stock companies are owned by stockholders who elect a board to direct the company's management. Mutual companies are owned by the policyholders who have the same rights as stockholders do in a stock company. Mutuals issue participating policies.

Banks

We study a population of banks at a *city* level (the borough of Manhattan in New York City) because banking has been restricted to local markets (states and, even more commonly, cities and counties) by government regulations. In analyses of subpopulations, we distinguish between commercial banks (including trust companies) and savings banks. Commercial banks targeted their services at business

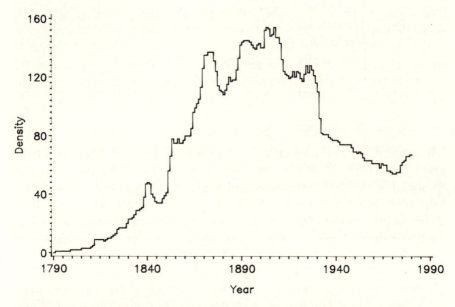

Figure 1.7. Historical evolution of the density of Manhattan banks

firms; savings banks sought the business of individuals and house-holds. Appendix A describes the differences in regulations that have governed the two subpopulations.

Figure 1.7 shows the evolution of density for the whole population. The number of banks increased rapidly for over a century from 1791. The panics of the 1840s and 1870s caused temporary drops in numbers which then resumed growth in the 1890s. The peak level of density was reached during the early years of the 20th century, followed by an abrupt decline during the Great Depression which continued until the end of the 1970s, with a slight rise during the 1980s.

Analytic Strategy

The shape of the typical time path of organizational density—initial slow growth, subsequent explosive growth, and stabilization—is especially interesting because it appears to be roughly regular. Without implying universality, we note that this general pattern of long-term growth characterizes a surprisingly diverse set of organizational populations in addition to those just discussed (see, for instance, Carroll 1984; Utterback and Suárez 1991). Although it is fairly easy to account *a posteriori* for the pattern for any one historical population in terms of historically specific features of the population and its environment, the commonality of the pattern cries out for a general explanation. How might the evolution of organizational density be explained?

Perhaps the regularity in growth paths of organizational density merely mirrors regularities in patterns of change in essential resources. That is, patterns of growth, stabilization, and possible decline in numbers might merely track resources essential to the functioning of the constituent organizations. Organizational populations may exploit ephemeral resources, growing rapidly while the resources abound and then declining as they fade. For example, firms serving immigrant communities may flourish during periods of peak immigration and then decline in numbers as immigration slows and ethnolinguistic populations assimilate. Such a process can apparently account for the history of foreign-language newspapers (Park 1929) and local life-assurance societies (Lehrman 1986).

An alternative explanation for the pattern concentrates on the implications of limits on the longevity of organizational forms. It suggests that organizational forms embody historically specific social and material technologies whose viability declines with the passage of time (Stinchcombe 1965). According to this view, the competitive edge of established organizational populations eventually erodes as new technologies emerge and social conditions change.[4] For example, the widespread distribution of electricity apparently eliminated many kinds of firms such as icehouses and local dairies. Changing political conditions and legal rulings eliminated many others such as slave plantations, proprietary medical schools, utopian labor unions, and opium dens.

---

[4] The obsolescence implied by this process may take a long time or it may never be reached entirely. Often the fears and anxieties of contemporary owners and operators do not prove well founded. The disappearance of newspapers, for instance, has been predicted each time new information transmission technologies emerge, first with the advent of radio, then television, and finally with the computer. Yet the newspaper industry remains large and, by most assessments, healthy.

A third possible type of explanation focuses on general sociological processes that govern the evolution of all kinds of organizational forms. Our version of this kind of explanation relies on two general sociological processes: legitimation and competition. As new organizational forms emerge, they must overcome legitimation obstacles and gain social acceptance if they are to proliferate. But proliferation triggers competition. When instances of the form become abundant (relative to resources), organizations in the population are locked into competitive struggles. So, in general, dynamics of organizational population growth are driven by opposing processes of legitimation and competition.

The three kinds of explanations are compatible with one another. Indeed, the details of the evolution of any particular organizational population likely depend on all three types of factors. Nonetheless, we concentrate here on a theory of density-dependent legitimation and competition.[5] We do so because sociologists have recently made considerable progress in relating these processes to vital rates in organizational populations. Moreover, processes of legitimation and competition serve as the main mechanisms of change in two of the most vigorous strands of contemporary organizational analysis: institutional theory (Meyer and Scott 1983) and ecological theory (Hannan and Freeman 1989). Our effort can thus be seen at a more general level as a synthesis of two theoretical perspectives that are commonly held to be in opposition to each other (DiMaggio and Powell 1983).

A Focus on Density Dependence in Vital Rates

Despite its heuristic utility, the rough empirical regularity in growth trajectories is a slim reed on which to build a general formulation. As the foregoing figures show, there is simply too much variation around the general pattern especially in timing. This variation should not be surprising, as the detailed time path of growth in an organizational population depends on the difference between its founding rate and the (average) mortality rate. These two rates operate at different levels of analysis and can be governed by very different processes. The organizational founding process operates for the population as

---

[5] We do, however, use some controls for resource fluctuations and historical obsolescence in our analysis, as we describe later and in Appendix A.

a unit because there is no clear-cut maternity function in organizational demography. (That is, organizations need not trace their origins to other organizations.) But mortality processes operate at the level of individual organizations. The implication of this difference is that heterogeneity in mortality rates within an organizational population can affect its trajectory of growth in density. Because the exact distributions of such heterogeneity presumably differ among populations, their trajectories of growth in density will differ even if the same overall process operates in all of them.

This argument is easiest to comprehend in the case of one possible source of variation—aging processes. Organizational mortality rates turn out to be affected strongly by the aging of individual organizations. Therefore, the average mortality rate in an organizational population, and hence the pattern of growth in density, depends on its age distribution. The age distribution depends in turn on the exact time path of foundings over the history of the population and on the strength of age dependence in the mortality rates. It is highly unlikely that any pair of populations have very similar histories of entries even if they have the same founding rates simply because of stochastic variation. Also, populations of different kinds of organizations are unlikely to have identical age dependence in mortality rates. As a consequence of such differences, even populations whose rates of entry and exit are the same can have quite different realized trajectories of population growth.

This reasoning suggests that social scientists should look for regularities in the vital rates of founding and mortality rather than in gross trajectories of growth and decline in numbers. Our theory and research reflect this understanding. We develop a theory that attempts to explain variation in founding rates and mortality rates as functions of organizational density. We translate this theory into mathematical models and use life-history data on all the organizations ever appearing in each of our historical populations to test the implications of the theory.

As we demonstrate in subsequent chapters, examining vital rates with appropriate stochastic models reveals a more robust regularity below the surface similarity in observable trajectories of growth and decline in organizational density. The deeper regularity involves the existence of a dependence of the vital rates on organizational density, especially the form of the dependence.

In the development of thinking about density dependence in vital rates of organizational populations, the basic theory was proposed before the empirical regularity had been uncovered. In particular, Hannan (1986a) posited a theory of density-dependent legitimation and competition, which we develop further in Chapter 2. This theory proposes that rates of organizational founding and mortality vary with the strength of legitimation and competition processes and that the latter depend on density in specific ways. More specifically, the theory assumes that the legitimation of an organizational population increases with its density at a decreasing rate and that competition within organizational populations increases with density at an increasing rate. As we explain in Chapter 2, these assumptions imply *nonmonotonic relationships between density and the vital rates.* The predicted relationship between density and the founding rate in an organizational population has the form of an inverted U. The symmetry of the argument implies that the relationship between density and mortality rates has a U shape.

Such a pattern of density dependence can generate the common pattern of growth of organizational populations. If the theory is correct, initial growth in density will trigger processes of legitimation that elevate founding rates and lower mortality rates. The result is rapid growth in density. However, eventually density grows high enough that competitive processes outweigh legitimation processes, depressing founding rates and elevating mortality rates. The result is that growth in density slows and density stabilizes.

Prior research, discussed in Chapters 4 and 6, and the research reported in this book confirm that there are regular patterns of non-monotonic density dependence in rates of organizational founding and organizational mortality. The theory discussed in the next chapter provides a framework for interpreting this regularity as reflecting the operation of general sociological processes of legitimation and competition.

Subsequent development of the theory sought to explain the common drop in density from its peak before rough stabilization. This feature of trajectories of density cannot be explained by the original version of the theory. Carroll and Hannan (1989a) suggested that drops from a peak could be explained by a certain kind of delayed effect of density on mortality rates. They argued that density at the time of founding has a permanent effect on mortality rates, that organizations founded during periods of high density have higher mortality rates at all ages. They cited two processes that could account for such a pattern of density delay (explained in greater depth in later chapters). "Liability of scarcity" refers to a situation in which intense competition due to high density at the time of founding makes it difficult for newly founded organizations to acquire the resources essential to constructing effective structures and routines. Organizations may also have great difficulty recovering from deprived initial conditions even if competition lessens in later periods. "Tight niche packing" refers to situations in which intense density-dependent competition at the time of founding causes new organizations to be pushed to the undesirable margins of the resource space and to become specialized to exploiting low quality resources, which diminishes life chances relative to those specialized to exploiting richer resources.

As was the case for the original theory, the prediction about density at founding has received strong support in initial work. It also receives strong support in the research reported in this book.

Research Strategy

The general strategy of theory building and empirical research reflected in this book differs from that of much contemporary work in the sociology and economics of organizations. Most other theories and research attempt to explain processes in the organizational world in terms of difficult-to-observe features of organizations. Prominent examples include organizational culture and transaction costs. Because of the cost of and difficulty in obtaining comparable measurements on large numbers of organizations (especially over time), theories that emphasize the causal primacy of such subtle features are rarely tested comparatively. As a result, progress in testing such theories lags far behind theoretical development and elaboration.

Our strategy puts complexity into the theories and models rather than into heroic requirements for observations. We concentrate on features of organizational populations that can be easily observed. And we relate covariation among the observables to theories and models that represent general sociological processes. Our research strategy requires only *counting,* albeit in a very comprehensive way. The strategy's simplicity allows comparison over time and across populations of dissimilar organizations.

Our use of seven different organizational populations to test arguments about density-dependent legitimation and competition may strike some as "overkill." However, we regard ease of replication as one of the attractive features of our theory and models. And we consider replication as essential to evaluating theoretical ideas.

We have three goals in conducting repeated tests. One is to rule out the possibility that some problem with the coverage of the histories of the organizational populations or with recording procedures might contaminate our analyses and findings. Even though we believe that the data we analyze are of high quality and that they accurately reflect the histories of the populations, we also recognize that the data are unlikely to be perfect. Archival sources spanning hundreds of years surely contain some errors. Random error presents no serious problems as long as it is infrequent and small relative to effects of measured variables; but systematic error might produce artifactual results. The advantage of replication in this context is that it is extremely unlikely—if not downright impossible—that the same type of systematic error would be present in the diverse sources for the five types of organizations including three national instances of one. Replication, therefore, allows us to have confidence in the set of findings that emerge from data that some may suspect are flawed.

The second goal of replication is to strengthen causal inferences. Specifically, we want to address the possibility that some feature of a population and its environment other than density dependence might account for a pattern of empirical results. In studies of any one population, it is difficult to make a convincing case that some time-varying factor not accounted for in the analysis does not actually account for the observed relationship between density and the vital rates. However, if the same relationship is observed for populations operating in different environments, the set of potentially spurious factors is greatly reduced. Replication helps verify the relationship between organizational density and the vital rates.

Our third goal in replication is to assess the generality of the relationship. Our primary argument (about density dependence and its sources) is intended to apply to all kinds of organizational populations. That is, the theory applies to populations of all types, in any time period, and in any society. Although the objective of ruling out spurious findings due to peculiarities of the history of a population can be met reasonably well by replications for a single type of population over many environments (say, brewing firms in many countries), the goal of assessing generality cannot. In order to establish the generality of patterns of density dependence, researchers must analyze data on different types of populations.

How different are the seven organizational populations that we study? Obviously they differ in national context and in the historical periods covered. They also span most of the two dimensions that organizational scientists typically regard as relevant: market exposure and institutional embeddedness. Several populations consist of classic business firms: beer brewers, banks (especially commercial banks) and life insurance companies (especially stock companies). The population of labor unions is a pure instance of nonbusiness or nonprofit organization. The other populations stand somewhere between these poles. Mutual life insurance companies and savings banks have often been tied to ethnic, religious, or occupational communities; and they have been structured legally as nonprofit organizations. Newspaper populations include some organizations that are every bit as profit oriented as banks or brewers are. They also contain others that are tied to social and political movements and whose goals are as much political as pecuniary.

Institutional theorists Meyer and Scott (1983) argue that some organizations operate in institutional sectors that abound with elaborate rules and requirements to which they must conform, whereas other organizations operate in technical sectors that reward efficiency. Combining the dimension of strength of institutional embeddedness with another dimension of degree of market exposure and efficiency testing yields four separate sectors within which organizations might be placed. How would the seven populations we study fall within such a classification? It seems clear that American labor unions have had low institutional embeddedness and low market exposure for most of the history of the population. But the institutional controls coming in the New Deal and the subsequent Taft–Hartley Act of 1947 made this population highly institutionalized. American brewers fall clearly in the category of high market exposure and low institutional embeddedness (with the ironic, and enormously important, exception of the periods of state and federal prohibitions). Newspaper populations probably ought to be placed in this category as well. Banks and life insurance companies face market pressures but are also highly embedded in regulation.

These populations also differ considerably in the life chances of individual organizations. Consider the typical lengths of organizational lifetimes as measured by their "half-lives." A half-life is the age by which half of the members of the population have experienced mortality.[6] Labor unions and banks have the greatest longevity, with half-lives of 16 and 15 years. Life insurance companies are next, with a half-life of 11.5 years. Then there is a drop in average longevity to brewers (8.5 years), San Francisco Bay Area newspaper publishers (7.5 years), and Irish newspapers (6.5 years). Finally, the half-life of nineteenth century Argentinean newspapers was less than a year.

This considerable diversity in terms of market situation, legal regulation, and longevity of individual organizations makes the empirical regularity in population growth especially striking. It also means that replications over populations are not trivial. If these populations exhibit exceeding diversity in sociological terms, then our research strategy of estimating the same structure for all will pose a serious challenge to the formulation.

Relation to Other Theory and Research

Explaining the evolution of density of organizational populations and the dependence of vital rates on density are research problems that contemporary organization analysis for the most part has not considered. With the exception of organizational ecology, all major sociological perspectives on organizations avoid the question by adopting the vantage point of a single organization, what Hannan and Freeman (1977) called "the focal organization perspective." These perspectives reason from the point of view of single organizations facing some set of internal and external conditions. In particular, they do not deal with the complexities arising from the possibility of joint actions by many different organizations. For instance, contingency theory concerns itself with identifying the most efficient organizational structure for different types of technologies and environments (Thompson 1967). Resource dependence theory addresses

---

[6] We take right censoring into account when calculating half-lives by using product-limit estimates of life tables and defining as the half-life the age at which the survival probability reaches 0.5.

the ways environmentally induced uncertainty might be overcome with interorganizational linkage mechanisms (Pfeffer and Salancik 1978). Transaction cost economics explains efficient organizational design in terms of the characteristics of the set of transactions and the social setting (Williamson 1975, 1985). Institutional theory concentrates on how normatively defined features of organizations are adopted and interpreted (Meyer and Scott 1983).

Our research questions apparently lie so far afield of other sociological theories that they strike some sociologists as questions more appropriate to economics. We disagree, and in subsequent chapters we attempt to demonstrate that sociological arguments have great relevance to these research problems. Moreover, the opinion that explaining the evolution of density falls within the purview of economics appears to exaggerate the relevance and applicability of economic theories of industrial organization to the issues under discussion.

By our assessment, economic theory has surprisingly little to say about the long-term evolution of organizational density. Although neoclassical economic theorists may have succeeded in explaining growth in markets, they have rarely attempted to treat systematically the organizational bases of such growth. Theories of economic growth, for instance, typically do not differentiate between market growth arising from the entry of new entrepreneurs and that emanating from the expansion of established firms. To the extent that economic research does address issues related to our research problem, such as market concentration, it tends to consider only part of the phenomenon (properties of one tail of the size distribution, for example, the market share held by the largest four or eight firms) or to be primarily interested in equilibrium outcomes. No developed economic theory adequately addresses the dynamics of complete organizational populations over long periods of time (see discussion of this point by Tirole 1988).

Another difference is that economic theory does not treat legitimation and competition—the main conceptual components of our theory—in the same ways that we do. Legitimation has no recognizable counterpart within economic theory. And although competition is fundamental to economic theory, economic treatments of organizations do not typically use competition theory to build models that can be estimated with comparative data on firms.

The latest fashion in industrial organization economics is applying game theory to competing firms in oligopolistic markets (see Shapiro 1989; Tirole 1988). This detailed and complicated approach has no doubt clarified the would-be rational behavior of rival firms in highly specific competitive situations. But the analytic results apparently lack robustness. For instance, the results show great sensitivity to the assumptions used in defining the situation (Fisher 1989). Even if this limitation can be overcome, game-theoretic approaches often will still not be soluble in the presence of a realistic number of competitors.

Organizational ecologists naturally wonder why the economics literature on industrial organization has not pursued the dynamic models of competition developed by population biologists, such as those deriving from the Lotka–Volterra (LV) framework. In fact, a leading proponent of game-theoretic modeling (Jacquemin 1987) considered the feasibility of applying a general version of the LV model to the study of industrial organization. But he argued that it could not be applied fruitfully to the business-firm context on the grounds that the model is too simplistic to depict real competitive situations among individual firms.

Because the models of density dependence that we develop here are extensions of the LV framework, we feel compelled to address Jacquemin's assessment. In our opinion, his view is on target as directed at organizational applications of the unmodified LV model, which is what he considered. However, instead of disregarding the model entirely, we think that the basic methodological strategy underlying it can and should be modified so as to apply to the organizational world. When this is done, the LV framework is capable of generating significant insight into competition processes.

What modifications of the LV framework are needed? First, the model should not be applied to the behavior of individual organizations but, instead, to classes of organizations defined by organizational form—that is, organizational populations. This would maintain a direct analogue with the LV framework, which treats the growth of entire populations rather than of individual members. Second, population growth rates should be decomposed into the constituent vital rates of organizational founding and mortality. These rates should be treated as stochastic, and observable heterogeneity among firms should be incorporated into analyses. Third, the formal specification of density dependence drawn from evolutionary population biology should be extended to take into account sociological and economic concerns. To be more precise, nonmonotonic density dependence can be used to represent the effects of legitimation and competition. At a general level, our efforts in this book can be seen as implementing these modifications and extensions of the analytic strategy of evolutionary population biology.

The Plan of This Book

We turn next, in Chapter 2, to a formal statement of the theory of density-dependent legitimation and competition. We emphasize the qualitative implications of the theory regarding the relationship between organizational density and rates of founding and mortality in organizational populations. Chapter 3 translates these qualitative implications into parametric models of density dependence. It develops the mathematical models that we actually estimate and provides the structure for relating empirical estimates to the general argument.

To avoid breaking the flow of the argument, we place most of the technical details about the research in a pair of appendices. Appendix A describes in more detail the seven populations to be analyzed. It also cites the sources of the data and describes the covariates used to control for temporal trends and changing social, economic, and political conditions. Appendix B describes the stochastic process representations of rates of founding and mortality along with the procedures we use to estimate the effects of density on the rates.

Chapter 4 provides the basic empirical results about density dependence in rates of organizational founding. It reports estimates of several empirical specifications built on different conceptualizations of the relationship between density and legitimation. It also develops the implications for the general theory of the estimates of the effects of density on founding rates. Chapter 5 continues this analysis but at the level of major subpopulations in populations of banks, labor unions, and life insurance companies.

In Chapter 6, the focus shifts to organizational mortality. Analysis of the effects of density on the rate of organizational mortality begins with what we call the overall rate of mortality, which treats the various types of ending events alike. Then it analyzes the effects of density on four distinct types of ending events. Comparison of effects of density on the rates of the various types of mortality clarifies the nature of the fundamental processes.

Chapter 7 addresses a series of complications, namely the choice of the proper unit of analysis for the study of competition and legitimation processes, reversibility of the processes, and consequences of faulty research design for estimates of effects of density on the vital rates. It addresses these issues in the context of the population of American brewing firms. It estimates density dependence in vital rates in populations defined at the national, state, and city levels, applies them to the reemergence of two old organizational forms—brewpubs and microbreweries, and shows what will happen if analysis is restricted to only the modern (post-Prohibition) period.

Chapter 8 integrates the empirical results on rates of founding and rates of mortality. It does so by using the estimates of effects on these rates to simulate the evolution of numbers in organizational populations. The results of these simulation studies show how density-dependent legitimation and competition might produce the common empirical pattern of growth, stabilization, and decline discussed in this chapter. Finally, Chapter 9 takes up the implications of the research for more general issues of social organization and change.

2

Theoretical Approach

The empirical work of this book relates density to rates of organizational founding and mortality with data on diverse populations. Some readers may wish to consider the models and empirical results directly on their own terms—as empirical regularities, instead of as implications of general theories of organizations. That is, readers may regard our research project as estimating complicated representations of the effects of density on these rates and no more. Such an interpretation appears to be warranted in that density serves as the key observable independent variable in our analyses.[1]

We prefer a different interpretation. We regard the mathematical models of density dependence (presented in the next chapter) as implications of a general theory of organizations. Our theoretical strategy centers on deriving models of density dependence in vital rates as implications of fundamental sociological processes. We think that this strategy offers two advantages. First, it provides theoretical and substantive meaning to the parameters that relate density to the vital rates. Second, it ties our empirical research to broad questions about the sociological forces that shape organizational populations. Because change in organizational populations entails structural change in society, the strategy provides a framework for developing the implications of our findings for general questions about social organization.

---

[1] Density dependence in the growth of human and animal populations holds great interest for mathematical demographers. For insightful treatments of density dependence in human demography, see Lee (1974, 1987), Tuljapurkar (1987), and Wachter (1988).

The core processes are legitimation and competition. This chapter discusses these processes as they bear on issues of density dependence and organizational evolution. Thus our theoretical treatment has a fairly narrow focus. We concentrate on the role of legitimation and competition in linking density and vital rates of organizational populations. We address two questions. First, how do organizational founding rates and mortality rates vary with the strength of legitimation and competition? Second, how do legitimation and competition vary with density? In addressing these issues, we build on existing theory (Hannan 1986a, 1989c; Hannan and Freeman 1989). However, we extend the theory in important ways and seek to clarify a number of important issues.

Competition Processes

Our first broad argument concerns competition, the central mechanism in most ecological theories. We discuss first the meaning of competition in an organizational context and then consider the relationship of competition and the vital rates.

In what sense do organizations and organizational populations compete? Our approach to defining competition differs from that of many other social scientists. Many want to think of competition as a property of observable social ties among identifiable organizations and as including conscious recognition by the parties to the relation (see Granovetter 1985, for example). According to this view, only organizations (or populations) that have explicit, tangible connections and recognize these ties can compete. A similar view, long held by many social scientists, equates competition with conflict or rivalry, which involve explicit social relations. Sociologists who favor either of these views speak of our approach as having "asocial" ideas about competition.[2]

---

[2] Much of the debate over the proper way to conceptualize competition strikes us as primarily rhetorical. For instance, although we do not use a network-based approach to conceptualizing competition, we do not deny that social networks have potentially important implications for organizations and populations of organizations. Nor do we find rivalry and conflict among organizations to be uninteresting phenomena. In fact, we

The ecological view of competition is indeed asocial—if that is the right term—in admitting the possibility that organizations (or other social actors) may compete even though they lack awareness of one another's existence and therefore cannot take one another's actions into account. We follow Georg Simmel and his student Robert Park in distinguishing between competition and conflict. Simmel (1908/1955) considered conflict to be a social relation in the sense that parties to conflict not only take one another into account but also orient their actions to one another. He conceived of competition as the indirect and diffuse (hence asocial) influences among actors that arise from their joint striving for the same limited outcomes. Whether two or more actors dependent on the same limited resources come to recognize their relation as competitors poses an interesting and possibly important question. But the absence of such recognition surely does not cause competitive constraints to dissipate.

Our view of competition parts company with much of sociology in another way. We assume that processes of intense competition may result in the *absence* of interaction across some boundary. This can be the case when two populations compete on a resource gradient and one can exclude the other through more efficient exploitation of resources or power. In such cases, the absence of interaction does not indicate that competition is lacking. Rather, the lack of observable interaction reflects the intensity of competition. Yet social scientists who regard tangible forms of interaction to be a necessary condition for actors to be in competition would regard such cases as involving no competition.

In our view, the utility of a view of competition depends on its capacity to deal with the sometimes diffuse nature of competition and with the possibility that intense competition can eliminate in-

---

would like to understand the conditions under which these different images of competition might coincide with the one we use (cf. Burt 1983). But we do not see a need to try to defend our conception as *the* primary sociological meaning of the process. As long as we are clear about our meaning, the value of our treatment ought to be evaluated by the insight and understanding that it generates and by the research questions that it permits to be analyzed and, ultimately, by the empirical findings pertinent to the questions.

teraction and overlap. An approach that combines the distinction of Simmel with the modeling strategy of modern niche theory seems to serve the purpose best (see Hannan and Freeman 1989).

The concept of niche provides a general way to express effects of environmental variations and competition on the growth rates of organizational populations (Hannan and Freeman 1977). Modern niche theories began in population biology with Hutchinson's (1957) abstract geometric treatment. Hutchinson formalized naturalistic images of the niche of biotic populations and defined the *fundamental niche* of a population as the hypervolume of environmental space formed by the set of points for which the population's growth rate (fitness) is nonnegative. In other words, the fundamental niche consists of the set of all environmental conditions in which the population can grow or at least sustain its numbers. By extension, the fundamental niche of an organizational form consists of the social, economic, and political conditions that can sustain the functioning of organizations that embody the form.

Hutchinson's geometric definition of the niche allows for identifying the intersection in the fundamental niches of different populations. If two organizational populations rely on completely different kinds of resources and depend on different kinds of social and political institutions, then their fundamental niches do not intersect. Otherwise, they do intersect, and so it makes sense to measure their similarity in terms of the degree of intersection or overlap.[3] Intersection in fundamental niches might be thought of as *potential competition.* In general, the potential for two populations to compete is proportional to the intersection of their fundamental niches. It follows that two populations compete if and only if their fundamental niches intersect.

When two or more populations with intersecting fundamental niches occupy the same system, the expansion of one population changes the conditions of the others' existence. In the case of competition, the presence of the competing population reduces the hy-

---

[3] McPherson (1983) used this perspective fruitfully in modeling the ecology of voluntary associations. However, he measures intersection in terms of realized niches, which raises the problem that a lack of intersection may result from intense competition rather than from differences in fundamental niches.

pervolume of environmental space in which another population can sustain itself. Hutchinson coined the term *realized niche* to refer to the restricted environmental space in which a population's growth rate is nonnegative in the presence of competitors. The realized niche is a subset of the fundamental niche and in most realistic cases it is substantially smaller than the fundamental niche.

Except in the highly unusual case of a population isolated from all competitors, all that can be observed in any empirical setting is the realized niche. Suppose that a pair of populations compete for a resource and that one of them can exclude the other from the full range of overlap of their fundamental niches. In this case, the realized niche of the stronger competitor coincides with the fundamental niche, but the realized niche of the weaker competitor is smaller than its fundamental niche. Interestingly, the two realized niches do *not* intersect in such cases. It follows from the general principles that the absence of an observed niche intersection does not imply the absence of competition in other portions of fundamental niches.

So far we have concentrated on *inter*population competition. However, much of the research reported in this book considers the evolution of density in single populations. Does the same kind of reasoning carry over to the case of *intra*population competition? These arguments hold *a fortiori* for intrapopulation competition, because members of the same population have (very nearly) the same fundamental niche.

Because observing competition usually proves to be difficult, empirically minded analysts look for ways to study competition indirectly. One way exploits the relationship between niche intersection and competition implied by classic bioecological competition theory. Population ecologists typically obtain indirect estimates of competition from analyzing the effects of densities of interacting populations on changes in their realized niches (defined in terms of observed utilization of resources). We follow a similar approach, concentrating on the effects of organizational density on the intensity of competition.

Mathematical models of ecological competition usually contain a representation for the "carrying capacity" of the environment for a population. This term refers to the numbers that can be sustained in a particular environment in isolation from other populations (that is, in the absence of competition and facilitation). A useful way to formalize the concept of competition builds on the idea that the presence of a competitor in the system lowers the carrying capacity for the focal population. Because the intensity of competition depends on the number of actors in the competing population, treatments of competition commonly parameterize the effect of adding a member to the competing population on the growth rate of a focal population. A parameter relating density of the competitor to a growth rate is called a *competition coefficient.*[4]

Bioecologists conventionally scale competition coefficients in a metric based on the effect of adding a member to a population on its own growth rate. This choice reflects the fact that ecological competition occurs both within populations and between populations. For the most part, we concentrate here on competition within populations. This focus greatly simplifies the problem of identifying competition because one can safely assume that members of the same population have very nearly the same fundamental niche. (The validity of this assumption depends, of course, on the precise marking of populations' boundaries.) It follows that members of a population compete in the sense that the life chances of any one member depend on the presence of the other members.

Competition and Vital Rates

Intense competition within an organizational population presumably depresses organizational founding rates. As the level of competition increases, more of the resources needed to build and sustain organizations have already been claimed by other organizations. Intense competition causes supplies of potential organizers, members, patrons, and resources to become exhausted. With intense competition, fewer resources go unclaimed, and markets are packed tightly. Given a finite carrying capacity set by environmental conditions, the more numerous the competitors are, the smaller the potential gains from founding an organization will be. Rational actors with the knowledge and skills to build organizations may hesitate to make attempts in densely populated environments and so look for better opportunities. This sort of process contributes to a negative relationship between competition and the founding rate. Capital markets

---

[4] MacArthur (1972) gives an insightful treatment of ecological competition, and Kingsland (1985) provides a fascinating intellectual history of the development of ecological theories of competition.

and other macrostructures often reinforce this tendency. For example, rational investors typically avoid participating in new ventures in highly competitive markets. Likewise, professional associations and government agencies often try to restrict entry under intense competition. These arguments point in the same direction.

Proposition 1. *The founding rate of an organizational population at time t, $\lambda(t)$, is inversely proportional to the intensity of competition within the population at that time, C_t. That is, $\lambda(t) \propto C_t^{-1}$.*

(We use the standard symbol $\propto$ to express proportionality rather than accumulate a series of constants of proportionality in algebraic representations of this and subsequent propositions.)

In the case of mortality, all relevant arguments imply that competition increases the rate. All organizations must maintain flows of resources from the environment in order to keep structures intact. As the competition intensifies, maintaining life-sustaining flows of resources becomes problematic for many, if not all, organizations in a population. Therefore, increasingly strong diffuse competition lowers the life chances of new organizations and those of existing ones by complicating the task of maintaining a flow of essential resources. In other words, when competition is already intense, further growth increases disbanding rates, after controlling for the environmental conditions that affect carrying capacities.

Proposition 2. *The mortality rate of organizations in a population at time t, $\mu(t)$, is directly proportional to the intensity of competition within the population at the time (contemporaneous competition). That is, $\mu(t) \propto C_t$.*

Our phrasing of Proposition 2 takes pains to indicate the time reference ("contemporaneous competition") because we also think that competition may have delayed effects on mortality rates (Carroll and Hannan 1989a). Consistent with Stinchcombe's (1965) well-known argument about organizational imprinting of the social conditions of founding, organizations may be particularly sensitive to competition at the time of their founding. Moreover, intense competition at their times of founding might have long-term effects on the mortality rates of "mature" organizations, for two reasons. The first concerns a *liability of resource scarcity*. Intense competition at the time of founding creates conditions of resource scarcity. When resources are scarce, new organizations that cannot move quickly from getting started to full-scale operation face very strong selection pressures. Those that survive the initial period of organizing presumably do not have the luxury of devoting time, attention, and resources to creating formal structures and perfecting stable, reproducible routines for making decisions and taking collective action. In cohorts of organizations facing such circumstances, staff members have little motivation for investing heavily in acquiring organization-specific skills. Such investment plays a crucial role in the development of reproducible organizational routines.

It might be difficult to recover fully from such deprived initial organizing. Inertial forces presumably operate in this context as well as others. More precisely, attempts at redesigning poorly fashioned structures may well entail survival risks stemming from fundamental change in core activities (Hannan and Freeman 1984). If so, cohorts of organizations that experience intense competition at founding will tend to be inferior competitors at every age.

A second consequence of intense competition at the time of founding concerns *tight niche packing.* With intense competition, resources are subject to intense exploitation and few resources remain unexploited. Because newly founded organizations can seldom compete head-to-head with established organizations, new entrants are pushed to the margins of resource distributions. Tight niche packing thus causes new organizations to attempt to use thinly spread and ephemeral resources. Even if they succeed at creating structures and routines for adapting successfully to the inferior regions of the resource space, in the course of doing so they commit themselves to persisting at the margins. The specialized learning of staff, the collective experience of the organization, and the organization's connections with the environment all become specialized to exploiting the inferior regions of the environment. Attempting to shift toward the richer center at some later time entails high risks of mortality during periods of protracted reorganization. If this reorganization succeeds, it will bring the organization into competition with others experienced in exploiting the center. In either case, these marginal organizations have higher than average mortality rates.

Arguments about the liability of scarcity and tight niche packing imply that mortality rates are elevated for all members of cohorts founded in periods of intense competition and that this higher rate persists over time. To establish notation, we denote the mortality rate at time t of organizations founded at time f by $\mu(t, f)$ and denote the intensity of competition at the time of founding by C_f.

Proposition 3. *The mortality rate at time t of organizations founded at time f, $\mu(t, f)$, is directly proportional (at any age) to the intensity of competition at the time of founding, C_f. That is, $\mu(t, f) \propto C_f$.*

Legitimation Processes

Our second broad argument deals with a process that has no counterpart in classical ecological theories (see, for example, Hawley 1950, 1986)—legitimation of organizational populations and the forms they embody. We claim that legitimation affects rates of founding and mortality and that legitimation varies systematically with density. This section describes our view of this institutional process and lays out our argument concerning the dependence of legitimation on density.

The literature on organizational sociology abounds with ideas about institutionalization and legitimation. The richest vein of institutional theory appears to be one developed by John Meyer and collaborators (Meyer and Rowan 1977; Meyer and Scott 1983). These sociologists have emphasized that the institutional environment of modern organizations has a largely normative character. More precisely, the institutional environment of organizations consists largely of normative prescriptions. Institutional norms are "rationalized and impersonal prescriptions that identify various social purposes as technical ones and specify in a rulelike way the appropriate means to pursue these technical purposes rationally" (Meyer and Rowan 1977, pp. 343–344). Such broad orienting rules are supplemented by myriad specific norms that prescribe organizational structures appropriate to particular realms of activity, for example, schooling, medical care, and manufacturing.

What does it mean for an organizational form to be institutionalized or legitimated? The most obvious—though not necessarily the most important—answer is that a form receives legitimation to the extent that its structure and routines follow the dictates of the prevailing institutional rules. In this sense, institutionalization means conformity with some set of rules, what DiMaggio and Powell (1983) termed "coercive" institutional isomorphism. A second meaning holds that an organizational form is institutionalized or legitimated to the extent that it has a taken-for-granted character (Meyer 1983; Meyer and Rowan 1977). A form acquires legitimation in this sense when there is little question in the minds of actors that it serves as the natural way to effect some kind of collective action.

These two conceptions of legitimation are quite different. They do not necessarily concur on interesting empirical situations. What a society's laws endorse and prohibit may not agree at all closely with what its members take for granted. For instance, even though most forms of gambling are illegal in most states in the United States, many organizations in the gambling business, such as those operating "numbers rackets," have a strongly taken-for-granted character. Indeed, they also frequently have strong institutional standing in the eyes of law-enforcement agencies as well by virtue of highly formalized arrangements of payoffs. What matters more, legal codes or the images and actions of consumers, police, and other key actors?

The idea of legitimation as taken-for-grantedness turns out to be more useful for our research problem because it has a clear-cut link with density. We discuss this connection in detail in the next section. So without implying that other forms of legitimation are irrelevant or unimportant, we use the term here to refer to taken-for-grantedness. Defined in this way, legitimation does not signify the formal legality of an organizational form. Indeed, our arguments should apply to organizations involved in illegal activities such as prostitution, gambling, and price fixing, as well as to those engaged in formally approved and legal activities.

Defining legitimation as taken-for-grantedness does not imply that legality can be ignored, however. Previous analyses of the data used in subsequent chapters show that the legality of an organizational form (or of an activity on which a population depends) strongly affects its emergence and persistence.[5] When the United

---

[5] In the analyses reported in subsequent chapters, we control for the effects of legality in those cases in which we found them to be important. We view legality in much the same way as we view other environmental constraints, and consequently, for the most part we refrain from discussing these effects in theoretical terms. We have shown in other studies that legality of an organizational form has much less predictable impact on vital rates than does density.

States government enacted legislation giving workers the right to organize and bargain for wages, the founding rate of labor unions increased and the mortality rate declined (Hannan and Freeman 1987, 1988a). Likewise, the various state and national bans on alcohol production dramatically affected the number of breweries founded and their eventual life chances. The national Prohibition not only forced many breweries to close, but it also depressed founding rates in the years before Prohibition (Carroll and Swaminathan 1991a). The years immediately following its repeal witnessed an avalanche of new entrants to the brewing market.

Despite the strong effects of changes in legality, we doubt that taken-for-grantedness depreciates rapidly when an organizational form is outlawed. National Prohibition, for example, lasted for 13 years; yet the American populace had no trouble recognizing and evaluating alcohol products and the establishments selling them during or after this period. Even more impressive, perhaps, is the large number of brewers who were prepared to enter the market the day after repeal (see Figure 1.5).

How broadly do legitimation arguments apply to the world of organizations? A common strategy in building theories of organizations divides the world of organizations into sectors and limits the scope of theories to particular sectors. The underlying rationale is that some theoretical mechanisms apply to some sectors and other mechanisms apply to others. Three "sectorizations" relevant to the consequences of competition and legitimation have been proposed. First, Meyer and Scott (1983) suggest that the world of organizations has been split into two sectors, a technical one in which survival depends on efficiency and an institutional one in which survival depends on isomorphism to institutionally approved ways of organizing. The second sectorization comes from DiMaggio and Powell (1983), who argued that organizational populations experience characteristic life histories with youthful periods in which efficiency properties govern survival and a mature period in which institutional isomorphism governs survival. Finally, ecologists Delacroix, Swaminathan, and Solt (1989) make a third sectoral claim, namely, that business organizations face only competitive pressures, whereas nonbusiness organizations are exposed to both legitimation and competition processes.

Hannan and Freeman (1989) argue against sectorization on the grounds that it hampers understanding of organizational diversity and evolution. They challenged the widespread view that institutional arguments necessarily contradict ecological arguments and their emphasis on selection processes. Consider, for instance, the claim that legitimation does not affect the life chances of business firms. Starting and maintaining firms requires that entrepreneurs mobilize capital, staff, and customers. The persons, corporate actors, and social networks comprising the sets of actors in each market presumably act on shared images of reality, including implicit definitions of appropriate organizational forms. Convincing a bank to provide start-up funds for an entirely new kind of venture, perhaps trying to start a new industry or to introduce a novel organizational form, encounters an additional layer of social resistance because the industry or form has not (yet) been legitimated. Similar conservative biases presumably affect the decisions of potential staff and customers.

It may turn out that creating sectors has theoretical value and that different parts of the organizational world operate according to different mechanisms. The best way to find out is by applying the same analytic structure to organizational populations in the various sectors. The previous chapter described why we follow this strategy here. We proceed on the assumption that these processes apply generally to *all* kinds of organizational populations and so apply them to populations of very different kinds of organizations.

Legitimation and Vital Rates

Legitimation of organizational forms affects the founding rates of populations using the form. Obviously, a taken-for-granted social form can be more readily visualized by potential organizers than one with dubious or unknown standing. Variations in the strength of institutional rules endorsing rational organization as the appropriate vehicle for attaining collective goals affect the ease of founding organizations. The capacity to mobilize potential members and resources increases greatly when those who control resources take the organizational form for granted. Reducing the need for such justifications lowers the cost of organizing.

Proposition 4. *The founding rate in an organizational population at time t is directly proportional to the legitimation of its organizational form at that time, L_t. That is, $\lambda(t) \propto L_t$.*

The link between legitimation and mortality is straightforward. Standard institutional arguments imply that legitimation enhances the life chances of organizations. Legitimation eases the problem of maintaining flows of resources from the environment and enhances the ability of organizations to fend off challenges (Meyer and Rowan 1977).

Proposition 5. *The mortality rate in an organizational population at time t is inversely proportional to the legitimation of its organizational form at that time. That is, $\mu(t) \propto L_t^{-1}$.*

Density, Competition, and Legitimation

The various arguments made to this point have numerous kin in the sociological literature on organizations. The distinctiveness of the theory under discussion lies not its assumptions about competition and legitimation but in how it combines these assumptions and especially how it relates competition and legitimation to density. The core idea in our strategy is to relate vital rates in organizational populations to competition and legitimation, two concepts that are difficult to measure directly over the full histories of organizational populations. Without ruling out the possibility that these key concepts may be measured directly in some cases, our general research strategy involves theorizing about the dependence of competition and legitimation on density, which can easily be observed.

The history of legitimation and competition for any organizational population arguably depends on idiosyncratic features of its form, the conditions under which it evolved, and the detailed texture of its time-varying environment. In other words, reconstructing the exact details of changing levels of legitimation and competition over the history of any one population demands attention to all of the unique features of that population's history. A key question in trying to understand organizational evolution concerns the importance of idiosyncracy. Do special features of populations and their histories dominate, or do population histories work out minor variations on common patterns? We are far from knowing the answer to this question. Lacking a clear-cut answer, we take the view that there is no hope of finding general processes unless we look for them, and we operate on the assumption of generality in the processes at work.

Testing its implications provides information about the utility of this assumption. If we are mistaken in thinking that the same general processes apply to all kinds of organizational populations, then orderly patterns are unlikely to result when we use the same analytic structure to analyze diverse populations.

A second strategic decision is choosing how many different kinds of processes to represent explicitly. In the previous chapter we described and defended our strategy of relying on observable features of organizational populations that can be compared over time and context. This strategy leads us to simplify and to consider a single numerical dimension: organizational density.

Our strategy been criticized for its reliance on analytic arguments rather than on direct measurements of all core concepts. For instance, Zucker (1989) charged that our strategy of theory testing yields inadequately specified tests, as we do not measure legitimation and competition directly.[6] We defend this feature of the approach on the grounds that it preserves comparability of procedures and findings across organizational populations and historical contexts. Indeed, this approach allows us to use data on diverse organizational forms from three countries over periods as long as four centuries, as we noted in the previous chapter (see also Carroll and Hannan 1989c).

Decisions about building theories of the role of competition and legitimation in organizational evolution do not turn on assessments of our current ability to measure variations in competition and legitimation directly. However, decisions about designing research to test such theories do turn on judgments about the utility of trying to measure legitimation directly in research on organizational populations. It is important to recognize that neither ecologists nor institutionalists have yet managed to measure directly legitimation as "taken-for-grantedness." Moreover, we doubt that direct measurement is feasible across the range of conditions that should be studied. A direct measure of legitimation as we define it requires learning what fraction of relevant individuals take a particular orga-

---

[6] This criticism of the indirect measurement strategy gives the impression that we ignored a well-codified approach to direct measurement, which is hardly the case. Indicators of legitimation tend to be indirect and open to multiple interpretations (Scott 1987a).

nizational form for granted. Leaving aside the obvious problems of reliability and validity in asking people questions about things that they may take for granted, such a research strategy severely limits the possible historical scope of organizational studies.

A less direct approach identifies one or more idiosyncratic events thought to be associated with the legitimation of particular historical instances of an organizational form. For example, Singh, Tucker, and House (1986) use the listing of a social service agency in a charitable registry as a measure of legitimation that is specific to the organizational form and the period of study. This indirect approach has some appeal. Yet we worry that it may be too tempting to choose such indicators *post hoc* (see, for example, Mezias 1990).

We are interested primarily in developing and testing general arguments, ones that apply to all kinds of contexts and that are not developed *a posteriori*. Relying on measures that build on idiosyncratic features of populations and their specificity of time and place impedes comparative analysis—a high price, as broad comparative analysis is essential to evaluating claims to generality. Moreover, it may well be that theories of legitimation and competition can be studied systematically and comparatively *only* by testing their implications for the relationships between other observables. If so, it makes sense to concentrate on observables that can be evaluated over long periods of time and in many contexts, such as density and vital rates. Put simply, the sociological problem may require what seems to be an indirect approach.

Competition and Density

It makes good substantive sense to concentrate on the relationship between density and competition because the intensity of competition depends on both the degree of intersection of fundamental niches and the numbers of competitors involved.[7] Even when two populations in the same system have highly intersecting fundamental niches, they presumably do not compete intensely if their numbers are very small relative to the abundance of resources. That is, organizational density, resource abundance, and competition are

---

[7] It may also depend on the sizes of the individual competitors, which we will discuss shortly.

tightly connected. Growth in organizational density relative to carrying capacity increases the likelihood and intensity of both direct competition between pairs of organizations within a population and diffuse competition among all or many of them. Individual organizations can easily avoid direct competition with others for members and scarce resources when density is low relative to abundances of resources. As density grows, the number of potential competitors grows. This makes avoidance more difficult, as can easily be seen by noting that there are $\binom{N}{2} = \frac{N^2}{2} - \frac{N}{2}$ possible pairwise competitive interactions in a population of N organizations. As density increases linearly, the complexity of the potential net of competition increases geometrically.[8]

Elementary considerations of congestion suggest that growing density intensifies competition at an increasing rate. In other words, variations in the range of high density (relative to abundance of resources) have more impact on strength of competition than do variations in the lower range. When numbers are few, an increase of population size by a single organization increases the frequency and strength of competitive interactions slightly if at all. But when density is high relative to the carrying capacity, the addition of another organization greatly increases the competition. Viewed from the viewpoint of the actions of a single organization, the difficulty of fashioning a strategy that works against all (or most) competitors becomes extraordinarily difficult when very many pairwise interactions must be considered simultaneously.

Proposition 6. *The intensity of contemporaneous competition, C_t, increases with density, N_t, at an increasing rate. That is, $C_t = \varphi(N_t)$; and $\varphi' > 0$ and $\varphi'' > 0$.*

(In our notation, $\varphi\prime$ indicates the first derivative of φ with respect to its argument, and φ'' indicates the second derivative.)

Earlier we distinguished an effect of density at founding from that of contemporaneous density. To complete our argument regarding density delay, we must introduce an assumption about the relationship between the density at the time of founding and the intensity

---

[8] This interpretation was suggested to us independently by both Ronald Breiger and John Padgett.

of competition at that time. Our arguments about tight niche packing and liability of resource scarcity suggest a proposition paralleling Proposition 6.

Proposition 7. *The intensity of competition at the time of founding, C_f, increases at an increasing rate with density at the time of founding, N_f. That is, $C_f = \psi(N_f)$, with $\psi' > 0$ and $\psi'' > 0$.*

Legitimation and Density

We argued that the legitimation of an organizational form also depends on its density. To expand this argument, it seems natural to ask what underlying mechanisms cause some organizational forms (but not others) to become taken-for-granted? Because institutional theory is decidedly phenomenological and little empirical evidence exists, the answer must be speculative (Scott 1987a).

It seems obvious, however, that the precondition to "social-fact-like" status is widespread identification and recognition, which are more likely when organizations in a population are numerous and occupy the centers of interorganizational networks. Likewise, endorsement by powerful actors and organizations aids in recognition and acceptance. Apparent stability of an organizational form also increases its recognizability, although this need not imply stability of individual organizations. For instance, individual restaurants come and go regularly, yet the form is stable and readily identified.

The process by which organizational forms gain taken-for-granted status encompasses at least two kinds of activity. One is collective action by members of the population to define, explain, and codify its organizational form and to defend itself from claims and attacks by rival populations. The second is collective learning by which effective routines and social structures become collectively fine-tuned, codified, and promulgated.

Intensity of both kinds of activities plausibly depends on density. In the case of collective action, low density hampers attempts to protect and defend the claims of a population or of some of its members (Hannan and Freeman 1986). Growth in numbers of organizations gives force to claims of institutional standing and also provides economies of scale in political and legal action. The capacity for collective action rises at least proportionately with density, and the process is no doubt self-reinforcing, at least initially. When founders organize collectively and form mutual benefit societies and trade associations, new entrepreneurs are enticed to enter the market. Those who do enter find that the association and its members provide useful guidance and assistance.

A bold version of this argument might hold that such social movement–like features play a necessary early role in the successful proliferation of any organizational activity (Olzak and West 1991). We are not prepared to make such a general claim at this point. But we do note with interest that ostensibly uncompetitive cooperative behavior characterizes the beginnings of many industries. More to the point of our theory, growth in density in the lower range can spark collective action and codification that contribute to the recognizability of an organizational form.

From the perspective of legitimation as taken-for-grantedness, it seems clear that extreme rarity of a form poses serious problems of legitimation. If almost no instances of a form exist, it can hardly be taken as the natural way to achieve some collective end. On the other hand, once a form becomes common, it seems unlikely that increases in numbers will have a great effect on its institutional standing. In other words, legitimation responds to variations in density in the lower range, but the effect has a ceiling. The ceiling might be interpreted as the point at which the percentage of relevant persons who take the form for granted reaches a sufficiently high level to make it a normative prescription. That is, at this point further increases in the percentage of persons who take the form for granted do not affect its cultural standing.

We want to consider two types of relationships between density and legitimation. The first, which comes from the first-generation version of the theory (Hannan 1986a, 1989c), assumes

Proposition 8. *Legitimation increases with density at a decreasing rate. That is, $L_t = \vartheta(N_t)$; and $\vartheta' > 0$, and $\vartheta'' < 0$.*

The argument that density increases legitimation at a decreasing rate implies that growth in the lower range of density has the biggest impact in conveying legitimation to an organizational population. In other words, according to Proposition 8, the strongest effect of density on legitimation occurs in tiny populations. This may not be sociologically realistic, however.

Perhaps, instead, increases in density convey little, if any, taken-for-grantedness when density is very low. But as density begins to grow large, increases in it might have strong impacts on legitimation over some range. In other words, legitimation grows with density at an increasing rate in some low range of density. But ultimately, the impact of growing density ought to decline at high density, as the original theory assumes (Hannan 1991). This revision of the argument assumes that

Proposition 9. *The relationship between density and legitimation is positive with a point of inflection $(\tilde{N}_\lambda)$ such that legitimation increases at an increasing rate with density to some point (the inflection point) beyond which legitimation grows with density at a decreasing rate. That is, $L_t = v(N_t)$; and $v' > 0$, and*

$$v'' \quad \text{is} \quad \begin{cases} > 0 & \text{if } N_t < \tilde{N}_\lambda; \\ < 0 & \text{if } N_t > \tilde{N}_\lambda. \end{cases}$$

The next two chapters contrast models in which legitimation increases with density at a decreasing rate over the entire range of density (in agreement with Proposition 8) with those in which this relationship has an S shape, with legitimation increasing greatly with density in its middle range (in agreement with Proposition 9).

A subtle issue that must be addressed explicitly concerns the behavior of density-dependent legitimation when density is close to zero. Density can actually equal zero in empirical cases after a population's initiation, because the early entrants perish before any additional organizations are founded. For instance, this was the case for the population of American national labor unions. We realize that legitimation does not drop to zero with density in such cases, at least not immediately. It seems reasonable to assume that legitimation is nonnegative at all levels of density (once a population's history has begun). What about competition at low density? When a population contains fewer than two organizations, intrapopulation competition does not exist—there are no potential competitors in the population. For this reason, we assume that legitimation exceeds competition at very low densities.

Proposition 10. *Legitimation is stronger than competition at very low densities. In particular,* $\vartheta(N_t) > \varphi(N_t)$, *and* $\upsilon(N_t) > \varphi(N_t)$ *when* $N_t < 2$.

Density Dependence in Vital Rates

The last step in constructing the theory is assembling the pieces so as to derive testable implications about density dependence in rates of founding and mortality. Starting with founding rates, Propositions 1, 4, 6, 8, and 10 jointly imply

Theorem 1. *Density dependence in founding rates is nonmonotonic,*

$$\lambda(t) \propto \frac{L_t}{C_t} = \frac{\varphi(N_t)}{\vartheta(N_t)},$$

and

$$\lambda(t)' \equiv \frac{d\lambda(t)}{dN_t} \quad \text{is} \quad \begin{cases} > 0, & \text{if } N_t < N_\lambda^*; \\ < 0, & \text{if } N_t > N_\lambda^*, \end{cases}$$

where N_λ^* denotes the turning point in the relationship (the density at which the relationship between density and the founding rate changes sign from positive to negative).

In other words, the relationship between density and the founding rate has the form of an inverted U. At low density, the marginal effect of density is positive—growth in density increases the founding rate. But at some level of density, N_λ^*, the relationship changes sign. Above the turning point, the marginal effect of density on the rate is negative—further growth in density depresses the founding rate. The legitimation process dominates at low density, and the competition process dominates at high density.

A parallel theorem results when the alternative proposition regarding the relationship of density and legitimation is used, that is, when Proposition 9 replaces Proposition 8.

Theorem 2. *Density dependence in founding rates is nonmonotonic,*

$$\lambda(t) \propto \frac{L_t}{C_t} = \frac{v(N_t)}{\vartheta(N_t)},$$

and

$$\lambda(t)' \equiv \frac{d\lambda(t)}{dN_t} \quad \text{is} \quad \begin{cases} > 0, & \text{if } N_t < N_\lambda^* ; \\ < 0, & \text{if } N_t > N_\lambda^* . \end{cases}$$

The main difference from Theorem 1 concerns the behavior of the relationship at low density. Theorem 1 states that the relationship increases at a decreasing rate at very low density (Proposition 8), and Theorem 2 postulates that the relationship increases at an increasing rate in this range (Proposition 9).

The argument yields a parallel theorem for the effect of contemporaneous density on mortality rates. Propositions 2, 5, 6, 8, and 10 imply a theorem for mortality rates parallel to Theorem 1.

Theorem 3. *Contemporaneous density dependence in mortality rates is nonmonotonic,*

$$\mu(t) \propto \frac{C_t}{L_t} = \frac{\vartheta(N_t)}{\varphi(N_t)},$$

and

$$\mu(t)' \equiv \frac{d\mu(t)}{dN_t} \quad \begin{cases} < 0, & \text{if } N_t < N_\mu^* ; \\ > 0, & \text{if } N_t > N_\mu^* . \end{cases}$$

Again, the key qualitative implication is nonmonotonicity in density dependence. In this case, the relationship has a U shape. At low density, growth in density lowers the mortality rate by increasing legitimation more than competition. But beyond the turning point, (N_μ^*), further growth in density increases competition more than legitimation and thereby raises the mortality rate.

Finally, the argument implies that a certain form of what has been called density delay. In particular, Propositions 3, 5, and 7 imply a theorem regarding density delay in mortality rates.

Theorem 4. *Density at founding permanently increases mortality rates. That is, the mortality rate at time t of organizations founded at time f is proportional to the density at that time,*

$$\mu(t, f) \propto C_f = \psi(N_f);$$

and

$$\mu(t, f)' \equiv \frac{d\mu(t, f)}{dN_f} > 0; \quad \mu(t, f)'' > 0.$$

The argument about density delay is interesting for two reasons. First, distinguishing between contemporaneous and delayed effects of density obviously helps clarify the mechanism by which density affects the evolution of organizational populations. Second, exploring this issue may help explain an important feature of the growth trajectories of diverse organizational populations noted in Chapter 1: The number of organizations in a population typically grows slowly initially and then increases rapidly to a peak (as we show later). Once the peak number of organizations is reached, density usually declines before stabilizing. If our theory of the effects of contemporaneous density is valid, it can account for the shape of the growth path to a peak, but it cannot explain the decline from the peak. Processes involving density delay may be able to do so. Specifically, if density has a delayed positive effect on mortality rates, then mortality rates will be especially high just after a population has reached its peak, and density will decline from the peak. Such a process may also engender cyclic variations dampening to an equilibrium.

A similar argument has received attention in the mathematical literature on population biology. Leslie (1959) hypothesized that mortality rates depend on contemporaneous density and conditions at the time of birth. Citing research on human mortality, Leslie (1959, p. 152) observed that "It appears that each generation of young tends to carry throughout life relative a degree of mortality peculiar to itself, and it is supposed that this characteristic mortality... represents the effect of environmental conditions experienced by each generation during the early years of its life in the population." For our purposes, the interesting aspect of Leslie's demonstration is that density delay (with an implicit interaction with age structure) produces dampened cycles in trajectories of growth even when the environment does not vary.[9] Such a process can generate the type of

---

[9] Much other theory and research has explored processes in which the effect of density on mortality is lagged by some constant or averaged over time. These processes, too, produce cyclic population growth in constant environments. Cushing (1977) reviewed the mathematical structure of these processes.

trajectory commonly observed for organizational populations.

In testing the claim in Theorem 3, we use a variant of Leslie's argument. The difference is that we argue that density at time of founding matters—not time of founding per se. For instance, two cohorts founded in different periods when density happened to be at the same level have the same rate according to our argument but not according to Leslie's.

Reversibility of Processes

An interesting, unexplored question concerns the reversibility of processes of density-dependent competition and legitimation. Consider a population whose density stabilizes above its initial level. Suppose that the population experiences some environmental catastrophe, such as a civil war or massive economic depression, and that the catastrophe diminishes the size of the population to a very low level. Does such a population have the legitimation of a new population with similar density, as would be the case if the (ahistorical) process were reversible?

Consider the examples of the populations of wineries and breweries in the United States after Prohibition (Carroll and Swaminathan 1991a; Delacroix, Swaminathan, and Solt 1989) or the population of newspapers in Argentina after the protracted repression of the Rosas' dictatorship (Delacroix and Carroll 1983). Does low density in such situations imply low founding rates and high mortality rates net of the level of demand for the products and services provided by the population? Whether a population of organizations facing these circumstances has low legitimation may depend on the length of the period of low density. At the repeal of Prohibition, many individuals still possessed skills in brewing and wine making. And the organizational forms for producing wine, beer, and distilled spirits were still widely known to potential investors and consumers. An analysis of American brewing firms over a period that spans Prohibition allows us to explore this issue empirically. We present a detailed analysis of this issue in Chapter 7.

In some other contexts, apparent reversals of the core processes—such as a resurgence of density after a decline—may be the result of population changes. For example, among American brewers, the century-long decline in the number of firms reached its nadir in 1983 when the number began to rise steadily again (see Figure 1.5). A simple-minded interpretation of this new trend in terms of the theory with reversible processes would explain it as the result of the enhanced legitimation of the brewing organizational form. Besides seeming implausible, this interpretation overlooks the fact that the new breweries consist entirely of microbreweries and the brewpubs. Because these organizational forms are new (at least in the modern era), the two types of breweries might experience their own separate processes of legitimation, perhaps tempered by their mutual occurrence and by the prior existence of the related mass production brewery. Failure to identify and distinguish new organizational forms undergoing their own evolutionary processes can lead to spurious conclusions about the combined populations—see Chapter 7.

Apparent reversals in the evolution of a population may also be the consequence of other organizational processes. In studying the long-term evolution of various organizational populations, we found that trends in density often coincide at least roughly with those of concentration. When the number of organizations declines, the market share held by the largest few firms often increases. This suggests to us that processes of legitimation and competition frequently interact with processes of niche width. More specifically, low density and low concentration (often occurring early in a population's history) seem to create conditions very different from low density and high concentration (often occurring late in the history). The primary difference pertains to the mix of generalist and specialist organizations. When concentration is high, specialist organizations often find small pockets of resources on which they can exist (Carroll 1985). This leads in turn to lower mortality rates and eventually to a larger population. Not recognizing and controlling statistically for such a process may again result in a misinterpretation of our theory of density-dependent legitimation and competition.

Conclusion

Before turning to specific representations of legitimation and competition, we shall summarize our general strategy: Putting together the processes of legitimation and competition yields a general sociological theory of organizational evolution. Density drives both, though in different ways. An important feature of our strategy of theory building is the *symmetry* with which we treat the determinants of rates of founding and mortality. The theory assumes that the same processes of legitimation and competition operate on each rate, though in inverse fashion. Such symmetry has obvious aesthetic appeal as a parsimonious way of explaining variations in the two rates. If it can be shown to be valid, such a theory is preferable to those that develop arguments specialized to explaining one or the other vital rate.

We argue that density increases legitimation at a decreasing rate but increases competition at an increasing rate. Legitimation increases founding rates and depresses mortality rates. Intensified competition lowers founding rates and heightens mortality rates. Taken together, these arguments imply that the relationships between density and the vital rates have specific nonmonotonic forms. Founding rates rise and then decline as a function of density. Mortality rates drop and then increase with rises in density. Empirical testing focuses on these straightforward and falsifiable predictions, which we shall specify in mathematical detail in the next chapter.

3

Models and Modeling Strategy

This chapter presents and motivates the mathematical models we use to represent the theory when testing its implications empirically. Thus this chapter serves as a bridge between the qualitative theoretical arguments of the previous chapter and the quantitative empirical analyses in the chapters that follow. In order to place the models in context, we begin by sketching a pair of classical deterministic models of population growth. We then present the models in considerable detail. The final section discusses potential challenges to our interpretation of estimates of parameters of the models.

The first chapter described a recurrent pattern of growth in populations of organizations: a gradual rise in density, followed by a rapid rise, and then stabilization (usually at a level below the peak). It may seem that such a pattern implies some particular dynamic process. Indeed, we have sometimes encountered the claim that the gross features of the population growth process impose a particular form of density dependence on the vital rates, perhaps even the specification we propose. Therefore, it is important to establish that this is not so. We assert that the gross pattern of growth in density does not impose any particular structure on the vital rates—such a pattern can be produced by many different processes.

Perhaps the most useful way of making this point is by contrasting our models with others that can also be broadly consistent with the observed patterns of growth in density. We discuss a pair of classical models of population growth that are consistent with at least some of the features of the observed patterns and whose mechanisms differ from ours: the well-known logistic and Gompertz models. Each has special interest because the growth paths of either one approximates the gross features of the growth phase of the observed trajectories of density of organizational populations (but not the decline from a peak before stabilization). These models provide a natural point of departure as well as a link with the literature of population dynamics in mathematical bioecology.

Classical Models of Population Growth

The logistic model of population growth in limited environments implies S-shaped growth of density to a steady state. A standard representation for the logistic model uses a quadratic relationship between density (N) and the instantaneous growth rate of density

$$\frac{dN}{dt} = aN_t - bN_t^2, \qquad a, b > 0.$$

Solving this differential equation—subject to the initial condition $N(0) = N_0$—yields the growth path (integral equation):

$$N(t) = \frac{a/b}{1 + \left(\frac{a/b}{N_0} - 1\right)e^{-at}}. \qquad (3.1)$$

This growth path of density has a symmetric S shape. It is symmetric around the point at which the growth rate is maximum ($N = a/2b$).

The connection between the logistic model and the models proposed in this book can be seen most clearly when the logistic is derived as the implication of *density dependence* in vital rates. In order to highlight these connections, we outline a derivation of the logistic model as a special case of compound growth. In particular, we consider a general compound growth process whose growth rate may depend upon density:

$$\frac{dN}{dt} = r(N_t)N_t \qquad (3.2)$$

where $r(N_t)$ is the density-dependent function for the (per capita) population growth rate. In applications to growth of biotic populations, it makes sense to specify the growth process in terms of the birth rate (r_b) and the death rate (r_d). In this case, the population growth rate equals the difference of the functions for the two vital rates: $r(N_t) = r_b(N_t) - r_d(N_t)$.

Malthusian arguments treat the two vital rates as constants. Then the overall growth rate is a constant; and the population will grow explosively if the birth rate exceeds the death rate and will fall exponentially to zero otherwise. The logistic model supposes instead that the vital rates are density dependent. In particular, it assumes that the birth rate falls linearly with density,

$$r_b(N_t) = b_0 - k_b N_t, \qquad b_0, k_b > 0,$$

and that the mortality rate rises linearly with density,

$$r_d(N_t) = d_0 + k_d N_t, \qquad d_0, k_d > 0.$$

Substituting these expressions into the compound growth process (Equation 3.2) yields

$$\frac{dN}{dt} = (b_0 - d_0) N_t - (k_b + k_d) N_t^2.$$

This process has steady states at 0 and at $K = (b_0 - d_0)/(k_b + k_d)$. Which steady state occurs depends on the sign of $r = b_0 - d_0$. If this quantity is negative, the population size will collapse exponentially to zero; if it is positive, the logistic growth process will generate S-shaped growth to the *carrying capacity*. The nonzero steady state is called the carrying capacity of the environment for the population.

In treatments of growth of biotic populations, the model is commonly reexpressed as

$$\frac{dN}{dt} = r N_t \left(1 - \frac{N_t}{K}\right),$$

which serves as the basis for the multi-population Lotka–Volterra formulation (see Wilson and Bossert 1971). In this parameterization, r (which equals $b_0 - d_0$) is called the "natural" rate of increase because it indicates the speed at which a population grows when no resource (or other) constraints apply, that is when density falls very far below the carrying capacity.

Deterministic models *without* density dependence can produce similar qualitative patterns of growth. One of the best known is the Gompertz model (Pitcher, Hamblin, and Miller 1978; Tuma and Hannan 1984, chap. 14). This model can also be regarded as the implication of a compound growth process, but one whose growth rate varies with time

$$\frac{dN}{dt} = r(t)N_t .$$

Suppose that the growth rate falls exponentially over time (the history of the population)

$$r(t) = r_0 \, e^{-ct} , \qquad c > 0 .$$

Substituting this expression into the compound growth process gives

$$\frac{dN}{dt} = r_0 \, e^{-ct} \, N_t .$$

Solving this differential equation—again subject to the initial condition $N(0) = N_0$—gives the growth path

$$N(t) = N_0 \exp\left(\frac{r_0}{c} \left[1 - e^{-ct}\right]\right) . \tag{3.3}$$

This growth path has steady states at 0 and at $N_0 \exp(r_0/c)$. It also has an S shape. However, the growth path of a Gompertz process does not have the symmetry of the logistic. Nonetheless, the growth paths of the two can be quite similar (see, for example, Tuma and Hannan 1984, chap. 14).

For our purposes, the main lesson of this review is that linear density dependence in vital rates or time dependence in growth rates without density dependence can explain some of the gross features of the trajectories of growth of organizational populations (such as those presented in Chapter 1).

The models we develop in this book are more complicated than either the logistic or the Gompertz models, as we show later in this chapter, they specify *nonlinear* density dependence. Yet, we have occasionally heard the ill-founded objection that the S-shaped growth of density constrains the vital rates to have the form of density dependence that we predict. It is very important in evaluating our work to recognize that many simpler models, say those with linear density dependence in vital rates, imply S-shaped growth trajectories as well. Moreover, models without any form of density dependence, like the Gompertz, also imply such a trajectory. Nothing in the common pattern of the observed population trajectories constrains the vital rates to have any particular form of density dependence, or even to depend on density at all, once environmental conditions and time trends have been taken into account.

Relating Vital Rates to Legitimation and Competition

According to Chapter 2, density dependence in vital rates of organizational populations is more complex than is assumed in classical representations of population dynamics such as the logistic and Gompertz.[1] The rest of the chapter discusses how we represent the effects of sociological processes on vital rates. In particular, we turn the previous chapter's qualitative arguments into parametric specifications of density dependence in rates of organizational founding and mortality.

Because we want to specify and test the theoretical arguments of the previous chapter, we concentrate on a limited class of models. This class has three properties. First, the models are consistent with plausible sociological arguments about legitimation and competition and with the theorems of the previous chapter. Second, they can be estimated with available data and statistical methods. Third, they allow the nonmonotonic pattern of density dependence introduced in Chapter 2, but they do not impose it on the data. In other words, our claims can be falsified—the models allow the data to determine the form of density dependence, depending on the signs and values of estimated parameters.

[1] There have been suggestions in the literature on population biology that growth rates rise and then fall with density. For instance, Allee (1931) argued that growth rates are low both below and above an optimum density. However, this line of argument does not appear to have had much impact on the subsequent development of mathematical models of population growth. In the past several years, mathematical biologists have reopened this question. Caswell (1989) provides a useful overview of this work.

In order to make this chapter reasonably self-contained, we re-state the main results of the previous chapter. For the founding rate, Theorem 1 postulates that

$$\lambda(t) \propto \frac{L_t}{C_t} = \frac{\varphi(N_t)}{\vartheta(N_t)}, \tag{3.4}$$

and the alternative (S-shaped growth) version, Theorem 2, holds that

$$\lambda(t) \propto \frac{L_t}{C_t} = \frac{\upsilon(N_t)}{\vartheta(N_t)}. \tag{3.5}$$

For mortality rates, combining Theorems 3 and 4 gives

$$\mu(t, f) \propto \frac{C_t \cdot C_f}{L_t} = \frac{\vartheta(N_t)\,\psi(N_f)}{\varphi(N_t)}. \tag{3.6}$$

The main task is choosing functional forms for the key relationships that are congruent with the qualitative restrictions stated in Theorems 1 through 4 and that also allow empirical estimation. The relationships to be considered are $\varphi(N_t)$ or $\upsilon(N_t)$, the effect of contemporaneous density on legitimation, $\vartheta(N_t)$, the effect of contemporaneous density on competition, and $\psi(N_f)$, the effect of density at founding on competition.

Density and Competition

Chapter 2 reviewed the ecological argument that changes in density in the upper range are critical to affecting the intensity of competition. When numbers are few, adding an organization to the population increases the frequency and strength of competitive interactions slightly at most. Adding an organization at high density strongly increases competition. In other words, the core qualitative assumption about competition is that growth in density increases competition at an increasing rate (Proposition 6).

Many parametric representations can be consistent with these restrictions. The simplest posit that competition rises as a non-linear function of density. For example, one might use a loglinear relationship $C_t = a \exp(b N_t)$ with $b > 0$, or a polynomial one $C_t = a + b N_t + c N_t^2$ with $c > 0$.

The original statement of the theory of density-dependent legitimation and competition (Hannan 1986a, 1989c) posited an equally simple relationship (with a single parameter other than a scaling factor)—an exponential relation between competition and the square of contemporaneous density,

$$C_t = \varphi(N_t) = c_t \exp(\beta N_t^2), \qquad \beta > 0, \qquad (3.7)$$

where c_t represents the effects of factors other than density that affect levels of competition. Two features of Equation 3.7 require explanation: loglinearity in parameters and choice of N^2 as the dimension of density. The choice of an exponential relationship (that is, one that is loglinear in parameters) rather than simply a linear relationship between competition and some function of density reflects the constraints imposed by the definition that rates of founding and mortality must be nonnegative (see Appendix B). The theory assumes that these rates depend on the level of competition. The choice of, for instance, a linear relationship between competition and a function of density would often imply that a rate is negative at some level of density, which violates the definition of a founding rate or mortality rate. However, the exponential relationship between the rate and a function of density is always nonnegative.

Why N^2 rather than, say, N? Hannan (1986a) made this choice on the grounds that it produces very rapid increases in the intensity of competition as density grows. Another possible reason for this choice comes from considering the network of possible ties among organizations in a population. Suppose that competitive pressure is proportional to the number of possible pairwise interactions among members in the population. The number of such pairs is

$$\binom{N}{2} = \frac{N^2}{2} - \frac{N}{2}.$$

As the population grows, the squared term dominates such that the number of pairs is approximately $N^2/2$. Hence the functional form in Equation 3.7 can be considered as representing the strength of intrapopulation competition as proportional to the number of possible pairwise interactions.

To the best of our knowledge, representing density-dependent competition in the form of Equation 3.7 does a reasonably good job of representing density dependence in competition as it affects rates of founding and mortality. It has served as the basis for all of the empirical work on the subject of which we are aware. Because we have no reason to doubt its utility, we did not tinker with it.

Next we consider *density delay.* The previous chapter argued that the intensity of competition at the time of founding has lasting effects on the mortality rates of organizations and that the intensity of such competition is proportional to the density of the population at the time of an organization's founding (Proposition 7). We specify this proposition with a simple loglinear relationship between the intensity of competition at the time of founding and the density at the time of founding:

$$C_f = \psi(N_f) = \exp(\delta N_f), \qquad \delta > 0. \qquad (3.8)$$

Density and Legitimation

Our discussion of legitimation as taken-for-grantedness in the previous chapter led to the conclusion that legitimation rises with density but that there are limits on the process. Once density and legitimation reach high levels, further increases in density convey little or no additional legitimation. The original version of the theory assumed that density increases legitimacy at a decreasing rate (Proposition 8). The first-generation model of density-dependent legitimation parameterized this qualitative assumption such that legitimacy increases with density according to a power law,

$$L_t = \vartheta(N_t) = l_t N_t^{\alpha}, \qquad 0 < \alpha < 1, \qquad (3.9)$$

where l_t represents the impacts of other time-varying factors. The inequality constraint ($0 < \alpha < 1$) ensures that legitimation increases with density at a decreasing rate, in agreement with the qualitative argument.

Numerous other parametric representations of the relationship of legitimation and density agree with the theoretical argument. Moreover, there are other ways of deriving nonmonotonic relationships between vital rates and density. We do not attempt to present an exhaustive account of feasible functional forms. Rather, we consider only adaptations of the logistic and Gompertz models to represent density-dependent legitimation because these well-known models agree with Proposition 9 and also have great substantive appeal in this context.

The previous chapter introduced the idea that very low density conveys little legitimation but that growth in density increases legitimation at an increasing rate. This idea is consistent with the notion that a very small population virtually escapes notice. Once density begins to grow, any increases might have strong impacts on legitimation over some range. But ultimately, the impact of growing density ought to decline at high density, as the original theory assumed.

This alternative view of legitimation suggests the use of S-shaped growth paths of legitimation (Proposition 9). Both the logistic and Gompertz models can generate such trajectories. However, instead of using them to represent the growth of density with time, we use them to represent the growth of legitimation with density. With such a modification, each relates the rate of change in legitimation over time to its current level and to a "ceiling on legitimation." The latter refers to a maximum level of legitimation that an organizational form can achieve in a given sociocultural environment. As we noted earlier, a ceiling may result from a saturation level of acceptance in the human population (that is, the percentage of persons accepting a form without question needed for a cultural definition to emerge). The ceiling presumably depends on various properties of the match between the organizational form and the social structure. We treat the ceiling, denoted by L^*, as unobserved but estimable. We assume further that L^* does not vary over time.

According to the logistic specification (see Equation 3.1), growth in legitimation with density from some initial level (L_0) to the ceiling (L^*) has the form

$$L_t = v(N_t) = \frac{L^*}{1 + \left(\frac{L^*}{L_0} - 1\right) e^{-\alpha N_t}}, \qquad \alpha, \ L_0, \ L^* > 0. \qquad (3.10)$$

The representation in Equation 3.10 conforms to the view that legitimation grows slowly with density when legitimation is low, then at some point grows rapidly, and finally slows near the upper limit.

The motivation for considering also a Gompertz version of the legitimation process is to relax a restrictive feature of the logistic model. Recall that the logistic model imposes the constraint that the growth path of legitimation be symmetric around the point of maximum growth rate, that is, that the S-shaped path be exactly symmetric. This requirement seems stronger than the qualitative reasoning demands.

The first section of this chapter noted that the Gompertz model can be derived as a consequence of time dependence in the growth rate of a compound growth process. We merely replace time with density in Equation 3.3 to obtain the model

$$L(N_t) = v(N_t) = L_0 \exp(c\left[1 - e^{-\alpha N_t}\right]), \qquad c = r_0/\alpha. \qquad (3.11)$$

For ease in comparison with the logistic model and for ease of estimation, we rewrite Equation 3.11 as

$$L(N_t) = e^c L_0 \exp(-ce^{-\alpha N_t}). \qquad (3.12)$$

According to the integral equation for the Gompertz model in Equation 3.12, the ceiling on legitimation (as N goes to infinity) is

$$L^* = e^c L_0. \qquad (3.13)$$

Therefore, Equation 3.12 can be expressed as

$$L(N_t) = L^* \exp(-ce^{-\alpha N_t}), \qquad \alpha, \ c, \ L^* > 0. \qquad (3.14)$$

The substantive import of the parameter c deserves comment. Equation 3.13 indicates that c equals the ratio of the ceiling on legitimation to its floor (in a logarithmic scale):

$$c = \ln\left(\frac{L^*}{L_0}\right).$$

A plausible interpretation is that c indicates something about the novelty of the organizational form that defines the population. The larger the value of c is, the more a population's taken-for-grantedness will rise once it reaches its peak density.

Density Dependence in Founding Rates

The next step in building parametric representations of density dependence in vital rates inserts these various parametric representations of density-dependent competition and legitimation into the basic theoretical equations for the vital rates (Theorems 1 through 4). This section completes the model for founding rates; the next section does so for mortality rates.

A Generalized-Yule Model

The model that initiated the line of research we follow combined a power-law relationship between legitimation and density with a loglinear relationship between competition and the square of density (Hannan 1986a). Replacing L_t and C_t in Equation 3.4 with the parametric representations as functions of density in Equations 3.7 and 3.9 yields the original model, an estimable specification of density dependence in founding rates

$$\lambda(t) = \frac{L_t}{C_t} = \frac{\varphi(N_t)}{\vartheta(N_t)} = \kappa_\lambda(t)\, N_t^\alpha \exp\left(-\beta N_t^2\right), \qquad \alpha, \beta > 0, \quad (3.15)$$

where $\kappa_\lambda(t) = l_t/c_t$. This model can be regarded as a generalization of the famous Yule process (see Appendix B; Yule 1924) in the sense that Equation 3.15 reduces to a Yule process when $\alpha = 1$ and $\gamma = 0$. For this reason, the model in Equation 3.15 has become known as a generalized-Yule (or GY) model.

It will simplify our presentation of empirical results to reexpress Equation 3.15 with coefficients having positive coefficients:

$$\lambda(t) = \kappa_\lambda(t)\, N_t^\alpha \exp\left(\gamma N_t^2\right), \qquad \gamma = -\beta. \qquad (3.16)$$

In terms of this parameterization, the hypotheses from Theorem 1 are

$$0 < \alpha < 1; \qquad \gamma < 0. \qquad (3.17)$$

Put simply, the predictions are that the first-order effect of density is positive (and less than one) and the second-order effect of density is negative.

If the estimates satisfy the inequalities indicated in Equation 3.17, then the relationship between density and the founding rate is *non-monotonic*. This relationship has the form of an inverted U according to the theory, because legitimation dominates at low density but competition dominates at high density. The relationship has a maximum at

$$N_\lambda^* = \sqrt{\frac{\alpha}{-2\gamma}} \ . \tag{3.18}$$

The founding rate rises as density increases until density reaches the level indicated in Equation 3.18; from that point on the founding rate falls with increasing density.

Plots of implied relationships between density and the founding rate aid in understanding the implications of the model. The solid line in Figure 3.1 shows the estimated relationship between density and the founding rate of national labor unions in the United States implied by estimates of the GY model in Equation 3.16. Note that the estimates imply that the founding rate rises very steeply with increasing density in the lower range of density, which follows as an implication of the assumption of a GY legitimation process. The founding rate reaches its maximum when density equals roughly 70, and then it flattens out over quite a broad range of density before dropping as the competition process takes over.

A Log-Quadratic Approximation

In earlier empirical research the most common alternative to the GY specification of density dependence in vital rates comes from the first application of the theory to organizational mortality rates. Hannan and Freeman (1988a) could not get iterative maximum likelihood estimates of a GY model to converge with data on the life spans of national labor unions. So they shifted to an approximation whose coefficients can have a similar qualitative interpretation: a log-quadratic approximation. This approximation has subsequently been used in some analyses of founding rates as well as mortality rates. In particular, Carroll and Hannan (1989b) found that it fit better than the GY model did in research on founding rates of newspaper populations.[2]

---

[2] This conclusion is not necessarily true when the problem of so-called overdispersion is taken into account, as we shall see in Chapter 4.

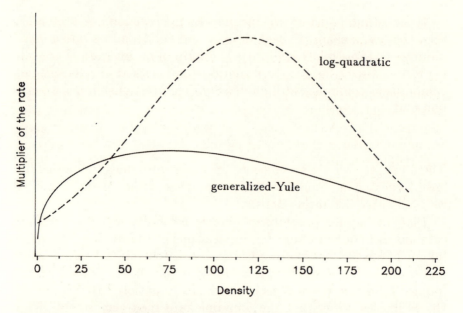

Figure 3.1. Effect of density on the founding rate of labor unions according to estimates of generalized-Yule and log-quadratic models

This log-quadratic (LQ) specification of density dependence in founding rates has the form

$$\lambda(t) = \kappa_\lambda(t) \exp\left(\theta_1 N_t + \theta_2 N_t^2\right) . \tag{3.19}$$

In terms of Equation 3.19, the predictions from Theorem 1 are

$$\theta_1 > 0 ; \quad \theta_2 < 0 . \tag{3.20}$$

If these inequalities hold, the log-quadratic approximation implies nonmonotonic dependence on contemporaneous density. The founding rate rises with density to the maximum given by

$$N_\lambda^* = -\frac{\theta_1}{2\theta_2} . \tag{3.21}$$

Above N_λ^*, the founding rate decreases with increasing density. Thus Equation 3.21 too can imply an inverted U-shaped relationship between density and the founding rate. Again, the main qualitative implication for empirical work is that the first-order effect of density be positive and the second-order effect be negative.

What substantive differences result from the slight change from the GY model to the LQ approximation? Carroll and Hannan (1989b) discussed two ways of motivating the latter. The former assumes that legitimation rises with density at an increasing rate (exponentially). Although this assumption may be correct, it does not agree with our views about legitimation, discussed at length in the previous chapter.

A second motivation comes from the idea that legitimation itself has a log-quadratic relationship with density, that is,

$$L_t = l_t \exp\left(\zeta_1 N_t - \zeta_2 N_t^2\right), \qquad \zeta_1, \zeta_2 > 0. \tag{3.22}$$

Because such a function implies that legitimation eventually declines at high densities, it contradicts the arguments of the previous chapter (Propositions 8 and 9) and the spirit of institutional theories of organizations. However, if we restrict attention to the range over which the log-quadratic relationship is positive, it will give a potentially useful approximation to the relationship assumed in the GY model. Over this range, the relationship between density and legitimation is roughly sigmoidal. Thus initial growth in density has a relatively small impact on legitimation relative to those at some intermediate level of density. (A more direct, but also more complicated, approach to representing such a relationship builds on the logistic and Gompertz models of legitimation discussed next.)

Figure 3.1 (dashed line) plots the relationship between density and the union founding rate implied by estimates of a LQ approximation. Although the overall relationship has the same nonmonotonic form as for the GY model, the details differ. The founding rate of the GY process grows modestly at low density—indeed, this function does not reach its maximum until density reaches roughly 100. However, the rate rises steeply with increasing density in the middle range of observed density before falling steeply at high density. The relationship has a more pronounced peak than does the one implied by the GY model. This difference between specifications may be important to the qualitative behavior of the population growth process. Consequently, we compare repeatedly the specification that builds on a generalization of the Yule process with the one in which density dependence has a log-quadratic form.

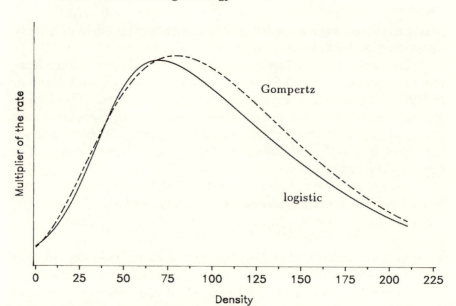

Figure 3.2. Effect of density on the founding rate of labor unions according to estimates of logistic and Gompertz models

Logistic and Gompertz Models

Finally, we explore the value of models that combine the two S-shaped legitimation functions, the logistic and Gompertz models, with our assumption about the relationship of competition and density. With a logistic legitimation process, the model of density dependence has the form

$$\lambda(t) = \frac{\upsilon(N_t)}{\vartheta(N_t)} = \left(\frac{L^*}{1 + \left[\frac{L^*}{L_0} - 1 \right] e^{-\alpha N_t}} \right) \exp\left(\gamma N_t^2\right), \qquad \gamma = -\beta.$$

(3.23)

In terms of this representation, the predictions from Theorem 2 are

$$L^* > L_O > 0; \quad \alpha > 0; \quad \gamma < 0. \qquad (3.24)$$

We report estimates of specifications with this form in Chapter 4 by treating L^* and L_0 as constants to be estimated from the data.

Replacing the logistic legitimation process with a Gompertz process (Equation 3.14) gives

$$\lambda(t) = \frac{v(N_t)}{\vartheta(N_t)} = L^* \exp\left(-ce^{-\alpha N_t}\right) \exp\left(\gamma N_t^2\right), \qquad \gamma = -\beta. \quad (3.25)$$

Now the predictions from Theorem 2 are

$$\alpha > 0; \quad \gamma < 0; \quad L^* > 0; \quad c > 0. \tag{3.26}$$

When estimating specifications with the form of Equation 3.25 in Chapter 5, we recover estimates of L_0 by using the definition of L^* in Equation 3.13 in conjunction with estimates of α and c.

Figure 3.2 compares the implications of the logistic (solid line) and Gompertz (dashed line) models of legitimation for founding rates of national labor unions. The two specifications agree closely—the Gompertz model can scarcely be distinguished from the logistic one in this case (and others we examined). Moreover, the relationships between density and the founding rate are quite similar to those of the LQ model in Figure 3.1 over the full range of density of unions.

Density Dependence in Mortality Rates

The procedure for forming estimable representations of density dependence in mortality rates parallels in an obvious way the procedure used in the previous section. Hannan's (1986a) original model of density dependence in mortality rates comes from combining the power-law relationship between legitimation and density in Equation 3.9 and the log-quadratic relationship between competition and density in Equation 3.6. Here we extend the original model by adding a delayed effect of density, as discussed earlier:

$$\mu(t, f) \propto \frac{C_t C_f}{L_t} = \frac{\vartheta(N_t)\psi(N_f)}{\varphi(N_t)}$$

$$= \kappa_\mu(t)\, N_t^\nu \exp\left(\beta N_t^2 + \gamma N_f\right), \quad \nu = -\alpha, \; t > t_f. \quad (3.27)$$

In terms of Equation 3.27, the predictions from Theorem 3 are

$$\nu < 0; \quad \beta > 0. \tag{3.28}$$

In other words, the first-order effect of contemporaneous density is negative due to the legitimating effects of initial growth in density. The second-order effect of contemporaneous density is positive, as is the effect of density at founding. Obviously, this model, too, implies a nonmonotonic relationship between contemporaneous density and the mortality rate, adjusting for age of the organization. According to Theorem 4 the effect of density at founding is positive

$$\gamma > 0. \tag{3.29}$$

The log-quadratic (LQ) approximation to Equation 3.27 has the form

$$\mu(t, f) = \kappa_\mu(t) \exp\left(\theta_1 N_t + \theta_2 N_t^2 + \theta_3 N_f\right). \tag{3.30}$$

The hypotheses of interest are

$$\theta_1 < 0; \quad \theta_2 > 0; \quad \theta_3 > 0. \tag{3.31}$$

This kind of approximation (often without the density delay effect) has been used in almost all published research on density dependence in organizational mortality. We find that it fits better than the GY model (in Equation 3.27) does for all seven populations. Thus we use this LQ approximation when analyzing density dependence in mortality rates. If the inequalities on coefficients indicated in Equation 3.31 hold, then the LQ specification of mortality rates yields an inverted U-shaped relationship between density and mortality rates in agreement with Theorem 3. That is, the mortality rate falls with initial increases in density but eventually a point is reached at which further increases in density raise the mortality rate.

Considerations of symmetry might dictate that we also use the logistic and Gompertz models of legitimation when analyzing mortality rates. But we have not attempted to do so, for two reasons. First, the LQ approximation always fits better than does the GY model for mortality rates. Recall that the LQ specification rises slowly initially and then speeds up with increasing density in a way that parallels the behavior of the logistic and Gompertz models in the range of low and medium density. Less can be gained by using the more complicated logistic and Gompertz models instead of the LQ approximation than if the GY model were the leading alternative.

The logistic and Gompertz models are also much more complicated to estimate than the others are. We have often found it a
formidable task to find initial values of parameters that would allow
iterative maximum likelihood estimators to converge when analyzing
the simple data on foundings. The data sets used in mortality analysis (organization-year records) are as much as 100 times larger than
those on foundings. (Appendix B explains why this is the case.) The
combination of complexity, delicacy in techniques of iterative estimation, and size of data sets suggests that it is not advisable to attempt
to use the logistic and Gompertz models in mortality analyses. For
these reasons, we report estimates of only the LQ specification of
density dependence in mortality rates.

Interpretations of Density Dependence

The models discussed in this chapter have engendered much interest
and at least some controversy in the sociological and organizational
studies communities. Friendly critics have pointed to several potential pitfalls in interpreting estimates of parameters as implications of
processes of legitimation and competition. This section explains our
position on interpreting effects of density and examines a number
of issues regarding the status of the theory in light of the current
debates.

Tautology?

The first section of this chapter developed the point that observed
trajectories of organizational populations over time do not imply any
particular form of density dependence. Indeed, density dependence
may not be implied at all by the commonly observed trajectory, as
this pattern can be produced by time dependence in rates. Yet the
suspicion that analyses of density dependence entail some sort of
tautology apparently lingers. Because the issue causes confusion, we
shall try to state the case plainly.

The suspicion of some kind of tautology in our claim that density affects vital rates seems to be based on an implicit scenario, as
follows: All organizational populations that we know begin small
(initial density is low). If the population grows large enough to be a
candidate for study, it must grow from the initial low level to some

higher density. For some initial period, the founding rate must exceed the mortality rate. Conversely, the other side of the argument claims that, because the populations that we studied have remained finite, mortality rates must eventually dominate (or at least balance) founding rates. The fact that founding rates dominate at low density and mortality rates dominate at high density suggests, according to this view, that the effects of density are not causal at all. Rather, the suspicion is that their patterns simply reflect the inevitabilities of finite growth.

We do not think that such a suspicion has a good foundation. Two issues deserve discussion, one particular, one general. The particular issue concerns the implications of our sociological theory for nonmonotonic density dependence in vital rates. Even if our scenario of tautological density dependence were accurate, nothing in it suggests—much less implies—that the relationship of density to the vital rates would be nonmonotonic. Because we contrast nonmonotonic density dependence with simpler monotonic alternatives, the scenario has no real bearing on our inferences.

The more general issue concerns the effects of exogenous conditions. Rates of founding and mortality presumably vary with external conditions facing organizational populations. These include abundances of resources, variations in political turmoil, and broad social, political, and economic structures. A truly simple account of population dynamics suggests that these conditions—not density—cause growth and decline in organizational populations. So, for example, one can obtain the observed patterns of growth, decline, and stabilization by assuming that some condition favoring the organizational form arises, for some time persists, and then wanes before stabilizing. Many accounts of organizational evolution take exactly this perspective. Accounts of life cycles of industries, for instance, assume that technical innovations and industry learning curves account for the rise, stabilization, and eventual decline in numbers in populations of firms with particular technologies.

We agree that external conditions affect rates of founding and mortality. When the data permit, we estimate stochastic models that incorporate the effects of social, economic, and political conditions as well as the effects of population dynamics. That is, we evaluate the effects of density on vital rates *net of the effects of specified environmental conditions.*

Legitimation and Competition As Processes

The role of legitimation and competition also deserves clarification. The theory of density dependence is sometimes interpreted as having two unobservable variables, degree of legitimation and level of competition, with density and squared density serving as "indicators" of the unobservables (Zucker 1989). According to this interpretation, we make progress by attempting to measure directly the levels of legitimation and competition rather than relying on estimates of effects of density on vital rates.

But this interpretation misses the mark (see Carroll and Hannan 1989c). In our view, legitimation and competition are processes that relate conditions facing a population to its vital rates.[3] Indeed, growth in density *controls* these processes—it does not reflect them, as the language of "indicators" connotes. Increasing density combines with other social processes in conveying institutional standing as taken-for-grantedness. Growth in density relative to the abundance of resources that sustains a population intensifies competition.

These contrasting interpretations of the role of density entail differing views of the effects of adding effects of covariates. If one accepts the view that density serves only as an indicator of competition, it follows that adding covariates that improve the representation of the strength of competitive interactions will diminish the estimated effect of the square of density. The reasoning is as follows: Adding covariates regarding abundance of resources and other conditions that affect the life chances of organizations will provide a more "direct" measure of the strength of competitive pressures than will density. Hence, an estimation of effects of both density and such

---

[3] The logic of general evolutionary ecology treats competition as a characterization of the parameter space in a dynamic model relating the growth of each population to its own density and the density of other populations in the system. Competition among a set of populations refers to the conditions under which the growth in each member of the set reduces the growth rates of the other members of the set. Therefore, competition should not be regarded as a state with levels ranging from "low" to "high." Put differently, competition is not a variable characterizing particular populations. Rather, it is a property of the dynamics of the system. These remarks also apply to legitimation—we regard it as a social process not a state.

covariates will attribute to the covariates the competitive effect of reducing founding rates and increasing mortality rates.

But according to the interpretation offered in this book, such procedures ought to sharpen estimates of the competitive effects of density. Increasing density implies intensifying competition only if the abundances of resources that sustain the population are fixed (or increase less rapidly than density). But many social and material resources fluctuate unpredictably. Such fluctuations introduce noise into the relationship between density and the vital rates. Unless such fluctuations are taken into account explicitly, one should not expect to obtain clear and precise estimates of the effects of density. Accounting for the effects of covariates that track such fluctuations therefore enhances the ability to detect effects of density.

Consider the same issue from the perspective of legitimation. If the theory is valid, increasing density in the lower range will increase legitimation and thereby increase the founding rate and decrease mortality rates. But suppose that a major economic depression, such as the depressions of the 1870s, 1890s, and 1930s, occurs when a population's density has reached the point at which legitimating effects are predicted to be strong. The depression may decrease the founding rate and increase mortality rates, as was the case for American labor unions (Hannan and Freeman 1987, 1988a). And these effects may be strong enough to dominate the effects of legitimation. If so, analysis that does not adjust for the effects of depressions is unlikely to obtain precise estimates of the first-order effect of density.

The two interpretations yield opposing predictions about the effect of taking account of environmental fluctuations on estimates of density dependence in vital rates (issues of statistical estimation aside). According to the view that density is an (indirect) indicator of basic processes of competition, adding such covariates will diminish—if not eliminate—the effect of density on rates of founding and mortality. According to our view that density determines legitimation and competition, adding such covariates will improve estimates of the effects of density, thereby reducing standard errors of estimate of the effects of density but not diminishing point estimates of the effects.

Yet there is a complication pertaining to statistical estimation with finite samples. In many cases, correlation between the set of relevant environmental covariates and density is high. Using many highly correlated covariates causes standard errors to be inflated. Therefore, it may turn out that adding many covariates will diminish the statistical significance of the effects of density, contrary to our expectations. For this reason, we cannot draw any substantive inferences from the effect of adding covariates. However, in the interest of obtaining precise estimates of effects of density, we do take account of effects of covariates in our analyses.

Density or Mass?

The theory of density-dependent legitimation and competition has another interpretation that seems natural to some colleagues with whom we discussed these issues. This interpretation differs from ours, but it does not necessarily deny the plausibility of our arguments. It posits that the estimated effects of density are reflections of the omitted effects of market size or total output in a population rather than of density per se (Winter 1990). In abstract terms, this interpretation pits mass dependence (the effect of the combined size of all members of a population) against density dependence (the effect of number of organizations in the population).

Without denying the potential importance of mass dependence, we offer two types of reasons for not accepting a mass-dependence interpretation of the models considered in this chapter. The first reason relies on empirical information. To the extent possible, given the constraint of using historical data spanning long periods, we attempt to control for the mass of individual organizations and the mass of the population. So, for example, when analyzing rates of founding and mortality of labor unions, we control for the effects of the aggregate of members in the entire population of unions. For breweries we use variables measuring market size, for example aggregate beer consumption and production. Admittedly these controls are imperfect and not historically comprehensive because of data constraints. We are encouraged by the fact that our conclusions about density dependence do not change when measures of mass are taken into account.

The second type of reason for not interpreting the effects of density as effects of mass follows from theoretical considerations. Given a certain level of mass, the number of organizations present makes a substantial difference in the processes of legitimation and competition. We used this logic earlier. But the issue has enough importance to merit expanding on it.

Consider the prediction that increases in density in the lower ranges depress mortality rates. Our theory explains this effect as a consequence of the legitimation process. We also suggested that processes of legitimation of organizational populations can be affected by at least two other kinds of processes: (1) collective action that affects a population's ability to defend itself and (2) collective learning by which effective routines and social structures are jointly fine-tuned over time. We argued that both sources of legitimation depend on density and also that density affects a population's capacity to generate potential organization builders by educating and training them in existing organizations. Although each of these factors might increase with the mass of an organizational population, we think that they are more tightly linked with density. To see this, imagine two extreme situations of two populations with the same mass but the first having only a single organization and the second having thousands of organizations. If each formal organization constitutes a relatively distinct arrangement of roles, routines, and resources, then the population that contains more "experiments" will have a higher probability of containing effective solutions to problems of adapting in a changing and uncertain world. Likewise, even though many newly founded organizations may fail, the number attempted coincides roughly with the number of persons or groups acquiring some experience and skill at founding and running an organization of this kind (Stinchcombe 1965). Finally, attempts to quash the organizational form are much easier to mount and probably more likely to succeed when directed at a single large target than when directed at many small ones (Carroll and Huo 1988). All of these reasons, which no doubt could be formulated in an underlying micromodel, lead us to think that density has special interest for studies of organizational sociology.

Size and Unobserved Heterogeneity

A different but related issue concerns the sizes of individual organizations, which can be thought of as unit-specific mass. According to one argument, density simply masks the well-known effects of organizational size (Winter 1990). When many organizations exist, most are small. Smaller organizations can be founded more easily, and their mortality rates are usually higher. It should be no surprise to find an empirical correspondence between density on the one hand and organizational vital rates on the other.

As typically stated, this argument is a more specific version of the general concern about unobserved heterogeneity and its possible correlation with independent variables. If a population consists of several types of organizations, each with its own type-specific mortality rate, there always will be the chance that an unlabeled mixture of the types will correlate spuriously with another variable. This result arises simply from the quicker disappearance of the higher mortality subpopulations, thus leading to their elimination from the base rate calculations. Such arguments are applied commonly to explain apparent age dependence in mortality rates, but in certain specific conditions, they may apply to density dependence as well.

Without denying the plausibility of such processes, we think it is incumbent upon those advancing atheoretical alternatives of this kind to demonstrate their plausibility under commonly observed situations. We also think that such criticism should specify the sources of unobserved heterogeneity. By doing so, critics allow research to progress, as collection and analysis of the effects of measures of the forms of heterogeneity would allow adjudication. In contrast, there is no satisfactory way to respond to a general claim about unobservable heterogeneity, because the sources of *all* differences among organizations can never be examined.

In the case of organizational size, we identified the source of spurious unobserved heterogeneity, and we can address the issue empirically. We do so in detail in Chapter 6 and so will not describe all our findings here. Suffice it to say now that we find that size does indeed affect organizational mortality rates but that controlling for this effect does not eliminate or diminish the effects of density.

A second specific form of unobserved heterogeneity has also received some attention. Petersen and Koput (1991a) argue that one part of one of the processes we study—the decline in mortality rates with increasing contemporaneous density in the range of low density—is consistent with the effects of a certain form of unobserved heterogeneity. We treat this claim in detail in Chapter 6 and suggest that there are strong reasons to question both its plausibility and substantive importance. We support this view with evidence from a more realistic simulation study.

Having stated the models to be estimated and having discussed possible interpretations of their parameters, we turn now to the estimation of these models and tests of the theory. In order to avoid breaking the flow for those who are interested mainly in the qualitative patterns of results, we placed the technical material concerning measurement, estimation, and testing in Appendices A and B. Those interested in the precise procedures that we use therefore might consult these appendices before reading the chapters on empirical work.

4

Density and Founding Rates

We turn now to empirical tests of the theory of density dependence. This chapter reports our main results on founding rates. It begins by reviewing the considerable volume of prior research. It discusses several potentially important methodological limitations of earlier studies and proposes an alternative way to conduct empirical analysis of this issue. This chapter also reports new results on the effects of density on founding rates in all of the populations of organizations introduced in the first chapter.

Our presentation of results centers on two main questions. First, do the qualitative predictions about density-dependent legitimation and competition receive support from analyses of these diverse populations? Recall that the theory states that founding rates vary with competition and legitimation, which in turn vary with the density of the population and environmental conditions. It implies that density has a *positive* effect on the founding rate at low densities and a *negative* effect at high densities. In other words, the theory predicts that density has a *nonmonotonic* effect on the founding rate. The first main objective of our study is to learn if this is so, once the effects of environmental conditions and period effects and several methodological complications have been taken into account.

For our second question, we investigate whether any of the representations of legitimation discussed in previous chapters consistently outperforms the others in our seven empirical tests. These are the generalized-Yule (GY), log-quadratic (LQ), logistic, and Gompertz specifications. All build on the same assumption about the form of density-dependent competition, but they differ in their assumptions about density-dependent legitimation. Therefore, learning about their relative performance provides indirect information about the nature of legitimation processes.

Prior Research

In the first test of the theory applied to founding rates, Hannan and Freeman (1987) estimated a GY model for the population of national labor unions in the United States over virtually its entire history, 1836 to 1985, and found the predicted pattern of nonmonotonic density dependence. Barnett and Carroll (1987) analyzed rates of founding of independent local telephone companies in several Iowa counties during the early history of this industry (1900–1917) and obtained similar results. However, Barnett and Amburgey's (1990) study of foundings of telephone companies in Pennsylvania between 1879 and 1933 found the same pattern only in specifications that did not contain the effects of environmental covariates; adding effects of such covariates actually reversed the signs of the effects of density.

Studies of foundings of brewing firms in the United States from 1634 to 1988 (Carroll and Swaminathan 1991a; Carroll and Wade 1991) and in Germany from 1900 to 1988 (Carroll and colleagues 1989, 1992) found the predicted nonmonotonic pattern of density dependence in founding rates. Ranger-Moore, Banaszak-Holl, and Hannan (1989, 1991) also found the predicted pattern of effects when analyzing the population of banks in Manhattan between 1792 and 1980 and of American life insurance firms between 1760 and 1937. Ranger-Moore (1991) obtained similar results in a study of foundings of life insurance companies in New York state over a longer period (1812–1985).

Carroll and Hannan (1989b) analyzed foundings in nine populations of newspapers, Argentina from 1801 to 1900, Ireland from 1801 to 1975, and seven metropolitan areas in the United States from 1801 (or the earliest date of publication if later) to 1975. They found the predicted pattern of signs of first-order and second-order effects of density for each of the nine populations. However, these effects were statistically significant for only six populations, including the three largest. Olzak and West (1991) found the predicted pattern for founding rates of ethnic newspapers and newspapers directed at immigrant populations and African-Americans in the United States from 1877 to 1914.

Two studies examined founding rates of cooperative associations. Lomi and Freeman (1990) found the predicted pattern of density dependence for foundings of cooperative banks and business organizations in Italy for the period 1963 though 1987. McLaughlin's (1991) study of foundings of cooperative purchasing associations in Saskatchewan from 1906 through 1988 also yielded the predicted pattern of effects.

A pair of analyses of founding rates of voluntary social service organizations (VSSOs) in Toronto from 1970 to 1982 obtained mixed support for the theory. Tucker and colleagues (1988) found the predicted pattern of density dependence for the full population only during times when public funding was increasing. But, when Tucker, Singh, and Meinhard (1990) considered founding rates of specialist and generalist VSSOs separately, the findings agreed with the theory. The Toronto study is limited, however, by the fact that it examined only a short slice of the population's history.

Three studies estimated effects of density on the rate of *entry* of firms into an industry. Processes of entry into an industry likely differ from founding processes because entry includes foundings and adaptive changes of firms that operated in other industries. Not surprisingly, the results of these studies are mixed. Mitchell's (1987) study of rates of entry into the medical diagnostic imaging industry (1959–1986) yielded the nonmonotonic pattern of density dependence predicted for founding rates. Wholey, Christianson, and Sanchez (1990) analyzed entry of health maintenance organizations (HMOs) into metropolitan statistical areas in the United States between 1976 and 1988. Entries into a local market includes the founding of local HMOs as well as the creation of local organizations by national or regional firms in the HMO business. These results also suggest that the theory of nonmonotonic density dependence applies to entry rates as well as the founding rates. When analyzing entries of HMOs over an earlier period, 1971 to 1982, Strang and Uden-Holman (1990) found that the model holds for the two main subpopulations but that effects of density within each population are dominated by the effects of the density of the other. Finally, Hannan and Freeman (1989) found that density dependence in the rate of entry into the semiconductor industry was simply monotonic, thus not agreeing with the theory as it might apply to entries.

According to our reading of evidence from studies of diverse organizational populations, the theory has received strong support, especially when populations are analyzed over long historical periods. In a thorough review of the literature, Singh and Lumsden (1990) provided a similar assessment. Given our current state of knowledge, one might conclude that no more research on this issue is needed. But, we disagree, for two reasons. First, some of the earlier studies used methods of analysis that are far from ideal. It is crucial to evaluating the theory and the weight of evidence to know whether the findings of prior research are robust, and especially whether they hold up when more appropriate methods of analysis are used. Second, as we noted, different studies used different parameterizations of density dependence. For an apparently successful theory to be developed further, an effort must be made to reconcile the various parameterizations.

Methodological Issues

The previous studies used a variety of methods of analysis, including some that are ill suited to the data. Most of the data sets analyzed to date contain only yearly counts of foundings. Some published analyses allocated events randomly (or uniformly) within years and analyzed the resulting interfounding times (see, for example, Carroll and Hannan 1989b; Wholey, Christianson, and Sanchez 1990).[1] Other research used conventional time series analysis without correcting for the nonnegativity of counts or for the discontinuous nature of count data (see, for example, Delacroix and Carroll 1983; Tucker and colleagues 1988).

When earlier research used stochastic process representations that are appropriate to counted data, it has relied mainly on Poisson regressions (Carroll and colleagues 1989; Hannan and Freeman

[1] The labor union data contain a mixture of exact dates of foundings and dates that are known only to the year. Hannan and Freeman (1987) analyzed these data in two ways. They allocated the events with unknown month within years randomly and then analyzed the interfounding times. Hannan and Freeman (1989) also ignored the partial data on exact timing and analyzed yearly counts.

1989). This approach assumes that, conditional on the values of the covariates, a time series of yearly counts of foundings is a realization of a Poisson process (see Appendix B). This assumption implies that the number of foundings per year (Y_t) is governed by the probability law

$$\Pr\left(Y_t = y_t \mid N_t, \mathbf{x}_t\right) = \frac{e^{-\lambda(N_t, \mathbf{x}_t)} \lambda\left(N_t, \mathbf{x}_t\right)^{y_t}}{y_t!}. \tag{4.1}$$

Here $\lambda(N_t, \mathbf{x}_t)$ is a regression function relating the founding rate to density and other covariates. (In our research, of course, the exact form of the regression function comes from the alternatives that were introduced in the previous chapter and will be restated shortly.) Poisson regression methods typically estimate the regression parameters by using the Poisson probability law in Equation 4.1 to form likelihood functions for the data and then use standard methods of maximum likelihood (ML) estimation. This approach has significant advantages over older ones based on conventional regression analysis. However, its value depends on the appropriateness of the Poisson assumption. For a series of counts of foundings to be a realization of a Poisson process, the stochastic process must consist of independent increments with constant rate (conditional on the values of covariates). This implies that the expected number of foundings in a year will equal the variance of the number of foundings in that year. Both of these assumptions (inherent in the use of Poisson regression with time-series data on counts of foundings) are problematic in the context of the present studies.

Empirical research in other sciences seldom finds that the mean equals the variance, even approximately, as the Poisson process implies. Instead, it has been common to find the condition called *overdispersion* in which the variance of event counts exceeds the mean, often by a considerable margin. Such a result can arise for a number of different reasons, including unobserved heterogeneity in founding rates and "contagion." In this context, contagion means that the occurrence of an event affects the rate of subsequent occurrence. Either unobserved heterogeneity or positive contagion can generate overdispersion.

Both interpretations of the source of overdispersion fit our research context. Founding rates likely fluctuate randomly over time, net of the effects of density and covariates, owing to unmeasured changes in environments. Autocorrelation in founding rates is also likely. Previous research generally finds that counts of foundings in the previous year generally have significant positive effects on founding rate. This is a form of contagion between years. There is every reason for suspecting that contagion does not also operate *within* years as well.

Indeed, our analyses yield clear evidence of substantial overdispersion in the data on organizational foundings, as we shall describe shortly. We shifted from Poisson regression to two approaches that allow us to deal explicitly with the problem of overdispersion. One approach uses the negative binomial probability law, particular assumed relations between the mean and the variance, and the method of ML estimation. Appendix B provides details on the derivation of the negative binomial regression as an implication of unobserved heterogeneity in Poisson regressions and describes our assumptions about the form of overdispersion (the relationship between the variance and the mean). The second approach specifies particular relations between the mean and the variance without specifying an exact probability law and uses the method of quasi-likelihood (QL) estimation. Appendix B also discusses this approach to estimating processes with overdispersion.

Another potentially important complication has so far escaped attention in research on organizational foundings—*autocorrelation.* It seems unlikely that the founding rate in one year is independent of the founding rate in the previous year, as is assumed implicitly in ML estimation of Poisson regressions and negative binomial regressions. Previous research on density dependence in founding rates implicitly assumed independence of observations from year to year. We take account of autocorrelation in order to check this assumption and the impact of its likely inapplicability on pattern of effects of density. (Appendix B explains the formulation we use.) This change in assumptions has major implications for estimation, even when one assumes a very simple structure of autocorrelation. In particular, the likelihood functions for such structures has not yet been derived. The most feasible approach at this point is to shift from ML estimation to QL estimation, as we describe in Appendix B.

The results reported in this chapter come from analyses that explicitly treat the problems of overdispersion and autocorrelation. We used both quasi likelihood and the more familiar method of maximum likelihood (and the negative binomial probability law) when analyzing founding processes with overdispersion only. Although the two estimators are not identical in this case, they yield very similar results. Importantly, a choice between them does not affect any of the substantive conclusions. However, once we allow autocorrelation, we can no longer use ML (given the current development of these methods). Instead, we use a generalization of QL developed by Zeger (1988), which is described in Appendix B.

As we noted, our ML analyses revealed that negative binomial regressions fit substantially better than do Poisson regressions for each population. The expected count of foundings does not equal the variance of foundings (conditional on the effects of covariates and periods) for any population. The results of QL estimation were the same. Moreover, taking account of overdispersion often makes a big difference in the findings. Specifically, estimates of density dependence from regressions with overdispersion often differ considerably from estimates from those that assume that the variance equals the mean (Barron and Hannan 1991). When this is case with our data, the correction usually makes the estimated effects smaller relative to standard errors, that is, less statistically significant. Therefore, the results of our reanalyses might diverge from those of prior studies.

We also found evidence of substantial autocorrelation of disturbances in most cases. Adjusting for this methodological complication also makes a real difference in some substantive conclusions, again reducing the statistical significance of effects in most cases. Hence, we also report estimates that adjust for autocorrelation and estimates of the autocorrelation parameter when autocorrelation is substantial, as explained later. When allowing autocorrelation does not improve the fit, we report estimates of processes without autocorrelation.

Experience in analyzing these data indicates the importance of controlling for the effects of environmental conditions when examining the effects of density on founding rates. We introduced such controls within the limits of information on environmental conditions for each population. Each of the effects of density reported in this chapter (and subsequent chapters) comes from analyses that control for the effects of covariates and period effects or time trends that have been chosen to represent the most important environmental influences.

Because the seven populations operated in quite different institutional contexts, the relevant environmental influences to be controlled also differ considerably. For instance, the founding rates of labor unions, banks, insurance companies, and brewing firms all have been affected strongly by legislative and regulatory events. However, the relevant legislation and regulations vary widely among forms. The crucial discontinuous environmental changes that affected brewing firms were the national Prohibition (the Twenty-first amendment to the Constitution and the Volstead Act) and various state prohibitions. The key events for labor unions were the passage of laws that facilitated or constrained union organizing. The key events for financial institutions were the imposition or relaxation of regulatory controls. We represent the effects of these and other legislative and regulatory changes by specifying that founding rates shift at the times that mark the onset of major changes in regulations.

These populations have also been affected by gradual changes in such environmental dimensions as scale (or productivity) of the economy or real wage rates. When data on gradually changing economic and social conditions are available, we introduce effects of metric covariates as well. Because the periods and relevant covariates differ by population and because the effects of these variables have been presented in the separate publications devoted to each population, we do not discuss them in this and subsequent chapters. Appendix A tells which covariates, period effects, and trends we used for each population.

A final point before turning to substantive findings concerns statistical inference: As will become clear, we place the most weight on the pattern of signs of effects over replications. But, we also present information about the likely random noise (sampling variation) in estimates. We report estimated standard errors of estimates of effects (in parentheses in all tables) as well as indications of statistical significance (at the 5% level). Given that the theory makes directional predictions for effects, we use one-tailed tests throughout. In the case of the GY model's first-order effect, this is not strictly appropriate, as the prediction is that the effect is positive and less than one. However, it is not misleading in this context to rely on the same directional tests in all cases.

Generalized-Yule and Log-Quadratic Models

The first question concerns the *signs* of the first-order and second-order effects of density. The most basic implication of our theory is that the founding rate increases with density in the lower range of density. This means that the first-order effect of density is positive. The general theory also assumes that density increases the intensity of competition at an increasing rate and that the founding rate is inversely proportional to the intensity of competition. Thus the second-order effect of density is negative.

The foregoing chapters made clear that the line of theory and research that we follow began with a generalized-Yule (GY) model of density-dependent legitimation and competition (Equation 3.16). The distinctive feature of the GY model is its assumption that legitimation increases with density at a decreasing rate. We estimated GY models with the form

$$\lambda(t) = N_t^\alpha \exp\left(\gamma N_t^2 + \mathbf{x}_t' \boldsymbol{\pi}\right) \epsilon_t, \qquad \gamma = -\beta, \qquad (4.2a)$$

where ϵ_t is a stochastic disturbance assumed to have the gamma distribution indicated in Appendix B. The theoretically motivated hypotheses are

$$0 < \alpha < 1; \qquad \gamma < 0. \qquad (4.2b)$$

At this first stage we also considered estimates of the simple alternative discussed in Chapter 3, the log-quadratic (LQ) approximation that assumes that legitimation increases with density at an increasing rate in the lower range of density. However, it does not sit as well with the theory, in that it assumes either that legitimation increases with density at an increasing rate over the full range of density or that legitimation eventually declines with increasing density. Nonetheless, as we noted earlier, some previous research has found that this approximation fits better than the GY model does. The LQ specifications as estimated have the form

$$\lambda(t) = \exp\left(\theta_1 N_t + \theta_2 N_t^2 + \mathbf{x}_t' \boldsymbol{\pi}\right) \epsilon_t. \qquad (4.3a)$$

In this case, the hypotheses drawn from the theory are

$$\theta_1 > 0; \qquad \theta_2 < 0. \qquad (4.3b)$$

Our strategy is to retain the GY model, which we prefer on theoretical grounds, unless the fit of the LQ approximation is clearly superior. Our interest in the GY model leads us to the following strategy in reporting findings. We report estimates of the GY model for each population and estimates of the LQ specification for four populations in which it fits better than the GY model does: unions and the three populations of newspapers. Finally, we also report estimates of the LQ specification for one case in which it does not improve the fit but still gives interesting results—brewers. All of the estimates appear in Table 4.1.

The pattern of estimates of the GY model agrees with the theoretical predictions in all seven cases. The estimated first-order effect (α) falls between zero and one in each case. The second-order effect of density (γ) is negative, as predicted, for five of seven populations. These estimates agree with the claim that founding rates are proportional to legitimation which increases with density at a decreasing rate. Estimates of the second-order effect support, albeit less univocally, the claim that founding rates are inversely proportional to competition, which increases with density at an increasing rate.

Yet the GY model does not always outperform the LQ approximation. As we noted, we obtain notably better fits from the latter for labor unions and the three populations of newspapers. In the context of the QL estimation, which underlies this analysis, better fit means smaller average residuals, as measured by Pearson's chi-square. Our decisions, however, are not based on these comparisons alone, as we conducted extensive ML estimation of parallel specifications without autocorrelation and find that comparative fits as judged by log likelihoods or likelihood-ratio tests versus constant rate processes lead to the same conclusions about relative fits over populations.

When the LQ specification fits better, the pattern of estimates of the effects of density still agrees with the theory. The first-order effect is positive and the second-order effect is negative in all four cases. It is interesting that the alternative LQ specification yields results that agree with the theory for brewers, in that the first-order effect of density is positive and significant and the second-order effect is negative and significant. We have not been able to determine the source of this discrepancy.

We noted earlier that prior research ignored potential problems of autocorrelation, which seems likely to be present in time-series data

Table 4.1. Effects of density on founding rates: QL estimates of generalized-Yule and log-quadratic models with overdispersion and auto-correlation

Population	Model	First-Order Effect	Second-Order Effect[a]	$\hat{\rho}$	X^2
Banks	GY	.642*	−.082*	−.491	199.7
(1792–1980)		(.188)	(.022)		
Brewers	GY	.611*	.0001	0	997.8
(1634–1988)		(.048)	(.0001)		
	LQ	.0024*	−.0006*	0	1196.9
		(.0008)	(.0001)		
Labor unions	GY	.326*	−.028*	−.572	127.2
(1837–1984)		(.076)	(.015)		
	LQ	.034*	−.145*	−.476	120.8
		(.006)	(.028)		
Life insurance cos.	GY	.768*	−.021*	−.213	220.0
(1760–1937)		(.227)	(.004)		
Newspapers					
Argentina	GY	.282*	−.004*	0	136.5
(1801–1900)		(.130)	(.002)		
	LQ	.009	−.097	0	131.8
		(.013)	(.077)		
Ireland	GY	.582*	−.002	−.366	240.9
(1801–1974)		(.132)	(.005)		
	LQ	.013*	−.033*	−.332	232.8
		(.004)	(.013)		
San Francisco	GY	.275*	.013	−.541	165.9
(1841–1974)		(.079)	(.011)		
	LQ	.005*	−.0063*	−.455	162.0
		(.002)	(.0037)		

*$p < .05$ (one-tailed);   [a] Coefficient multiplied by 1000.
Note: Standard errors are given in parentheses; X^2 is the Pearson chi-square statistic. All models contain effects of covariates, time trends, or period effects—see Appendix A for details. The specification with a quadratic relationship between mean and variance is used for all populations.

on event counts. We find evidence of substantial autocorrelation in ϵ_t in five of seven populations. Table 4.1 reports estimates of the autocorrelation parameter, ρ, for these populations. In all cases, $\hat{\rho}$ is negative. This result is perhaps surprising, though it should be remembered that these all these estimates are obtained from analyses that control for the effect of the lagged number of foundings. In most cases, autocorrelation is also substantial, and taking it into account improves fit greatly. But despite the apparent strength of autocorrelation, density dependence has the predicted pattern. The pattern of density dependence, reported in previous research, appears to be robust with respect to potential confounding effects of autocorrelation.

Logistic and Gompertz Models

Do models that specify an S-shaped relation between density and legitimation provide a clearer picture of the process? Recall that the logistic and Gompertz models of legitimation imply that the initial growth of density away from zero has merely a slight impact on legitimation. But they also imply a ceiling on the growth of legitimation in agreement with the GY model but in opposition to the LQ approximation.

These more complicated models represent the growth of legitimation as a function of density in terms of three parameters: L_0, the level of legitimation at zero density (the floor on the process); L^*, the maximum level of legitimation (the ceiling on the process); and α, the rate at which legitimation grows from floor to ceiling as density rises.

We estimated logistic models of the form

$$\lambda(t) = \left(\frac{L^*}{1 + \left[\frac{L^*}{L_0} - 1\right] e^{-\alpha N_t}}\right) \exp\left(\gamma N_t^2 + \mathbf{x}_t'\boldsymbol{\pi}\right) \epsilon_t, \qquad (4.4)$$

and Gompertz models of the form

$$\lambda(t) = L^* \exp\left(-ce^{-\alpha N_t}\right) \exp\left(\gamma N_t^2 + \mathbf{x}_t'\boldsymbol{\pi}\right) \epsilon_t, \qquad c = r_0/\alpha. \quad (4.5)$$

Our initial work with logistic and Gompertz models of legitimation included a detailed comparison of the estimates of the two models for national labor unions (Hannan 1991). This and subsequent comparisons for other populations revealed that they agree rather closely. They yield similar estimates of floor and ceiling levels of legitimation and they imply very similar relationships between density and founding rates. We concluded that little of substance will be gained from reporting estimates of both of them.

Moreover, reliable discrimination between these two models of legitimation requires a huge number of observations, many more than are available in our studies. The reason is that their growth paths differ only in the mid-range of density, where data are very sparse. The sparsity of data in the mid-range of density follows as an implication of the pattern of population growth. That is, after a period of slow growth at low density, the numbers grow very rapidly during a brief period before stabilizing. Such a growth pattern makes the distribution of observed density quite unusual. Whereas we normally expect to find observations clustered in the center of a distribution and for the tails to be thin, the pattern is reversed for the density of organizational populations. Because these populations spent much time at low density and at relatively high density and relatively little time in making the transition between them, most years of observation have either low or high density.

More generally, the theory underlying this research implies that such sparsity is endemic to the phenomenon, because founding rates rise and mortality rates fall in the mid-range of density, because of the effects of density-dependent legitimation. Therefore, growth in density is most rapid in the mid-range because density rises when foundings exceed mortalities. Hence, populations tend to traverse the mid-range of density quickly, if the theory is correct, producing few years of observation on behavior in this range. This implies that it may be inherently difficult to distinguish sharply among models of density dependence in organizational evolution whose main differences concern behavior in the mid-range of density.

For these reasons, we now focus solely on the Gompertz model because it is less restrictive (in not imposing symmetry in the S shape of the growth path) and easier to estimate. Even though it is relatively easy to estimate, we never succeeded in obtaining convergent ML estimates of the Gompertz model (or, for that matter, the

Table 4.2. Gompertz models of founding rates: QL estimates of regression models with overdispersion and autocorrelation

	$\hat{\alpha}$	$\hat{\gamma}^a$	$\hat{c}$	$\hat{\rho}$	X^2
Labor unions	.178*	−.014	2.31*	−.541	116.8
	(.085)	(.015)	(.544)		
Life insurance cos.	.055*	−.018*	6.09*	−.347	194.6
	(.012)	(.004)	(1.64)		

*$p < .05$; ^{a}Coefficient multiplied by 1000.

Note: Standard errors are given in parentheses; X^2 is the Pearson chi-square statistic. All models contain effects of sets of covariates, period effects, and/or time trends—see Appendix A.

logistic model) for the population of breweries. We also learned that the Gompertz actually fits less well than the simpler LQ specification for the Argentine and Irish newspapers and about as well as the simpler, best-fitting model for San Francisco Bay Area newspaper publishers and Manhattan banks. The improvement in fit with the Gompertz is substantial for life insurance companies and moderate for labor unions.

Continuing the strategy of retaining complications only when they improve fits, we report estimates of the Gompertz model just for labor unions and life insurance companies (Table 4.2). Both first-order effects of density, $\hat{\alpha}$, are positive and significant, as predicted. Both second-order effects of density are also negative as predicted; however, this effect is not significant for unions.

Figure 4.1 compares the implications of estimates of the Gompertz model (Table 4.2) with those of the generalized-Yule and log-quadratic models (Table 4.1) for founding rates of labor unions. The three specifications agree that the founding rate rises substantially and then falls substantially over the observed range of density. In other words, estimates of each model tell that the relationship between density and the founding rate of labor unions has an inverted-U shape, as hypothesized. But, the details of the relationships differ. The Gompertz and generalized-Yule functions turn from positive to negative at a considerably lower density than the LQ function and do not rise as much. More generally, the two specifications preferred on

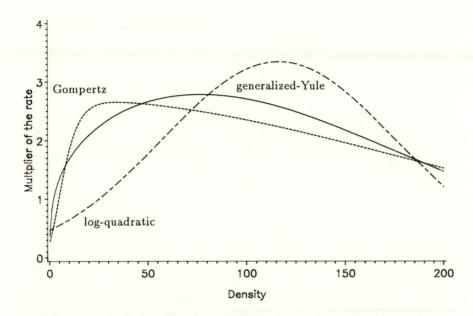

Figure 4.1. Effect of density on the founding rate of labor unions according to generalized-Yule, log-quadratic, and Gompertz models

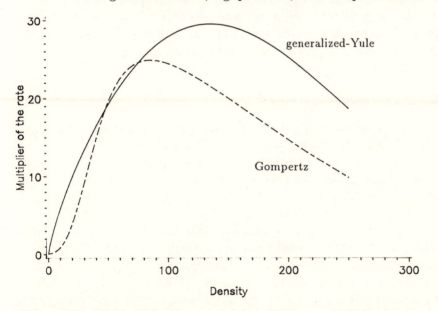

Figure 4.2. Effect of density on the founding rate of life insurance companies according to generalized-Yule and Gompertz models

theoretical grounds (GY and Gompertz) turn out to be quite similar over the full range of density.

Figure 4.2 compares the implications of the GY and Gompertz models for the relationship between density and the founding rate for life insurance companies. The two give similar qualitative patterns as was the case for labor unions. Note, however, that the GY function rises more rapidly initially and rises to a higher peak than the Gompertz function does. Assuming an S-shaped relation between density and legitimation dampens the strength of the estimated effect of legitimation on this founding rate.

Theoretical Implications

Because we presented several sets of estimates, it may be helpful to summarize the results in a simple table. Table 4.3 indicates which specification best fits each population. When simple models fit nearly as well as more complicated ones do, we give preference to the simpler ones. The remainder of the table reports the signs of the first-order and second-order effects of density, whether these effects are statistically significant and whether the pattern of density dependence has the predicted nonmonotonic form. This summary table helps organize our answers to the questions that motivated our research.

The Qualitative Predictions

The most important question asks, Do the implications of the qualitative theory hold for these diverse populations? The summary table reveals a strong tendency for density dependence to have the predicted nonmonotonic pattern. Only one of 14 preferred estimates has the "wrong" sign—the second-order effect for brewers. In our view, this is the most important of our results on founding rates.

Others with whom we discussed these findings put more weight on tests of statistical significance of parameter estimates than on the pattern of signs. If statistical significance is the central issue, then it might appear that we have a somewhat weaker case. One way— the natural way for many—of reading Table 4.3 is as indicating that "only" ten of the 14 estimated effects are statistically significant individually. In this vein, a more accurate summary would distinguish

Table 4.3. Summary of effects of density on founding rates

Population	Model	First-Order Effect	Second-Order Effect	Non-monotonic
Banks	GY	+*	−*	yes
Brewers[b]	GY	+*	+	no
Labor unions	Gomp.	+*	−	yes
Life Insurance cos.	Gomp.	+*	−*	yes
Newspapers				
Argentina	LQ	+	−	yes
Ireland	LQ	+*	−*	yes
S.F. Bay Area	LQ	+*	−*	yes

*$p < .05$ (one-tailed test);
[b] Both first-order and second-order effects of density are in the predicted direction and significant when the LQ model is used for this population.

the two effects. Then it is clear that the first-order effect works as predicted in that six of seven of the estimates are individually significant. But just four of the seven estimates of the second-order effect are significant. Should we then accept the portion of the theory dealing with density-dependent legitimation but reject the part dealing with density-dependent competition?

Given our strategy of replication, we think that rejecting part of the argument based on these results would be a mistake. It would seem to make more sense to consider the set of results jointly than singly. A joint test seems more appropriate here than seven (or 14) individual ones. We are unsure how to construct a formal joint test that takes account of the differing variability of estimates across studies because the sets of covariates used in each analysis differ. However, one can easily design some informal joint tests that give a sense of the likely result. For instance, consider the set of signs of the two effects of density. As we noted, 13 of 14 agree with the predictions of the theory. Now consider the null hypothesis that the theory is mistaken, which presumably implies that positive and negative effects are equally likely in samples of data. Then a simple application of the binomial theorem gives the probability of 13 "successes" in 14 trials as .00085. Using this reasoning, fewer than one time in a thousand would one obtain signs of effects over seven independent replications that agree so closely with the theory simply by chance.

The signs can agree with the predictions of the theory without the relationships changing sign over the observed ranges of density. For instance, the founding rate might simply rise with density at a decreasing rate over the range but never actually turn down. Do the estimated relationships between density and the founding rates actually change slope from positive to negative within the observed ranges? Table 4.4 provides the relevant information. The first and second columns report the observed minimum (N^{min}) and maximum density (N^{max}) for each population. The third column reports the maximum in the estimated relationship between density and the founding rate (N^*). The figures in this column indicate the densities at which the estimated founding rates reach their maximum levels (net of effects of covariates, time trends, and period effects). When the first-order effect of density is positive and the second-order effect is negative, the founding rate is a maximum at this level. At densities below N^*, the founding rate rises with increasing density; above N^*, the founding rate decreases with increasing density. We can see that N^* falls within the observed range of density for each population; the estimates of the best-fitting models do indeed imply that the relationship between density and the founding rate has the form of an inverted U within the range of observed variation in density for five populations. For a sixth, the San Francisco Bay Area newspaper publishers, the maximum falls just beyond the range of the data, and the function relating density to the founding rate is flat at the upper range of the data.

Pattern of Density Dependence

There appears to be little doubt that density has some form of non-monotonic relationship with organizational founding rates, although the summary table reveals that no one mathematical model of this relationship dominates empirically. Consider the one with which this research program began, the GY model, which builds on the assumption that density increases legitimation at a decreasing rate. The GY model fits best only for banks and brewers. For labor unions and

Table 4.4. Qualitative implications of estimates of density dependence in founding rates according to estimates of best-fitting models

	Model	$N^{\min}$	$N^{\max}$	N^*	$\widehat{\lambda}^*$	$\dfrac{\widehat{\lambda}(N^{\max})}{\widehat{\lambda}^*}$
Banks[a]	GY	0	154	62	10	.35
Brewers[a]	GY	0	2726	2071	20	.74
Labor unions[c]	Gompertz	0	211	35	6.1	.54
Life insurance cos.[c]	Gompertz	0	432	85	25	.03
Newspapers						
Argentina[a]	LQ	0	125	46	1.2	.56
Ireland[b]	LQ	0	224	197	3.6	.98
San Francisco Bay Area[b]	LQ	0	395	398	2.7	1.0

[a] Calculations based on the estimates of the GY model in Table 4.1.
[b] Calculations based on the estimates of the LQ model in Table 4.1.
[c] Calculations based on the estimates of the Gompertz model in Table 4.2.
Note: $N^{\min}$ and $N^{\max}$ denote the minimum and maximum values of density observed, respectively. N^* denotes the maximum in the relationship between density and the founding rate implied by the estimates; $\widehat{\lambda}^*$ denotes the multiplier of the founding rate at the maximum, that is, when density equals N^*; and $\widehat{\lambda}(N^{\max})$ denotes the estimated multiplier of the rate when density is at its observed maximum.

life insurance companies, the fit can be improved substantially by assuming that legitimation has an S-shaped relationship with density. For the three newspaper populations, the best fit comes from the LQ approximation, which we regard as less well motivated than the others. Our investigations suggest, however, that the LQ representation sometimes fits well because it agrees qualitatively with the logistic and Gompertz models that legitimation grows slowly with density when density is very low. It seems that differences among populations and their environments affect the details of processes of density-dependent legitimation and competition. It is therefore premature to settle on one of the parametric models.

Strength of Density Dependence

A final consequential issue concerns the strength of the effects of density on legitimation and competition. There are at least two meaningful ways to assess and compare effects of density. One considers the "direct" effects of density on the values of the functions for legitimation and competition; the other considers the relative strength of legitimation to competition. Figure 4.3 helps demonstrate how absolute and relative comparisons relate to the estimated effects of density on founding rates. It plots a hypothetical set of relationships, which agree with the implications of the theory under test. The top panel plots illustrative growth paths of legitimation (L) and competition (C) as functions of density: legitimation rises with density at a decreasing rate and competition rises with density at an increasing rate. The curves cross at a density denoted by N^{**}.

Recall that the theory assumes that the founding rate is proportional to the ratio of legitimation to competition. The bottom panel plots the relationship between density and the founding rate as implied by the curves in the upper panel. The maximum rate, λ^*, represents the point (level of density) at which legitimation has its strongest effect relative to competition. In the bottom panel of Figure 4.3, this occurs at density N^*. Recall from Chapter 3 that N^* denotes the turning point in the relationship, the level of density at which the marginal effect of adding an organization to the population on the founding rate changes from positive to negative.

But even when the marginal effect of density on the founding rate is negative (that is, $d\lambda/dN < 0$ which is the case when $N > N^*$), the legitimation process may still dominate the competition process in *absolute* terms. That is, there are values of density at which the marginal effect of density is negative but the level of the founding rate is nonetheless higher than the founding rate at low density. In fact, it is not until the multiplier of the rate drops below unity that competition dominates in an absolute sense. In Figure 4.3, this occurs at density N^{**}.

It should be clear from the figure that either legitimation or competition can be large in absolute terms but small relative to the other. For instance, increasing density may generate large increases in legitimation over some range of density, but these gains may be swamped by even bigger increases in competition. The large positive impact

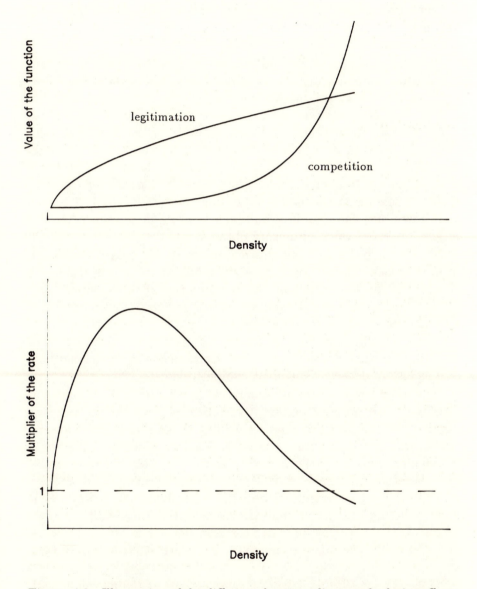

Figure 4.3. Illustration of the difference between direct and relative effects of density

of density on legitimation is lost in relative calculations, which emphasize the bigger effect on competition in such cases. Although the curves representing legitimation and competition will always cross at some level of density according to the assumptions of Chapter 2, this need not occur within the range of density observed empirically for a population.

It is not obvious which evaluations—relative or absolute—ought to be used in comparing effects of density across populations. But, because the theory treats legitimation and competition as opposing forces, it seems consistent with the theory to rely mainly on relative comparisons. We concentrate on two aspects of the estimated relationships between density and founding rates. The first is the magnitude of λ^*, which tells the maximum level of the relative strength of legitimation to competition. The second is the ratio of the multiplier at the empirical maximum of density $\lambda(N^{max})$) to λ^*, which tells how much the founding rate falls from its maximum when the largest observed value of density obtains.

We begin by examining the maximum of the relative strength of density-dependent legitimation. The fourth column in Table 4.4 reports the effect of density on the founding rate at the maximum, $\widehat{\lambda}^*$. Although the baselines of comparison differ slightly for the different specifications,[2] the ratio of the founding rate at its maximum to the rate in a very small population for each is given by $\widehat{\lambda}^*$. A larger value of $\widehat{\lambda}^*$ implies that density-dependent legitimation is much relatively stronger than density-dependent competition.

The populations vary considerably in the relative strength of density-dependent legitimation. This effect is generally stronger for populations composed of what we usually think of as firms: brewers, banks, and life insurance companies. (As we noted in Chapter 1, newspapers have often been tied to social and political movements and therefore sometimes differ from classical firms.) The weakest effect in this set of "business" populations is for banks, whose maximum founding rate is ten times that near zero density, and the maximum rate relative to the rate near zero density is 20 for brewers, and 25 for life insurance companies. By contrast, this ratio ranges

[2] For the GY model, this index compares the rate at the maximum with that in a population with one organization. For the LQ and Gompertz models, the point of reference is a population of size zero.

from 6.1 to 1.2 for unions and newspapers.

Thus the upper bounds of the strength of the legitimating effects of density relative to its competitive effects are *stronger* for the populations whose organizations are classical business firms as for those whose organizations are tied to social movements. In this particular sense, our results discredit the claims of Delacroix, Swaminathan, and Solt (1989) that legitimation processes operate only for non-business organizations.

Given that density drives founding rates upward strongly in most cases, does density-dependent competition depress the rates when density is high? An easy way to answer this question is by examining the relative strength of density-dependent competition at high density. The fifth column of Table 4.4 reports the ratio of the estimated founding rate at the highest density actually observed for each population, $\widehat{\lambda}(N^{max})$, to its maximum rate, which occurs at N^*. The comparison tells how much the founding rate declines from its peak as density reaches its observed maximum value.

At its peak, density-dependent competition has been strong relative to legitimation for all but the populations of newspapers. At one extreme, the founding rate of the population of life insurance companies dropped by 97% from its peak and that for banks fell by roughly 80% from its peak. Competition dominates in an absolute as well as relative sense in both of these cases. At the other extreme, our estimates imply that the relationship of density to the founding rate is relatively flat from the peak to the point of maximum density for the Irish newspapers and San Francisco Bay Area newspaper publishers. Interestingly, there is no clear ordering of strength of the relative effect of competition in terms of location on a continuum from firm to social movement. For instance, the (relative) competitive effect is stronger for "nonbusiness" labor unions than for brewers.

The results regarding the strength of the relative effects, like those regarding the consistency of signs of estimates of key parameters, provide valuable information for assessing the theory. These results tell that processes of density-dependent legitimation and competition have been powerful enough to have played major roles in shaping the evolution of these populations.

5

Interactions Between Subpopulations

So far we have considered only single-population theory and have estimated single-population models. Put differently, our arguments and empirical analyses have concentrated on intrapopulation competition and legitimation, the effect of a population's density on its vital rates. Restricting attention to such processes makes most sense when an organizational population has been effectively isolated from interaction with other populations or when the effects of other populations can be summarized well in terms of fluctuations in carrying capacities. For instance, growth in populations of certain kinds of firms such as commercial banks may improve the life chances for other populations by stimulating the flow of resources into a system. Such an effect can be represented by taking account of growth in available resources as long as interest focuses on populations that benefit indirectly from the actions of other populations.

In other cases, the impact of the growth (or decline) of particular populations has very specific implications for the life chances of other organizational populations. Then it does not suffice to attend solely to the indirect and diffuse (resource-based) effects of these dynamics. Rather, analysts must consider directly the specific interdependencies among populations. Incorporating these types of relationships among populations (or subpopulations) into the structure developed so far makes our modeling framework directly analogous to the general Lotka–Volterra framework of bioecology, discussed in earlier chapters. It also provides a way to represent a variety of sociological processes as well as historical arguments regarding the details of the evolution of particular populations, as we shall demonstrate.

Multi-Population Models

Interdependence among populations has considerable interest and importance when their fundamental niches intersect substantially. Although there are many diverse situations in which niches of interacting populations intersect, we focus on an important special case. This is the situation in which a population of organizations can be divided into two or more subpopulations on the basis of some differences in organizational form that can be argued to have implications for resource utilization. The fact that the two (or more) subpopulations can be considered subsets of a single population means that their niches intersect. But differences in organizational form allow the possibility of complicated interrelationships of the dynamics of the subpopulations.

When attention focuses on vital rates of populations (and subpopulations), two populations can be thought of as interacting if the density of one affects the vital rates of the other. The institutional histories of the pairs of subpopulations provide suggestions that links between them may have been complex. For example, the initial growth of one population might stimulate foundings of the other by legitimating the broad organizational form that defines the whole population of which these are subunits. But, the continued growth of the initial population might eventually depress the founding rate of the other by exhausting the finite resources needed for organizing. So it makes sense to consider both monotonic and nonmonotonic interdependencies.

In the simplest case, which Hannan and Freeman (1989) suggested might be common empirically, interdependence among populations can be represented by the monotonic effects of the density of each population on the vital rates of the other. If so, the growing density of one population will either increase or decrease the founding rate (or mortality rate) of another population, and the effect will be monotonic. Pure competition between a pair of populations means that the density of each decreases the founding rate and increases the mortality rate of the other. A mixed legitimating and competitive interaction occurs when the growth of one population legitimates the other, but the growth of the second worsens the life chances of the first by eroding its resource base. If the cross-effect involves only legitimation, the density of each population will increase the founding rate and lower the mortality rate of the other. Finally, interdependence may be asymmetric: One relation is present and the other does not exist.

The reasoning laid out in Chapter 2 and in the preceding discussion suggests that interdependence between subpopulations may be nonmonotonic. Indeed, Hannan and Freeman (1989) found this to be the case for subpopulations of independent and subsidiary firms in the semiconductor industry. The growing density of one population may legitimate another until its growing numbers become sufficiently large that competitive interactions come to dominate. In other words, the form of interpopulation effects of density might parallel those of intrapopulation density.

To represent such processes formally, we must respecify the intensity of competition. Let C_{ij} denote the competitive pressure on the ith subpopulation in the (possible) presence of subpopulation j. Then assume that $C_{ij} = g(N_i, N_j)$. Substituting this extended version of the competition process into the single-population generalized-Yule (GY) model (Equation 3.16) yields a model in which the founding rate of the ith subpopulation depends on its own density and the density of the second subpopulation.

We explored several ways of parameterizing the cross-effects. First, we contrasted results of analyses that specify monotonic cross-effects with those that allow possible nonmonotonic cross-effects. Adding a second-order effect of the density of the other population does not substantially improve fits for any of the populations we study. Therefore, we report estimates of simple monotonic cross-effects.

Second, we contrasted the fits of two representations of monotonic cross-effects: One uses a loglinear relationship and the other a power-law relationship. It turns out that choice of one or the other does not alter conclusions about the presence or absence of cross-effects. Because a simple loglinear relationship produces a better fit in most cases, we concentrate on it.

We expected that the representations of the effects of own density that fit best for the various complete populations (as reported in Chapter 4) would also fit best for the subpopulations. Nonetheless, we explored the fits of the three contending models. In two cases, banks and life insurance, we found that this assumption was accurate. However, this turned out not to be the case for labor unions.

As we shall explain, the log-quadratic approximation fit better than the Gompertz model did for founding rates of the subpopulations of craft and industrial unions.

We report estimates of models with the general form

$$\lambda_i(t) = \kappa_{\lambda_i}\, \varphi_i(N_{it}) \exp\left(\gamma_i N_{it}^2 + \zeta_{ij} N_{jt}\right), \qquad \zeta_i = -\beta_i, \qquad (5.1)$$

where $\varphi_i(N_{it})$ is one of the forms of density-dependent legitimation considered in previous chapters. For banks, we specify cross-effects within a GY model of the effect of own density. For unions, we embed the cross-effect in a log-quadratic (LQ) approximation of the effect of own density. For life insurance companies, we use the Gompertz model.

If subpopulation j competes with i, then $\zeta_{ij} < 0$. But if the relationship is symbiotic, this coupling parameter is positive. Finally, if the two subpopulations do not interact, then the coupling parameter is zero. Because we do not make any directional predictions about cross-effects, we use two-tailed tests of significance.

Empirical Results

Four of the data sets allow us to explore interactions between subpopulations: labor unions, brewers, banks, and life insurance companies. For labor unions, the forms are craft unionism and industrial unionism, the two forms that have dominated American labor organization. For banks and life insurance companies, the alternative forms are standard capitalist forms (commercial bank and stock life insurance company) and a mutual or cooperative form (mutual savings bank and mutual life insurance company). For all these cases, the pairs of subpopulations coexisted over most of their histories. The fourth case, brewers, differs considerably in that two new forms reemerged during the last decade or two of the 350 year history of the larger population. Explaining late resurgence entails some complications not shared by the other studies. For this reason, it makes sense to analyze the case of brewing separately, and we do so in Chapter 7. This chapter considers subpopulations of unions, banks, and life insurance companies.

We focus primarily on two questions. First, does own density have a nonmonotonic effect on founding rates within subpopulations?

Second, does the density of one subpopulation in a pair affect the founding rate of the other? Because the pattern of links between subpopulations turns out to differ among studies, it is simplest to consider the results for unions, banks, and life insurance companies separately.

Craft and Industrial Labor Unions

The population of national labor unions in the United States contained two main organizational forms over most of its history. The distinguishing feature of the craft form is that definitions of jurisdictions and target memberships are based on the boundaries of crafts or occupations. Craft unions sought to organize some, but usually not all, workers at a work site and in an industry, for instance carpenters but not other construction workers. The industrial form defines jurisdictions in terms of a set of crafts or occupations. Industrial unions attempted to organize all production workers in an industry or set of industries, regardless of job title or skill level. The difference between craft and industrial forms coincided fairly well with a crucial difference in political orientation. Craft unions were inclined by and large to engage in "business unionism." Industrial unions were much more likely to propose radical transformations of the organization of work. Most historical accounts of the American union movement conclude that these two forms of organization were indeed very different. This difference was crystallized in structures and strategies of their respective national federations, the American Federation of Labor (AFL), a federation of craft unions begun in 1886, and the Congress of Industrial Organization (CIO), a federation of industrial unions that broke from the AFL in 1933. For these various reasons we find it interesting to consider the dynamics of subpopulations of the two forms.

The craft form began first and grew large in numbers long before the subpopulation of industrial unions grew appreciably. Even after the New Deal reforms of the 1930s and the surge in industrial unionism, there were still many more craft unions in the United States. The maximum density of the craft subpopulation was 156, but the maximum number of industrial unions was 50 (see Figure 5.1).

How did the two populations interact? Leaders of craft unions and their federation tried to discourage industrial unionism and sought to incorporate unskilled and semiskilled workers into craft

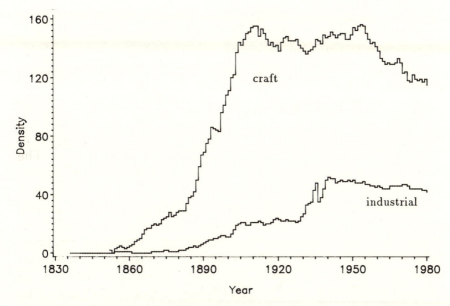

Figure 5.1. Historical evolution of the density of craft and industrial labor unions in the United States

unions as second-class citizens. Historical accounts of the American labor movement have emphasized asymmetric competition. Namely, the success of craft unionism had nearly succeeded in competitively excluding industrial unionism before the New Deal whose legislation changed the rules of the game. However, Hannan and Freeman (1987, 1989) found that the density of craft unions had a *negative* effect on the founding rate of industrial unions once the effect of the New Deal has been taken into account.[1] They also found that density of industrial unions had a strong, significant negative effect on the founding rate of craft unions. This appears to be an instance of symmetric competition.

We now report new results on these issues. We use a different functional form for the effect of own density (LQ approximations rather than the GY models estimated by Hannan and Freeman).

---

[1] This effect was significant when a partial-likelihood estimator was used; it was not significant in an analysis that involved maximum-likelihood estimation of Poisson regressions applied to yearly counts of foundings.

Table 5.1. Craft and industrial labor unions: QL estimates of effects of density on founding rates in log-quadratic models

Variable	Craft		Industrial	
	(1)	(2)	(3)	(4)
N_i	.057*	.060*	.073*	.067
	(.013)	(.013)	(.044)	(.094)
$N_i^2/1000$	−.286*	−.274*	−2.30*	−2.23*
	(.064)	(.064)	(.817)	(1.24)
N_j		−.029		.001
		(.027)		(.012)
Observations	149	149	133	133

*$p < .05$ (one-tailed except for cross effect).
Note: Standard errors are given in parentheses. N_i is the density of own subpopulation, and N_j is the cross-effect of density of the other subpopulation. Specifications for both populations include overdispersion and autocorrelation in addition to covariates and time trends and/or period effects—see Appendix A.

We also use somewhat different procedures.[2] And we use different stochastic assumptions (allowing overdispersion and autocorrelation) and a different estimator (quasi likelihood rather than maximum likelihood).

We began by estimating LQ and Gompertz specifications for each population. We tried both because there was little difference in fit between them when applied to the complete population of unions. Because the LQ approximation fit better than the Gompertz did for both subpopulations, we report estimates of the former here.

We begin with estimates of the LQ approximation whose estimates appear in Table 4.1 for the combined population of unions.

[2] The difference concerns treatment of the start of the series. Hannan and Freeman treated the first observed count as an outcome to be analyzed, which Chapter 4 argued is inappropriate. Therefore, we drop the first year of observation for each subpopulation and the string of zero counts for prior years for the shorter-lived population.

The first and third columns of Table 5.1 report estimates of the effects of own density (denoted by N_i) for the craft and industrial subpopulations. Own density has the predicted nonmonotonic effect for each subpopulation: The first-order effect is positive and the second-order effect is negative. Thus the basic theoretical argument is supported when the subpopulations of labor unions are considered separately.

The first-order effects of density are almost identical for the craft and industrial subpopulations (Table 5.1, columns 1 and 3). In terms of the theory, this means that the legitimating effect of each additional union (relative to the competitive effect) was the same in each subpopulation. But the second-order effect of own density is an order of magnitude greater for the industrial population than for the craft subpopulation. The fact that the relative effect of competition was much stronger for industrial unions depressed the density in this population.

Next we add the cross-effects of density of the other subpopulation to the basic single-population model (columns 2 and 4 in Table 5.1). The growing density of industrial unions depressed the craft founding rate; and the growing density of craft unions boosted the founding rate of industrial unions. But, neither cross-effect is statistically significant. Considering just the signs of the cross-effects, something like a predator-prey relationship characterizes the interactions between these forms. The growth in craft unions stimulated the foundings of industrial unions. But the growth of industrial unions depressed the founding rate of craft unions. Yet one cannot reject the null hypothesis that the founding rates of each subpopulation did not depend on the density in the other.

Figure 5.2 displays the qualitative implications of our estimates of the effects of own density on the founding rates of craft unions (solid line) and industrial unions (dashed line). This figure has two vertical axes; the right vertical axis gives the scale for the craft subpopulation and the left vertical axis gives the scale for the industrial subpopulation, which makes it easier to compare the forms of the relationships. It is clear that the relationship between density and the founding rates is strongly nonmonotonic in each subpopulation.

When evaluating Figure 5.2 (and those that follow), the different scales on the two axes must be kept in mind. The maximum multiplier for the craft subpopulation is roughly an order of magni-

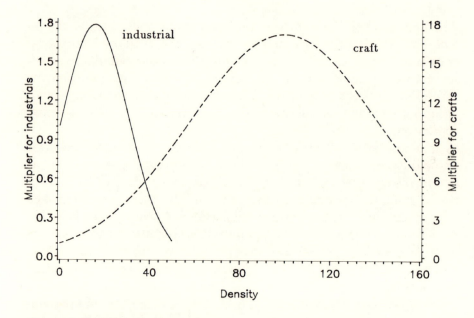

Figure 5.2. Effect of own density on the founding rates of craft and industrial labor unions

tude greater than that for the industrial one. The former reaches a maximum of 17 when the density of craft unions equals 100; the latter reaches a maximum of only 1.7 when the density of industrial unions equals 16. The reason is that the larger second-order effect of own density for industrial unions causes its founding rate to drop strongly when the population's density is quite low, keeping the number of industrial unions low (the effects are plotted exclusively over the observed ranges for each subpopulation).

This pattern makes sense historically. Industrial unions have broader niches than craft unions do, and thus they had more niche overlap within the subpopulation at the same density than the craft unions did. As a result, adding an industrial union to the population has a bigger relative impact on the population of industrial unions than would be the case in the craft population. Put differently, variations in the strength of density-dependent competition relative to legitimation explain why craft unions have always greatly outnumbered industrial unions in the United States.

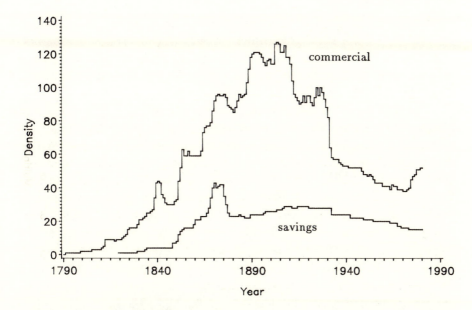

Figure 5.3. Historical evolution of the density of commercial and savings banks in Manhattan

Commercial and Savings Banks

Next we address the issues of density dependence within and links between subpopulations in the context of two types of business organizations, banks and life insurance companies. Following historical accounts of American banking, we analyze foundings of commercial banks and savings banks.

Federal and state governments traditionally made a strong distinction between commercial and savings banks in the ostensible interest of protecting the investments of two different types of customers. Commercial banks developed to facilitate business transactions, including those of the federal and state governments. Savings banks targeted their services at individuals and households. The rise in number of savings banks in New York resulted from a social movement to provide minimal financial security for households. During the early nineteenth century, social reformers sought the government's sanction for a form of banking that could provide such services. An alternative to commercial banks was favored because the latter were widely distrusted and because social reformers feared that reliance on them would tie workers more closely to economic cycles. When the state government began to charter savings banks, it distinguished them unambiguously from commercial banks by requiring that savings banks have a nonprofit status and by limiting the types of deposits that they could accept.

The first banks in Manhattan were commercials.[3] This form has always been more numerous than savings banks, and the trajectory of density of commercial banks has the same form as that of the composite population (see Figure 5.3). Density in this subpopulation peaks around 1910 at 127. The first savings bank in Manhattan was founded in 1819. The trajectory of subsequent growth of savings banks differed considerably from that of commercial banks. The number of savings banks initially grew slowly, grew rapidly in the post–Civil War period to a peak of 43, then declined abruptly during the panics of the 1870s and remained at a stable lower level.

Our survey of the institutional histories of the populations under study provided some conjectures about the likely forms of linkage between subpopulations. None has been drawn so clearly as to deserve the label *hypothesis*. In the case of Manhattan banks, state regulation sought to maintain a barrier between the subpopulations of commercials and mutuals. To the extent that such regulation succeeded, we ought not to find evidence of coupling between the two subpopulations. Yet regulation did not rule out interlocks between boards of directors of commercials and mutuals until the mid-nineteenth century and then merely proscribed such interlocks in cases in which the savings bank maintained deposits in the commercial bank. Indeed, Olmstead (1976) argues that differences in regulations applying to the two kinds of banks caused commercial banks to develop cooperative relations with savings banks in order to use them to engage indirectly in certain kinds of transactions forbidden to commercial banks, especially so-called call loans, those whose repayment could be demanded at any time. If this conjecture is correct, the growth in commercial banks stimulated the founding of savings banks.

[3] In defining commercial banks, we included trust companies that offer banking services. Because the management of personal estates requires such banking services as investing and holding deposits, New York State has always allowed trust companies and commercial banks to provide the same services.

Table 5.2. Commercial and savings banks: QL estimates of effects of density on founding rates in generalized-Yule models

Variable	Commercial		Savings	
	(1)	(2)	(3)	(4)
$\log N_i$	.627*	.653*	.902*	1.10*
	(.212)	(.219)	(.410)	(.527)
$N_i^2/1000$	−.114*	−.115*	−.943*	−.855*
	(.034)	(.034)	(.523)	(.534)
N_j		−.010		−.081
		(.016)		(.134)
Observations	189	189	161	161

*$p < .05$ (one-tailed except for cross effect).

Note: Standard errors are given in parentheses. N_i is the density of own subpopulation, and N_j is the cross-effect of density of the other subpopulation. The specification for commercial banks includes both overdispersion and autocorrelation; the specification for savings banks includes only overdispersion because the effect of autocorrelation is not significant. All models contain effects of environmental covariates and period effects—see Appendix A.

The distinction between commercial and savings banks has blurred in the twentieth century as commercial banks sought the accounts of individuals and savings banks have been granted wider powers to invest and offer time deposit accounts. At the same time, their roles in the larger economy have become more and more similar. Yet over the long period we study, the niches of the two forms surely differed. Consequently, it makes sense to consider separately the dynamics of the subpopulations defined in terms of this dimension of form.

Again we begin with the basic single-population model of density dependence applied to each subpopulation using the GY model, which fit best in this case (columns 1 and 3 in Table 5.2). As was the case with unions, the predictions of the theory of density-dependent legitimation and competition are supported for both subpopulations. Both first-order effects of own density are positive, and both second-order effects are negative. Each of these effects is also statistically

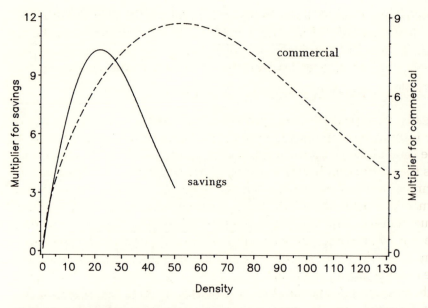

Figure 5.4. Effect of own density on the founding rates of commercial and savings banks in Manhattan

significant. Once again we find that the implications of the theory hold for subpopulations as well as for the combined population.

According to these estimates, the founding rate of commercial banks (dashed line) reaches a maximum when its density reached 52, at which point the rate is 8.7 times higher than at zero density (Figure 5.4, right vertical scale). The founding rate of savings banks (solid line) reaches a maximum when density equals 22. At this density, the founding rate for savings banks is 10.3 times higher than the rate at zero density (Figure 5.4, left vertical scale). Thus the effect of legitimation relative to competition was about half again more powerful for the population whose growth had more the character of a social movement. The effect of competition drives down the founding rate in each population by roughly half from the peak when density reaches its observed maximum.

We find no evidence of interdependence between these subpopulations. Adding the cross-effect of the density (N_j) scarcely improves the fit for either subpopulation. Despite the plausible claims that interlocking directorates between commercial banks and savings banks would have created links between the density of commercials and the founding rate of savings banks, the efforts by state regulators to maintain institutional barriers between the subpopulations triumphed in practice, at least insofar as founding rates are concerned.

Mutual and Stock Life Insurance Companies

Finally, we repeat the same procedures for the two subpopulations of life insurance companies. Historical accounts of the industry emphasize the difference between the stock and mutual forms, which parallels the distinction between commercial and mutual savings banks in terms of form of ownership (see Appendix A). Stock companies are owned by stockholders (who elect a board to direct the company) and issue "nonparticipating" insurance, which means that policyholders are not owners and therefore do not share in profits. Mutual companies, on the other hand, are owned by the policyholders who have the same rights as stockholders do in a stock company, including the right to shares of revenue. Beside differing in terms of property rights and forms of governance, the two forms also differed historically in terms of capitalization at the start of the business. Stalson (1942) indicates that stock companies usually began with much more operating capital than mutual companies did. North (1952) argues that capital reserves were crucial to the success of insurance companies in the rapidly expanding industrial economy of the late nineteenth century.

Unlike the two kinds of banks, stock and mutual life insurance companies conducted the same kinds of business in the same consumer markets, differing solely in form of ownership. The similarity of their business practices presumably meant tighter links between the two subpopulations than was the case for commercial and savings banks. The links may have been either positive or negative, depending on whether growth of one population tended to legitimate the other or to exhaust its resource base. The literature does not offer any clear indications on this issue.

The distinction between stock and mutual form was recorded for all but 76 of the 1064 companies founded before 1938. We did not include the foundings of these firms (7.2% of the total) in our analysis. Three other companies were excluded because their dates of starting and ending were not reported. These exclusions left 985 foundings to be analyzed. Some life insurance companies switched from mutual to

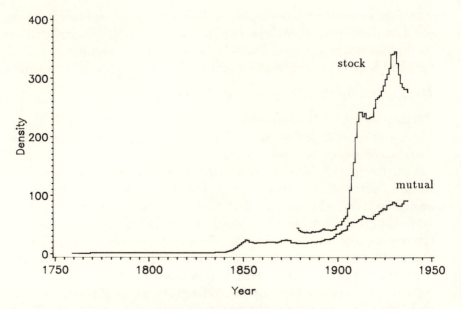

Figure 5.5. Historical evolution of the density of mutual and stock life
insurance companies in the United States

stock or vice versa. Although Stalson's counts of density do not take
account of such transitions, he provides an exhaustive list of all such
switches occurring during the lifetimes of firms still in existence in
1937. We did not treat these transitions as founding events, but we
did use them to correct the population densities that Stalson (1942)
recorded.[4]

Yearly counts of densities of these subpopulations are given in
Figure 5.5. The first American company to sell life insurance was
a mutual, the Presbyterian Ministers Fund founded in 1759. The
first stock company to sell life insurance, the Baltimore Fire Company, began in 1787. Although the stock population began later, its
numbers surpassed those of mutuals by 1818. The stock companies

---

[4] An exhaustive review of the New York Insurance Report ranging over
the years 1860 to 1971 indicates that such transitions were uncommon
in general and were almost unknown before 1900. We conclude that the
number of transitions for firms in the national population that failed
before 1937, a figure unobtainable from the data, is almost certainly very
small.

Table 5.3. Mutual and stock life insurance companies: QL estimates of effects of density on founding rates in Gompertz models

	Mutual		Stock	
Variable	(1)	(2)	(3)	(4)
N_i	.372*	.373*	.089*	.090*
	(.202)	(.197)	(.021)	(.026)
$N_i^2/1000$	−.510*	−.404*	−.023*	−.026*
	(.157)	(.242)	(.007)	(.006)
N_j		−.234		.039*
		(.312)		(.019)
Gompertz parameter	7.53*	7.74*	4.76*	3.60*
	(2.32)	(2.34)	(.929)	(1.10)
Observations	178	178	150	150

*$p < .05$ (one-tailed except for cross effect).
Note: Standard errors are given in parentheses. N_i is the density of own subpopulation, and N_j is the cross-effect of density of the other subpopulation. For stock companies, the model has overdispersion and autocorrelation. Because overdispersion was insignificant for the mutual subpopulation, the model specifies that the variance equals the mean (and that there is no autocorrelation). All models contain effects of environmental covariates and period effects—see Appendix A.

experienced a small peak in the late 1830s, and the mutuals peaked in the early 1850s. An increase in the number of stock companies from 1860 to 1870 caused the total population to rise before the panics of the 1870s. Likewise, the decline in stock density accounts for much of the decline in the size of the total population during the 1870s. After that, the numbers in each population resumed growing, though stock density rose more rapidly, peaking at 341 in 1930. Mutual density peaked at 96 in 1935.

Starting again with single-population models for each subpopulation, we find that the best fit comes from a Gompertz model, as was the case for the whole population of insurance companies. The founding rate of each subpopulation depends on density in the pre-

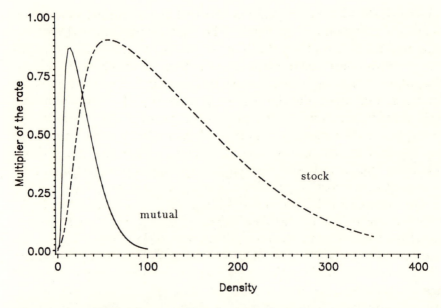

Figure 5.6. Effect of own density on the founding rates of mutual and stock life insurance companies in the United States

dicted nonmonotonic fashion (columns 1 and 3 in Table 5.3). Both the first-order and second-order effects of own density (N_i) agree in sign with the theoretical prediction. For mutuals, the pioneer subpopulation, both first-order and second-order effects of own density are significant. Only the second-order effect is significant for stock companies (column 4).

Figure 5.6 shows that the qualitative implications of these results correspond to those for the subpopulations of labor unions and banks.[5] Again the effect of own density is strongly nonmonotonic over observed ranges of density for each subpopulation. For mutuals (solid line), the turning point in the density dependent founding pro-

[5] In the Gompertz specification, the pure density dependence effect reaches a maximum multiplier of unity, so there is no need for separate axes for the two subpopulations. Differences between subpopulations in founding rates then appear as differences in the constants, period effects, and effects of covariates. For this reasons, the density multipliers for the Gompertz specification differ from those of the GY specifications used by Ranger-More, Banaszak-Holl, and Hannan (1991).

cess occurs at a density of about 25, and the empirical population reaches a maximum of 96 firms. The legitimation effect drives the rate up strongly and then the effect of competition within the population drives down this multiplier to the level in a very small population when density equals its historical maximum. The turning point for stock companies (dashed) occurs at a density of roughly 60 firms. This value falls well below the empirical maximum (341). Again, the multiplier of the rate rises to unity and then falls close to zero within the observed range. Put simply, both legitimation and competition processes appear to have operated strongly for both subpopulations.

Results for cross-effects differ greatly for the two forms of insurance company. For mutuals, adding the cross-effect (column 2) does not make any noticeable difference. Therefore, the subsequent growth of the population of stock companies did not affect the founding rate of mutuals. But for stock companies, adding the cross-effect does make a big difference. The density of mutual companies has a strong and significant positive effect on the founding rate of stock companies. The legitimating effect in this case comes from the other subpopulation, which pioneered the industry. This result makes sense in light of our view that these two subpopulations have been quite similar in business structure and market. The more similar the subpopulations, the more likely that the initial expansion of one will legitimate the other.

6

Density and Organizational Mortality

We turn now to density dependence in rates of organizational mortality. Even though the main questions are the same as those in Chapter 4, this chapter's structure differs in three main ways. First, the relevant stochastic processes have different state spaces. Founding, as we defined it, denotes a unitary event. (Recall that we do not regard starts by mergers or secessions as foundings.) Each founding means the creation of a new organization from scratch, and each presumably responds to the same causal processes. Mortality, as we shall see, is not a unitary event because organizational lifetimes end in several different ways. The rates of different types of mortality may be governed by different causal processes. Therefore, we pay considerable attention to different types of organizational mortality. We argue that the theory of legitimation and competition does not apply to all types, and we conduct empirical analyses to learn whether this is so.

A second difference is that we do not explore the fits of different specifications of the legitimation function in the context of organizational mortality. As we shall explain later, we settled on one specification. Among other advantages, this allows us to contrast results across different types of mortality in a straightforward manner.

Third, the units to which events occur differ for founding and mortality. We regard foundings as events to the organizational population (see Appendix B). But mortality involves the ending of identifiable organizations. This difference in units means that more kinds of covariates come into play in studies of mortality. Instead of studying exclusively the characteristics of populations, such as density, and those of environments, we must also consider the effects of organizational characteristics. The analyses reported in this chapter control for the effects of (1) aging, (2) recent foundings and mortalities, (3) organizational characteristics, (4) temporal trends and periods, and (5) environmental conditions. Finally, we use data on organizational size and industry output in an attempt to rule out mass dependence interpretations of the estimated effects of density. Appendix A gives the specifications for each population.

According to Theorem 3 in Chapter 2, contemporaneous density has a nonmonotonic effect on mortality rates. The strength of legitimation relative to competition causes the organizational mortality rate to fall with increasing density in the lower range but increasing competition eventually causes the rate to rise with density, when levels of relevant resources have been taken into account. In other words, the effect of density on the mortality rate is predicted to be *negative* at low density and *positive* at high density. If so, the mortality rate will fall with increasing density up to a point (the neighborhood of the carrying capacity) and then rises with increasing density. As in the preceding chapters, we are mainly concerned with evaluating the success of these predictions for the various populations.

For estimation purposes, we break each organization's age span into a set of nonoverlapping segments. This procedure is known as spell splitting in the literature on event-history analysis. It allows us to represent the effects of density and other variables that change over time. We associate with each subspell the appropriate levels of the organization's age at the start of the subspell, the density of the population at the start of the subspell, and so forth. Because many measures of environmental conditions are available as yearly time series and because density is known accurately only to the year (owing to imprecise dating of events within years), we split life spans into yearly subspells. When analyzing subspells, we assume that the covariates remain fixed within subspells, as is now conventional in such research.

We use only one parameterization for assessing the qualitative predictions about the nonmonotonic effect of contemporaneous density. This decision is based on comparisons of fits of generalized-Yule (GY) and log-quadratic (LQ) specifications of the effect of contemporaneous density, which revealed that the latter fits better for all seven populations. We also showed in Chapter 3 that complexity of the logistic and Gompertz models of legitimation precludes their use in analyses of mortality. Thus we concentrate on log-quadratic approximations. Recall from Chapter 4 that this approximation can agree closely with models of density dependence based on the assumption of logistic or Gompertz legitimation processes. For this reason, limiting our attention to the LQ specification is less restrictive than it might seem.

We thus report estimates of log-quadratic specifications of the effect of contemporaneous density:

$$\mu_i(t) = \exp\left(\theta_1 N_t + \theta_2 N_t^2 + \theta_3 N_{f_i}\right) \cdot f(\mathbf{x}_{it}, \tau_p, a_i). \tag{6.1}$$

Here $\mu_i(t)$ denotes the mortality rate of organization i at time t; N_t is contemporaneous density, the density of the population at the start of the year (in historical time) during that year; and N_{f_i} denotes density at the time of organization i's founding. The vector $\mathbf{x}_{it}$ is a set of relevant organizational characteristics and environmental conditions measured at that time; τ_p are period effects; and a_i is the age of the organization.

In terms of Equation 6.1, the key theoretical predictions about the effects of contemporaneous density are

$$\theta_1 < 0; \qquad \theta_2 > 0. \tag{6.2}$$

We also investigate whether the estimates of these parameters are such that the function relating mortality rates to density actually changes from negative to positive within the range of variation in density observed.

The original studies of density dependence in organizational mortality rates examined only variations in contemporaneous density. Chapters 2 and 3 pointed out that organizations may be especially sensitive to density at the time of their founding. Such an effect would be consistent with Stinchcombe's (1965) argument about the imprinting of social conditions at founding. It also follows from our arguments in Chapter 2 about the liability of scarcity and tight niche packing.

We specify a variant of Leslie's (1959) model of density delay in Equation 6.1, which claims that what matters is the density at the time of founding. Arguments about the liability of scarcity and tight niche packing suggest that the effect of density at founding is monotonic and *positive* (Theorem 4). It seems likely to us that such an effect has the same relative effect at all ages, which implies that the absolute effect is largest at young ages, because the mortality rate is highest at those ages. We estimate an effect of density delay with this property. We hypothesize that density at the time of founding has a positive effect on the age-specific mortality rate and that its effect persists over time. In terms of Equation 6.2, the hypothesis concerning density delay is

$$\theta_3 > 0. \tag{6.3}$$

Other social scientists, in discussing our work, have suggested a different scenario regarding density delay, one that might be called the "trial-by-fire" hypothesis. This leads to a different prediction, namely, that high density at the time of founding increases the mortality rate of new organizations but does not affect the mortality rates of individual organizations conditional on their level of frailty. But because frailty cannot be observed, the implications of this scenario for the relationship between density and the unconditional mortality rate after the founding period are far from obvious. An effect of density at the time of founding on mortality rates is an instance of an effect of contemporaneous density. Net of the effect of contemporaneous density, would founding density affect later mortality? The answer seems to depend on one's view of the length of the period of the trial by fire. We presume here that this trial lasts for the year of founding. Because the trial-by-fire hypothesis assumes that high founding density causes mortalities over a broader range of frailty, one interpretation is that the unconditional mortality rate is lower after the founding year for cohorts founded in periods of high density than for others. In terms of Equation 6.1, this counterargument implies that the persisting effect of founding density on the mortality rate is negative rather than positive as in Equation 6.3.

Prior Research

Density dependence in mortality rates has been studied in a great deal of earlier research. The first test again used national labor unions in the United States. Hannan and Freeman (1988a) were unable to estimate the basic GY model of density dependence in mortality rates with data on life histories of unions; the iterative maximum likelihood programs that they used did not converge to stable values.[1] Instead they shifted to a log-quadratic approximation. With this revision, their results strongly support the hypothesis that the relationship between density and disbanding rates (rather than overall mortality rates) has an inverted-U shape, net of the effects of age, period effects, and many different covariates.

Barnett and Carroll's (1987) analysis of independent local telephone companies in several Iowa counties between 1900 and 1917 and Barnett and Amburgey's (1990) analysis of all telephone firms in Pennsylvania between 1879 and 1933 found similar results.[2] Carroll and Hannan's (1989b) study of mortality in nine populations of newspapers found that the predicted pattern held in six of nine populations but that the point estimates of the effect of density were significant only for the largest populations: Argentina, Ireland, and the San Francisco Bay Area. Additional support comes from studies of trade associations (Aldrich and colleagues 1990), Manhattan banks and American life insurance companies (Banaszak-Holl, Ranger-Moore, and Hannan 1990; Banaszak-Holl 1991), savings and loan associations in California (Haveman 1990), medical diagnostic imaging companies (Mitchell 1987), American brewers (Carroll and Swaminathan 1991a; Carroll and Wade 1991), and West German brewers (Carroll and colleagues 1992; Wiedenmayer and Ziegler 1990). Hannan and Freeman's (1989) study of rates of exit of firms from the American semiconductor chip manufacturing industry also yields results that agree with the predictions.

Three analyses failed to find nonmonotonic density dependence: Tucker and colleagues' (1988) study of mortality rates of voluntary social service organizations in Toronto from 1970 to 1982, Staber's (1989) study of failure among Atlantic Canada worker cooperatives from 1940 to 1987, and Delacroix, Swaminathan, and Solt's (1989)

---

[1] In our reanalysis with different software, we obtained convergent estimates of the GY model with union data, which we will discuss later.

[2] Inclusion of a quadratic effect of population mass makes the effects of density nonsignificant in the latter analysis. However, the first-order and second-order effects of density still have the predicted signs.

analysis of mortality rates of California wineries from 1940 to 1985. As we demonstrate in Chapter 7, the negative results of Delacroix, Swaminathan, and Solt are very likely a consequence of their failure to obtain data on the period before Prohibition. In particular, we show that the predictions of the theory are supported for the population of American brewers when the whole history of the population is analyzed but do not when analysis is restricted to the post-Prohibition period. Likewise, this finding leads us to question the value of the evidence from the Toronto study and the Atlantic Canada study, which consider merely 13 years and 47 years, respectively, both late in the history of the population.[3]

The argument that density at founding increases mortality rates of organizations net of the effects of contemporaneous density was confirmed in Carroll and Hannan's (1989a) analyses of American labor unions, Argentinean newspapers, Irish newspapers, newspaper publishers in the San Francisco region, and American brewers. These results have since been replicated in studies of banks in Manhattan and American life insurance companies (Banaszak-Holl, Ranger-Moore, and Hannan 1990).

An important motivation for additional research on the effects of density on mortality rates is to clarify potential ambiguities arising from the possibility of multiple types of organizational mortality. Some previous research, such as Hannan and Freeman's study of unions, considered just one type of mortality—disbanding. However, most previous research did not distinguish among types of mortality events (for example, acquisition and merger) but instead estimated effects of density on a overall mortality rate. We think that some inconsistencies among findings from prior studies might be explained as consequences of differences in definitions of mortality events.

Results

The Overall Rate of Mortality

We first consider the rate of *overall* mortality. This choice has the advantage of being comparable for all seven populations. (The data

[3] The Staber study also apparently fails to model density as a time-varying covariate.

on newspapers and newspaper publishers do not allow distinctions among types of mortality.) But this choice has the potential disadvantage that aggregating over processes with differing dynamics and causal structures may obscure some of the processes of interest. Previous research on some of these populations indicates that density's effect on the rate of merger differs greatly from its effect on the rate of disbanding (Banaszak-Holl, Ranger-Moore, and Hannan 1990; Hannan 1989a). We follow our analysis of overall rates of mortality with one that distinguishes separate forms of organizational mortality for those populations for which the data allow such distinctions.

All analyses considered in this chapter include effects of organizational aging. For all except the newspaper populations, we use a Weibull representation of age dependence because it fits better than the Gompertz representation used in much of the earlier research. For the newspaper populations, we use a Gompertz specification of age dependence, because it generally fits the data better (see Carroll and Hannan 1989b).

We estimated the parameters of both Weibull and Gompertz models using maximum likelihood methods that take right censoring into account. (See Appendix B for details.) Because we have discussed elsewhere the effects of aging, environmental conditions and secular trends on the mortality rates of these populations, we focus here on the effects of density. We also report the coefficients for organizational age because of their importance to the overall population dynamics.

Table 6.1 presents the estimates of the effects of density on the rate of overall mortality for the seven populations. The hypotheses about nonmonotonic density dependence fare remarkably well for each population.[4] The first-order effect of contemporaneous density is negative for each population; and the second-order effect is positive

---

[4] Because the data on brewing firms before the nineteenth century may not be as reliable as those for the nineteenth and twentieth centuries, we also analyzed data for this population for the period from 1800 to 1988. The point estimates were very similar to those in Table 6.1, but the standard errors were slightly larger (the three effects of density were still significantly different from zero, nonetheless). See Carroll and Swaminathan (1991a).

Table 6.1. Overall rates of organizational mortality: ML estimates of effects of contemporaneous density (N_t), density at founding (N_{f_i}), and age

Population	N_t	N_t^2	N_{f_i}	Age
Banks (1791–1980)	−.035*	.189*	.010*	−.091*
	(.014)	(.064)	(.002)	(.037)
Brewers (1633–1988)	−.0010*	.255*	.00050*	−.180*
	(.0001)	(.027)	(.00003)	(.010)
Labor unions (1836–1985)	−.024*	.056	.007*	−.109*
	(.010)	(.037)	(.001)	(.041)
Life insurance cos.	−.035*	.191*	.010*	−.129*
(1759–1900)	(.010)	(.061)	(.003)	(.062)
Newspapers				
Argentina (1800–1900)	−.050*	.160*	.014*	−.194*
	(.010)	(.046)	(.004)	(.013)
Ireland (1800–1975)	−.015*	.027*	.002*	−.027*
	(.004)	(.012)	(.001)	(.002)
San Francisco Bay Area	−.015*	.018*	.004*	−.021*
(1845–1975)	(.002)	(.003)	(.001)	(.002)

*$p < .05$ (one-tailed test).
Note: Standard errors are given in parentheses. N_t^2 is measured in thousands for all populations except brewers for which it is measured in millions. All models contain effects of sets of covariates, period effects, and/or time trends—see Appendix A. Age dependence has a Gompertz form for newspaper populations and a Weibull form for all others.

for each population. Thus Theorem 3 receives support from the results for all populations.

Our density-delay hypothesis about the effect of density at founding (Theorem 4) also receives support for all the populations we studied. Density at time of founding has a significant positive effect on mortality rates in each population, as arguments about the liability of scarcity and niche packing predict.

Competing Risks of Mortality

What happens when we disaggregate mortality events by type? We investigate this question for different types of mortality in those populations for which it is an issue and for which the data allow us to do so: banks, brewers, and unions. Our research strategy uses the conventional competing risks framework for estimating the effects on different forms of organizational mortality. Briefly put, this approach treats all organizations as "at risk" for any given type of mortality until the organization is recorded as having experienced another type of mortality, at which point it is treated as though it were censored. As we explain in Appendix B, we do not attempt to analyze the underlying event-specific survivor functions for which the assumption of independence of competing risks (or some other strong assumption) is required. Rather we analyze the cause-specific rates directly, which does not require such an assumption.

We consider four forms of mortality, in different combinations for different populations according to the availability of the data: disbanding, absorption, equal-status merger, and suspension of operations. Disbanding means the cessation of the organization with its structure being dissolved rather than incorporated by another organization. (In the case of business firms, the legal event associated with disbanding is often bankruptcy.) Absorption by merger means that an organization ceases to exist as an independent corporate actor and its structure (including membership and resources) is incorporated by another organization. Equal-status merger means that two or more organizations join to create a new organization that combines elements of each. In such cases, each partner to the merger is considered to have ceased to exist as an independent actor, and a new corporate actor is considered to have begun. Suspension of operations, which applies here only to brewing firms, means that a brewing firms ceases operations because of the imposition of a legal prohibition (at either the state or federal level). Suspension, unlike the other events, depends entirely on the actions of other organizations.

The theory of density-dependent legitimation and competition was developed to explain disbanding rates (and founding rates, as we already discussed). It does not necessarily apply to other kinds of mortality. Both forms of merger, absorption and equal-status merger, contain a complication. The possibility of absorption depends on the availability of potential absorbers, and the possibility of merger depends on the availability of potential merger partners. The rate of each type of merger is presumably a positive function of density. At low density, the scarcity of potential absorbers and merger partners depresses rates of absorption and merger. Increasing density in the lower range presumably increases these rates. Such a force opposes the hypothesized process of density-dependent legitimation. Therefore, the estimated first-order effect of contemporaneous density on rates of absorption and merger combines two effects of opposite sign. The predictions of the theory need not hold in such cases even if it is correct for other forms of mortality.

Equal-status merger entails another complication. Organizations enter mergers for diverse strategic reasons, and merger does not necessarily signal organizational weakness or failure. The theory as stated in Chapter 2 does not provide any reason for suspecting that processes of legitimation and competition affect the rate of merger or, if they do, that they operate in the same way as for rates of disbanding and absorption. Finally, there is also no reason for thinking that the theory can explain a suspension of operations, prompted as it is (at least for these populations) by exogenous environmental events. We conclude that the predictions of the theory will receive less support for rates of absorption than for rates of disbanding and not at all for rates of equal-status merger and suspension. Therefore, when considering the separate forms of organizational mortality we are primarily interested in two questions. First, does the prediction of nonmonotonic density dependence hold for the rate of disbanding? Second, does the nonmonotonic pattern fail to hold for the rates of merger and suspension?

We present the key results—estimates of the effects of density (both contemporaneous and delayed) and of age—for the different outcomes in one table (Table 6.2) so that the patterns of effects across types of mortality can be compared easily. The general patterns of effects do indeed differ for different types of outcomes.

The predictions about contemporaneous density are supported strongly for the rate of *disbanding* for all three populations. That is, the first-order effect of contemporaneous density is positive and significant; and the second-order effect is negative and significant. As was the case in analysis of the rate of overall mortality, the effect

Table 6.2. Rates of specific forms of organizational mortality: ML estimates of effects of contemporaneous density (N_t), density at founding (N_{f_i}), and age

Outcome	Population	N_t	N_t^2	N_{f_i}	Age
Disbanding					
	Banks	−.034*	.132*	.015*	−.263*
		(.017)	(.079)	(.003)	(.058)
	Brewers	−.0009*	.022*	.00061*	−.226*
		(.0001)	(.003)	(.00003)	(.011)
	Unions	−.045*	.134*	.014*	−.122*
		(.014)	(.053)	(.002)	(.059)
Absorption					
	Banks	−.039*	.281*	.010*	.052
		(.023)	(.110)	(.002)	(.056)
	Brewers	−.0047*	.093*	.0011*	.563*
		(.0006)	(.029)	(.0002)	(.104)
	Unions	−.046*	.154*	.006*	−.039
		(.020)	(.075)	(.002)	(.083)
Merger					
	Banks	−.043	.319	.001	.321*
		(.041)	(.220)	(.004)	(.150)
	Unions	.035	−.184	.001	−.125
		(.021)	(.078)	(.002)	(.078)
Suspension					
	Brewers	−.0003	−.0005	.00001	−.107*
		(.0002)	(.0072)	(.00005)	(.025)

*$p < .05$ (one-tailed test except for Age).
Note: Standard errors are given in parentheses. N_t^2 is measured in thousands for all populations except brewers, for which it is measured in hundred-thousands. All models contain effects of covariates, period effects, and/or time trends—see Appendix A.

of density delay is also positive and significant for each of the populations. The implications of the theory hold strongly when applied to the rate of disbanding, as we expected. Indeed, in one way, confirmation of the theory is stronger in the case of disbanding rates than for overall rates of mortality. The second-order effect of density on the overall mortality rate was not significant for labor unions (Table 6.1); however, the parallel effect on the disbanding rate is significant. The greater consistency of effects of density on the rate of disbanding provides powerful support for the theory.

Effects of contemporaneous and delayed density on the rate of absorption are fairly similar to those on the rate of disbanding. The pattern of signs of effects on the two rates is the same. Contemporaneous density has a significant nonmonotonic effect on each rate for each population. And density at founding has a positive and significant effect on each rate for each populations. Roughly the same structure of density dependence applies to rates of disbanding and rates of absorption. Put differently, absorption and disbanding are similar outcomes from the perspective of density dependence.

But what about the effect of density on the rate of merger? Table 6.2 reports results for merger rates of banks and unions. Just one of the six effects of contemporaneous and delayed density on the rate of merger is statistically significant—the second-order effect of contemporaneous density for unions. However, this effect has the opposite sign of the parallel effect on the rates of disbanding and merger. Finally, as predicted, density does not affect the rate of suspension of brewing firms. In summary, the results in Table 6.2 agree with the argument that processes of density-dependent legitimation and competition apply to the rate of disbanding but *not* to rates of equal-status merger and suspension.

Controls for Size and Total Mass

In Chapter 3 we noted that some social scientists have advanced mass-dependence interpretations of our findings of density dependence (Winter 1990). Typically, these arguments take one of two forms. Either the observed effects of density are assumed to reflect effects of the mass of the population (the aggregate size of all organizations in the population) or they are thought to be due to organizational size, possibly confounded through aggregation. Although we cannot control for population mass and organizational size over much of the long periods studied, we can do so for certain shorter periods for which such data are available. If the effects of density remain strong and consistent with previous findings once such controls are introduced, then we are fairly confident in dismissing the suggestion that mass dependence masquerades as density dependence.

We analyze the effects of organizational size and population mass for brewers, labor unions, and life insurance companies. In each case we use the natural logarithms of population mass and organizational size as covariates in the loglinear specification of effects of covariates on the mortality rates to allow the possibility that effects of size have a ceiling or floor. We specify that each dimension of size has a power-function relationship to the mortality rate. That is, we estimate specifications of the form

$$\mu_i(t, f_i) = \exp\left(\theta_1 N_t + \theta_2 N_t^2 + \theta_3 N_{f_i} + \zeta_1 \log S_{it} + \zeta_2 \log M_t\right)$$
$$\cdot f(\mathbf{x}_{it}, \tau_p, a_i), \qquad t > f_i, \tag{6.4}$$

where S_{it} denotes an organization's size in the year in question and M_t denotes the total mass of the population at that time.

For brewers, the measure of total population mass refers to production in the industry, namely, the total tax-paid withdrawals of malt beverages in millions of gallons. This variable has been recorded from the various issues of the *Brewers Almanac* and is available for the period 1863 to 1984. For organizational size of individual brewers, we use the comprehensive listing of brewery production levels in 1878 and 1879 provided by Salem (1880). This allows us a rare examination of mass dependence in a period of high density, but it has the disadvantage of a short observation window. We introduce population mass and organizational size in separate analyses in order to allow each variable to have its maximum possible effect.

The first row of Table 6.3, which uses data only for the years 1878 and 1879, reveals that organizational size does indeed have a strong effect on mortality. (Because there are just two years of observation, there is too little variation in contemporaneous density to estimate its effect.) Smaller brewers go out of business at a much higher rate than large brewers do. Yet adding an effect of organizational size does not eliminate the effect of density delay. Founding density continues to exert a positive and significant effect on mortality.

Table 6.3. Effects of contemporaneous density (N_t), density at founding (N_{f_i}) on rates of disbanding controlling for organizational size (S) and population mass (M)

Population	N_t	N_t^2	N_{f_i}	$\log S$	$\log M$
Brewers					
(1878–1880)			.0008*	−.243*	
			(.0002)	(.041)	
(1878–1988)	−.0074*	.0022*	.00041*	−.127*	
	(.0006)	(.0002)	(.00005)	(.016)	
(1863–1985)	−.0011*	.00030*	.00044*		.00008*
	(.0001)	(.00003)	(.00003)		(.00003)
Labor unions					
(1836–1985)	−.041*	.116*	.015*	.045	
	(.017)	(.066)	(.003)	(.054)	
(1890–1985)	−.026	.090	.013*		
	(.049)	(.160)	(.003)		
(1890–1985)	−.021	.103	.015*	.043	−.518
	(.060)	(.190)	(.003)	(.062)	(.348)
Life insurance	−.058*	.234*	.009*		$.29 \times 10^{-4}$
cos.	(.015)	(.009)	(.003)		$(.39 \times 10^{-4})$

*$p < .05$ (one-tailed test).
Note: Standard errors are given in parentheses. N_t^2 is measured in thousands for all populations. All models contain effects of sets of covariates, age with a Weibull specification, period effects, and/or time trends—see Appendix A.

The result of our attempt to obtain useful estimates of the effects of contemporaneous density net of the effects of organizational size appears in the second row of Table 6.3. This analyses treats organizational size as fixed at its 1879 level and analyzes the lengths of lifetimes of all brewers operating in 1878–79, each followed for as long as possible. This approach allows us to introduce contemporaneous density but it has the disadvantage of not treating size as a time-varying covariate. So these estimates should be regarded with caution, especially the coefficient for size. Nonetheless, the findings are very encouraging for the theory of density-dependent legitimation and competition. Despite a strong and significant negative effect of size, both contemporaneous density and founding density show significant effects in the directions predicted by the theory and seen in Table 6.1.

The third row in Table 6.3 shows the result of adding an effect of total industry production. Population mass has a positive but non-significant effect on organizational mortality. Most importantly, the effects of density remain strong and consistent with findings from simpler analyses considered earlier and with the theoretical predictions.

For unions, the available measure of organizational size consists of a count of members at (or near) the time of the founding of the union. Because this measure is available for 507 of the 621 unions, we lose about a fifth of the union-year observations when we include size at founding as a covariate; the number of observed disbandings falls from 191 to 146. The fourth row of Table 6.3 shows that adding size at founding does not eliminate the significant first-order and second-order effects of contemporaneous density (even though the number of events and observations are considerably smaller). Moreover, the effect of density at founding remains positive and significant.

The available measure of total mass of the population of national labor unions is a count of total membership across all national unions. Unfortunately, the series from which these data were taken begins in 1890 when the density of unions was near its historic peak. Estimating an effect of total mass therefore requires analysis to be restricted to the period after density had finished its historic rise. The fifth row in Table 6.3 presents estimates of the basic specification (Equation 6.1) for the period for which a measure of population mass is available, 1890 to 1985. It shows that restricting attention to this late period makes it difficult to obtain precise estimates of the effects of contemporaneous density. (We treat in detail the implications of left truncation in Chapter 7.) The estimated standard errors are more than triple those in Table 6.2. As a result, neither effect of contemporaneous density is significant. (The effect of density at founding remains significant and positive, however.) Hence, the result of adding our measure of total mass, the total membership of all unions, cannot be very informative. Adding the effects of total mass and size at founding (sixth row) does not alter this pattern.

Each of the effects of density has the predicted sign, but only the effect of density delay is significant.

Finally, for life insurance companies, we measure population mass in terms of the aggregate assets of all life insurance firms in the population (in thousands of dollars in constant 1860 prices). The seventh row of Table 6.3 reveals that adding the log of total assets of the population does not affect estimates of contemporaneous and delayed effects of density. We continue to find that contemporaneous density has a significant nonmonotonic effect on the rate of disbanding (that is, bankruptcy) and that density at founding has a significant positive effect on this rate.

In assessing the claims of critics such as Winter (1990), then, we conclude that they have merit in suggesting that organizational size and population mass can be important determinants of organizational mortality. This is the case only for the population of brewers, however. More to the point of this book, we found no evidence that introducing these factors eliminates—or even diminishes—the effects of density.[5] Processes of density dependence appear to be separate and distinct from processes of mass dependence. Although we would prefer to be able to control for mass dependence in all of the analyses we report, data limitations frequently prevent us from being able to do so. We take consolation in the tentative conclusion that such omission has not contaminated estimates of effects of density in those cases in which we could control for mass.

Implications of Unobserved Heterogeneity

As we mentioned in Chapter 3, Petersen and Koput (1991a) claim to have discovered a related general problem in our interpretation

---

[5] As this book went to press, Banaszak-Holl (1991) reported findings for the population of Manhattan banks over the full two hundred year history of the population. With size of bank (assets) treated as a time-varying covariate in analyses of rates of bankruptcy, she finds that size of bank has a powerful negative effect on the rate. Including this effect essentially eliminates the effect of age of organization. However, contemporaneous density still has the predicted pattern of effects and is still statistically significant even when size of bank and mass of the population are taken into account in the model.

of tests of density-dependent legitimation and competition in rates of organizational mortality. They argue that the negative first-order effect of density is consistent with a simpler and thus preferable alternative explanation, one that relies on the operation of a certain form of unobserved heterogeneity instead of legitimation. In particular, they assert that unobserved heterogeneity produces spurious negative effects of density that persist even when organizational age is controlled. The relationship to the argument about mass-dependence is that the most likely source of unobserved heterogeneity is organizational size or mass.

Petersen and Koput (1991a) back up this claim with results from one trial of a simulation of the lifetimes of 10,500 organizations over 21 years.[6] They constructed a single population of 10,500 organizations consisting of five subpopulations with very different mortality rates that are constant over time and hence independent of density. Equal numbers of organizations are created in each frailty class in each year, so that the mortality rate falls over time because differential mortality leads to increasing underrepresentation of the high mortality subpopulations. And, in the simulation structure, density rises as time passes because density is just a monotonic transformation of time. This form of unobserved heterogeneity, when coupled with the special form assumed for the founding process, can apparently reproduce the negative first-order effect of contemporaneous density on mortality rates.

Because others are likely to think up scenarios in which our results might be due to the operation of some simple structure of unobserved heterogeneity, we consider this issue in some detail. We elsewhere questioned the generality of Petersen and Koput's finding and especially its substantive importance (Hannan, Barron, and

[6] They actually report estimates of one trial each of two simulation structures. Because the second simulation, which introduces a structural positive effect of density squared, does not introduce any new analytic issues, we concentrate on their first simulation. Curiously, a footnote to the concluding section of Petersen and Koput's (1991a) article reveals that they actually ran four trials of the first structure and that density dependence was significant in only two of the four. However, they do not otherwise acknowledge the inconsistency between the strong statement of their methodological claim and the weakness of the evidence on which it is based.

Carroll 1991). Using their computer programs, we showed that the result they report is *not* typical. We found that the effect of density was significant once age was controlled in just three of ten trials, even though the number of organizations analyzed in each trial is huge—10,500. Petersen and Koput (1991b), in replying to our analysis, argue that the logic of statistical inference requires only a very few trials to be significant in order to support their claim. Although their application of this logic is twisted in our view, we do not see any reason to rebut it because, as we demonstrate below, a more realistic simulation never produces evidence in their favor.

We also pointed out that our empirical research, and that of the other investigators cited in this chapter, controls for forms of (historical) time variation in mortality rates. This kind of control obviates the problem of spurious density dependence in the structure they studied because the average hazard of mortality declines monotonically with time and density rises monotonically with time under the structure they simulated. For example, age of population and density are so collinear in the simulated data that we were unable to estimate specifications with effects of these two variables that we could not invert the Hessian. In cases like the one in the simulated structure, researchers using the standard approach of controlling for temporal trends would not have been misled into reporting spurious effects of density because they would not be able to estimate any of the parameters. Weakening the association between density and time would allow estimation; but it would very likely also mean that controlling for temporal trends would eliminate the spurious effect.

Most important, the presence of unobserved heterogeneity does *not* create any pattern of spurious effects of density in a more realistic structure. We showed this by introducing stochastic variation in number of foundings in each frailty class for each year and analyzing smaller numbers of organizations over much longer periods. We modified Petersen and Koput's own simulation program to allow such variability. Because most of the empirical studies find many fewer organizations than 10,500 and consider periods longer than 21 years, we also modified the vital rates and length of study period to come closer to what researchers have encountered. Our revised structure still uses five frailty classes, but with each class having its own random flow of foundings. Thus we made what would seem to be a mild departure from the structure used to challenge our interpreta-

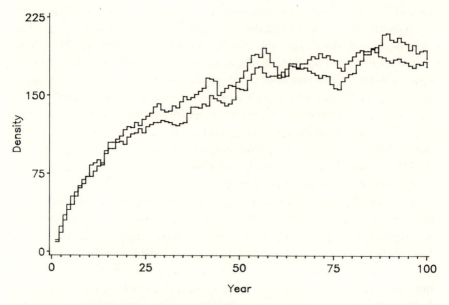

Figure 6.1. Illustration of two growth paths of density produced by the simulation of unobserved heterogeneity

tion of density dependence. Specifically, we assumed that foundings in each class follow a Poisson process with the same constant rate. We set the rate in each class to 2, so the expected number of foundings per year in each class is 2 with variance of 2. The expected total number of foundings is 10 which also equals the variance. We made the hazard of mortality constant over time in each frailty class, and we tried two sets of hazard rates. In what we call Simulation 1, the hazards were set at .05, .075, .10, .125, and .15. In this case, the average hazard in any founding cohort is .10, which implies an expectation of life of 10 years. In Simulation 2 we set the hazards at .025, .05, .075, .10, .125, with an average hazard of .075 and an average life expectancy of 13.3 years.

We simulated histories of 20 populations of organizations over 100 years, ten for each quintuplet of hazards of mortality.[7] We obtained paths of population growth over time that are reasonably close to

[7] The simulations and estimation were run using GAUSS programs (Aptech Systems 1991), the former written by David N. Barron, the latter supplied by Petersen and Koput.

those of empirical populations that we and others were studying, except that they involve much more rapid growth in density during the early histories of the populations.[8] There is fairly steady growth to a maximum over roughly 50 to 60 years followed by random fluctuation over the remainder of the simulated histories. Figure 6.1 gives an example of two growth paths of density from Simulation 2. Each trial generates histories of 1000 organizations on average over 100 years. The number of organization-years of data ranges from 10,200 to 11,140 over ten replications for Simulation 1 and from 12,903 to 14,859 for Simulation 2. (There are more observations in the latter because the mortality rates are lower.)

Because the key issue is whether density has a sizable and significant spurious negative effect net of the effect of organizational age, we concentrate on the specification with effects of density and age. Shifting to random founding rates (and analyzing fewer organizations over much longer periods) makes a very big difference. As shown in Table 6.4, slightly more than half (11 of 20) of the estimates of the effect of density in this situation are *positive* (in opposition to Petersen and Koput's story). Only one of the 20 estimates is statistically significant at the .05 level—just what one expects by chance when the effect is really zero. In this one case, the effect is positive, not negative. In data structures resembling those used in empirical research on density dependence, there is *no consistent spurious effect of density once age has been controlled.*

We also experimented with analyzing only the first 50 years of history produced by Simulation 2 (the one with more unobserved heterogeneity) in order to learn whether this decision affects our results. Specifically, we generated histories of ten more populations over 50 years using the same founding rates and mortality rates as in Simulation 2. In estimates of models of mortality rates with effects of density and age, the estimated effect of density was positive for five populations and negative for the other five. Considering only the growth phase does not alter the qualitative conclusion. We also experimented with more realistic founding processes. Overdispersion in founding rates weakens still more the association between density and the average hazard of mortality.

[8] We think that this difference reflects the operation of density dependence in the founding rates of real organizational populations.

Table 6.4. Effects of density and age on density-independent mortality rates with unobserved heterogeneity in two simulations

Replication	Simulation 1		Simulation 2	
	Density	Age	Density	Age
1	.344	−.097*	.082	−.144*
	(.188)	(.021)	(.102)	(.023)
2	.024	−.052*	−.119	−.120*
	(.166)	(.024)	(.111)	(.023)
3	.331	−.068*	−.129	−.105*
	(.212)	(.027)	(.142)	(.024)
4	−.0004	−.110*	−.080	−.151*
	(.182)	(.022)	(.102)	(.023)
5	−.097	−.059*	.096	−.129*
	(.165)	(.025)	(.096)	(.022)
6	.569*	−.076*	−.060	−.124*
	(.250)	(.022)	(.120)	(.021)
7	−.110	−.040	.171	−.118*
	(.161)	(.024)	(.122)	(.022)
8	.086	−.074*	.097	−.125*
	(.174)	(.023)	(.117)	(.023)
9	.171	−.081*	−.058	−.119*
	(.209)	(.023)	(.140)	(.022)
10	−.241	−.065*	.195	−.127*
	(.222)	(.024)	(.113)	(.022)

*$p < .05$.
Note: Standard errors are given in parentheses. Density is measured in hundreds.

Perhaps the most important factor in evaluating the implications of the unobserved-heterogeneity challenge is the *symmetry* of the theory of density-dependent legitimation and competition—it applies to both mortality rates and founding rates. As we understand it, Petersen and Koput's conjecture does not apply to density dependence in founding rates. The plausibility of their alternative explanation relative to the one implied by the sociological theory is a matter of judgment. We tried to demonstrate here that in the usual research context, the alternative advanced by Petersen and Koput is less plausible. In replying to our work, Petersen and Koput (1991b, p. 416) come close to retracting their original claim: "We accept these [Hannan, Barron and Carroll's] simulations as evidence that controlling for organizational age under a more realistic founding process may totally alleviate the problem of unobserved heterogeneity."

But what Petersen and Koput (1991b, p. 416) give with one hand they take back with the other: "However, . . . to make the simulations more realistic, construct them within the context of models with true age dependence."[9] So we conducted a simulation to investigate this suggestion. We modified the framework outlined above to introduce true age dependence of a Weibull form. We set the Weibull age dependence parameter to .5, which is typical of estimates obtained from studies of organizational populations (Hannan 1989a; Hannan and Freeman 1989). We chose the second parameter of the Weibull model so that the mortality rates within each frailty class at five years of age were equal to the constant rates used by Petersen and Koput and we used ("Simulation 2"). Then we estimated models in which the hazard of mortality depends on age and density, as in the work described above.

We conducted 20 trials of this structure. It turned out that the estimated effects of density were more systematically negative than was the case without true age dependence—the effect is negative in 16 of 20 trials. Yet, there is no suggestion that researchers would often be misled to conclude that there was structural density dependence. The average of the 20 estimates of the effect of density is −.036 and the standard deviation is .069, Clearly, the most likely result is that the effect of density would be nonsignificant. In our 20 trials, three estimated effects of density were significant. But two are negative, and one is positive. Thus even the extreme outcomes do not tell a consistent story.

Of course, ruling out one class of explanations based on the operation of unobservables does not rule out the larger class of such explanations. Explanations based on unobservables are sufficiently protean to be able to explain any empirical pattern if not disciplined by theory or evidence from other studies. Still, we think

[9] This is a curious idea, as age dependence itself is likely to reflect unobserved heterogeneity as we have already mentioned.

that addressing the specific form proposed by Petersen and Koput helps shore up the foundations of the research program on density-dependent legitimation and competition.

Theoretical Implications

Although the structure of this chapter is less complex than the main chapter on founding rates (Chapter 4), it is still helpful to collect the main qualitative results in a summary table. We do so in Table 6.5, which reports the signs and statistical significance of the effects of contemporaneous and delayed density on the overall mortality rate for all populations and on the rate of disbanding for the three populations for which we could make this distinction. In the case of the overall rate of mortality, the signs of effects agree with the predictions in 14 of 14 cases. Moreover, 13 of the 14 are statistically significant. (We continue to use the .05 level and one-tailed tests.) The effect of density at time of founding is positive and significant for each population. For rates of disbanding, the signs agree with the predictions in nine of nine cases, and all nine effects are statistically significant. In terms of the binomial joint tests across populations proposed in Chapter 4, the null hypothesis that positive and negative effects are equally likely for each of these effects is extraordinarily improbable given these results.

Qualitative Implications

What do these estimates of the effects of contemporaneous and delayed density imply about the form and strength of density dependence? The point estimates of the impact of contemporaneous density imply that both the overall rate of mortality and the rate of disbanding fall with density in the lower range and then eventually rise with increasing density at some point. How much do the rates fall, and when do they begin to rise? Table 6.6 answers these questions. The column labeled N_t^* indicates the turning point in the relationship between contemporaneous density and the two mortality rates. When N_t falls below N_t^*, increases in density decrease mortality rates; when N exceeds N_t^*, increases in density elevate mortality rates. The turning point in the overall mortality rate falls within the observed range for banks, brewers, and life insurance companies.

Table 6.5. Summary of effects of density on rates of organizational mortality

Population	Rate	N_t	N_t^2	N_{f_i}
Banks	Overall	$-^*$	$+^*$	$+^*$
	Disbanding	$-^*$	$+^*$	$+^*$
Brewers	Overall	$-^*$	$+^*$	$+^*$
	Disbanding	$-^*$	$+^*$	$+^*$
Labor unions	Overall	$-^*$	$+$	$+^*$
	Disbanding	$-^*$	$+^*$	$+^*$
Life insurance cos.	Overall	$-^*$	$+^*$	$+^*$
Newspapers				
Argentina	Overall	$-^*$	$+^*$	$+^*$
Ireland	Overall	$-^*$	$+^*$	$+^*$
San Francisco Bay Area	Overall	$-^*$	$+^*$	$+^*$

$^*p < .05$ (one-tailed test)

The turning point for the rate of disbanding lies within the observed range of density for all three populations for which this event could be analyzed, banks, brewers, and labor unions.

One reason that turning points may fall outside the observed range of density is that legitimation processes may outweigh competition processes over the full ranges of variation in density. A natural way of assessing the strength of density-dependent legitimation (relative to competition) in the context of our formulation is by recording the drop in the mortality rate as density ranges from zero to its minimum level. For banks, brewers, and life insurance companies (for which the turning point falls within the range of the data), the relevant measure of relative strength of legitimation is $\hat{\mu}(N_t^*)$. (Again we focus on a multiplier because the model contains the effects of delayed density, age, and other covariates, and the effect of

Table 6.6. Qualitative implications of density dependence in rates of overall mortality and of disbanding implied by the estimates in Tables 6.1 and 6.2

Population	Rate	$N_t^{\max}$	N_t^*	$\widehat{\mu}(N_t^*)$	$\widehat{\mu}(N_t^{\max})$	$\widehat{\mu}(N_{f_i}^{\max})$
Banks	Overall	154	93	.20	.40	4.7
	Disband	154	129	.11	.12	10
Brewers	Overall	2726	1960	.38	.44	3.9
	Disband	2726	2045	.40	.44	5.3
Labor unions	Overall	211	214	.08	.08	4.4
	Disband	211	168	.02	.03	19
Life insurance	Overall	129	92	.20	.26	3.6
Newspapers						
Argentina	Overall	125	156	.02	.02	5.7
Ireland	Overall	224	278	.12	.13	1.6
San Francisco	Overall	395	417	.04	.04	4.8

Note: N_t^* denotes the minimum in the relationship between contemporaneous density and the mortality rate. $\widehat{\mu}^*$ denotes the minimum multiplier of the overall rate of mortality, that is, when density equals N_t^*; $\widehat{\mu}(N_t^{max})$ is the multiplier of the rate when density is at its observed maximum; and $\widehat{\mu}(N_{f_i}^{max})$ denotes the multiplier of the rate for organizations founded when density is at its observed maximum—this is the maximum value of the density at founding multiplier.

contemporaneous density is multiplied by the effects of these other variables in determining the mortality rate.) For the other four populations, the relevant minimum is $\widehat{\mu}(N_t^{max})$—the multiplier of the rate at the observed maximum of density. In either case, the smaller the multiplier is, the stronger the effect of density-dependent legitimation will be relative to that of competition on the rate of overall mortality.

Legitimation had an exceedingly strong effect in all cases. For the four populations for which the turning point in the overall mortality rate falls outside the observed range of density, the minimum multiplier of the mortality rate is .08 for unions, .02 for Argentine newspapers, .12 for Irish newspapers, and .04 for San Francisco newspaper publishers. These numbers tell that the age-specific mortality rate falls with density by 88% to 98% net of the effects of delayed density and the covariates, trend, and period effects. It may well be that the turning points fall outside the sample ranges of density because legitimation has such a powerful relative effect on mortality rates in these populations.

For the three populations with U-shaped relations between density and the overall mortality rate over the observed range of density, the multipliers are .20 (banks), .38 (brewers), and .20 (life insurance companies). In other words, density-dependent legitimation lowered mortality rates by 60% to 80% for these populations. Although these effects are weaker than for unions and newspapers, they are nonetheless strong.

Legitimation processes have clearly dominated competition processes in regard to the effect of contemporaneous density in each population. But the competitive effect of density delay must also be considered. The estimated effects of density at founding are extremely powerful. A natural way to express the strength of density delay is in terms of the density-delay multiplier at the highest levels of density at founding, $\hat{\mu}(N_{f_i}^{max})$, for each population. These effects are huge relative to a baseline in most cases. The weakest effect, for Irish newspapers, is 1.6, which implies that the age-specific mortality rate of Irish newspapers founded when density was at its peak are 60% higher than for those founded at zero density. The multipliers of the overall rate of mortality for the other six populations ranges from 3.6 to 5.7. That is, organizations founded at the peak have age-specific mortality rates that are 3.6 to 5.7 times higher than those founded at zero density. Density at founding has an even stronger effect on the rate of disbanding—more than double the effects on the overall rate of mortality. Recall that our specification of density delay imposes the restriction that elevation of mortality rates due to high density at time of founding persists for an organization's entire lifetime. That is, they are effects on age-specific mortality rates. These estimated effects are large for permanent effects.

The strength of the effect of density delay is the main source of the failure of relationships between contemporaneous density and mortality rates to turn within the observed range of density and to have a more pronounced U shape. The effect of density delay picks up much of the competitive effect. Taken together, the combined effects of contemporaneous density and density at founding involve a very strong relative legitimation effect and a very strong direct effect of competition. In particular, these effects are powerful relative to the effects of aging and of covariates. They have been strong enough to exert a major influence on the evolution of numbers in these populations.

7

Complications

The preceding chapters discussed a variety of issues that could confound the analysis of organizational density. Foremost among these are questions about (1) the appropriate level of analysis, (2) the reversibility of processes of legitimation and competition, and (3) the use of left-truncated observation schemes. This chapter examines these concerns in detail by analyzing further the data on American brewing firms.

We focus on the brewers because questions of level and reversibility are especially pressing for this population. Although the brewing industry in the United States now has a national (or even global) scope, in years past its scope was much more local. During the nineteenth century and earlier, brewers produced beer for markets no larger than cities or even neighborhoods. Among other things, the lack of mechanical refrigeration drastically limited the geographical scope of a brewer's market. Recognition of changing limits on the scope of brewing firms leads naturally to the first research problem we address here: Should processes of density dependence for the population of brewing firms be specified at city, state, or regional levels of analysis instead of the national level reported in earlier chapters?

Density in the American brewing population has recently risen after a long period of decline (see Figure 1.5). After falling to a low of 43 in 1983, the number of brewing firms rose to 123 in late 1988. Did density begin to rise again because the effects of density are reversible and the industry is now undergoing renewed legitimation? Or is there another explanation?

When discussing this problem in Chapter 2, we noted that the resurgence of density late in a population's history can be caused by the effects of other sociological processes. Once controls for these other processes are introduced into the analysis, there may be no need to make the absurd assumption that the legitimation process has been reinvigorated. For the brewing industry in the recent period, we investigate two additional sociological processes that might account for the pattern in Figure 1.5. First, we examine whether the industry has evolved into several distinct organizational forms in this period. If so, then we expect that the resurgence of density can best be understood by treating the dynamics of each subpopulation separately, with each subject to its own processes of legitimation and competition. Second, we investigate the extent to which resource partitioning might have occurred in the industry during this period. Resource partitioning implies that the market has become segmented into generalist and specialist submarkets. The key variable for this process is overall market concentration. Carroll's (1985) model implies that concentration enhances the life chances of specialists but diminishes the life chances of generalists.

The third complication concerns the validity of results from heavily left-truncated observation schemes.[1] This issue arises because Delacroix, Swaminathan, and Solt (1989) challenged the applicability of the theory to populations of business firms after analyzing the recent history of wineries in California. Our chief complaint about their study is that it uses only data that span 1940 to 1985, despite an obviously longer prior history of the wine industry (in California and other states—see Pinney 1989). We want to learn how such

---

[1] There is a subtle difference between left truncation and left censoring. We follow Cox and Oakes (1984, p. 177): "Left truncation arises when individuals come under observation only some known time after the natural time origin of the phenomenon under study. That is, had the individual failed before the truncation time in question, that individual would not have been recorded." By contrast, these authors also say that "censoring on the left arises if observation does not start immediately and some individuals have already failed before it does. For those individuals the fact that they failed, but not the failure time, is known" (Cox and Oakes 1984, p. 178). As will become clear later, the observation schemes that we find problematic for studying density dependence are treated as left truncated even though on occasion there is enough information in the data set to treat it as left censored.

left truncation affects estimates of density on vital rates for a population for which the pattern of nonmonotonic density dependence holds strongly when its entire history is analyzed. Although data on any of the populations analyzed above might be used to address this question, the case of brewers is ideal because of its obvious parallel to wineries. In particular, the national Prohibition confounded the evolution of the population of wineries and may justify an analysis of the post-Prohibition period. But if so, it should do the same for brewers, as they were equally subject to the ban.

In order to explore the possible consequences of left truncation in the observation plan, we report analyses of effects of density on vital rates of the national population of brewers using exclusively post-Prohibition data. Unlike the winery study, we can isolate the consequences of a design that excludes most of the history of the population because we can compare the post-Prohibition findings for brewers with those reported in Chapters 4 and 6, in which complete historical data were analyzed.

Our exclusive focus on the brewing population in studying these three complications does not signify that we consider the issues to be limited to this population. On the contrary, we believe that they commonly arise in the analysis of all kinds of organizational populations. Our efforts here are intended to be illustrative, to show ways in which these common problems might be addressed and resolved. We are fortunate in that the brewing data allow us to do so in such a clear way.

Levels of Analysis

As the beer industry developed across the centuries, some American brewing firms increased in scale and expanded their geographical scope. What was a locally based craft during the seventeenth, eighteenth, and early nineteenth centuries evolved first into a regionally based production system by World War II and later into a unified national market dominated by a few large multiplant producers by the 1980s (Elzinga 1986). What consequences, if any, does this transformation have for the relevance of processes of density dependence in organizational evolution?

To this point we have treated the entire set of brewing firms in the United States as a single organizational population evolving according to unified density-dependent processes of legitimation and competition. An assumption underlying such analysis is that the population and its associated institutional arena and competitive arena—its market—are primarily *national* in scope. Because the market eventually evolved to this level (and, along the way, selection pressures were severe), we believe that analyzing processes of density dependence at the national level makes substantive sense. This assumption is buttressed by the strong consistency in the pattern of density dependence in analyses at the national level. But we are also curious to know whether the predictions will also be supported when applied to populations defined for smaller geographical areas. Given the history of the industry, it would be surprising if the processes of legitimation and competition did not operate (in some degree) at the regional, state, and city levels. Moreover, one might expect that the processes would actually be stronger at those levels, at least during certain periods.

We think it likely that competition was more localized than legitimation, at least during the early portion of the history of the industry. Information, especially that generating the sense of taken-for-grantedness of an organizational form, could flow relatively freely through the national system while product markets were still localized. Internal migration presumably played a strong role in spreading images of appropriate organizational and institutional forms. And mass migrations occurred much earlier than the development of national product markets for beer. If so, estimates of the second-order effect of density (which is associated primarily with the direct effect of density-dependent competition) will be more powerful at more local levels over the broad period studied. More precisely, the difference in strength between estimates based on "local" density and those based on "nonlocal" density will be greater for the second-order effect of density than for the first-order effect.

We take a straightforwardly empirical approach to investigating these issues. Following Carroll and Wade (1991), our strategy is to estimate the density dependence in rates of organizational founding and mortality for different subsets of the brewing firm data, with density, previous events, and outcomes defined for populations bounded by region, state, and city (see also Swaminathan and Wiedenmayer

1991). We start by examining the processes for the U. S. Census Bureau's nine regions. We then analyze data on the populations in three large states: Illinois, Pennsylvania, and Wisconsin. Each state developed a large market for beer and a sizable number of brewing firms emerged as well. Finally, we analyze rates of founding and mortality for brewers in the major urban centers in these states: Chicago, Philadelphia, and Milwaukee.

We use and compare analyses that involve two different definitions of density. In the first, we relate vital rates to the density of firms within the relevant locality. So, for instance, we relate vital events in the population in the New England region to "regional density," which means the number of brewing firms located in New England. We also relate events in this population to "nonregional density," which denotes the density in the rest of the country (excluding New England). If there is no national level process, then we should not expect nonregional density to have systematic effects. In analyses of events within state populations of brewers, we relate events to "state density" and "nonstate density," which is the density in the rest of the country. Finally, in analyses at the city level, we relate events to "city density" and "state (noncity) density."

Regional Analysis

The largest numbers of brewers appeared in the regions in the Northeast (Middle Atlantic and New England) and the Midwest (East North Central); the fewest in the South (East South Central and West South Central). Remarkably, the long-term pattern of growth, stabilization and decline in density occurred in all regions (see Carroll and Wade 1991). We find it especially interesting that the timing of this rise and fall is somewhat (although not exactly) similar among regions. Figure 7.1 illustrates this pattern for three of the regions: Middle Atlantic, Pacific, and Mountain (see Carroll and Wade for plots for the other regions). This pattern suggests that the processes may indeed have operated at the national level, with each region displaying merely minor variations on the national pattern.

Effects of regional density on the founding rates within each of the nine regions can be found in Table 7.1. (We use the log-quadratic specification for all analyses of brewer founding rates reported in this chapter.) The first row for each region gives the effects of regional

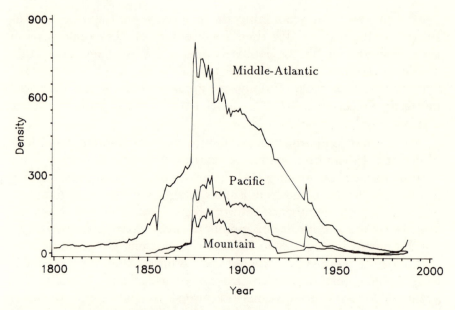

Figure 7.1. Historical evolution of density for selected regional populations of brewing firms

density. The first-order effect of regional density is positive as predicted for all nine regions. This effect is significant for seven of nine regions. The second-order effect of regional density is negative as predicted for eight of nine regions (all but the Mountain region). This effect is significant for four of nine regions.

The second row for each region in Table 7.1 reports the effects of "nonregional" density (density in the rest of the country excluding the density of the region in question). The first-order effect of nonregional density is positive for each region except Mountain and Pacific; this effect is significant in six instances. The second-order effect is negative for eight regions (the exception is the Mountain region); the effect is significant for four of the seven regions with a negative effect. Overall, the results for nonregional density agree with the implications the theory for eight regions, although only four of these have significant first-order and second-order effects.

According to results of both regional and nonregional analyses, the prediction of nonmonotonic density dependence fares least well for regions with fewer brewers. This result agrees with the finding

Table 7.1. Founding rates of brewing firms by region: ML estimates of the effects of regional and nonregional density

Region	Specification	N_t	N_t^2
Middle Atlantic	Region	.0136*	−.0130*
(1800–1988)	Other regions	.0055*	−.0022*
New England	Region	.0667*	−.5147
(1800–1988)	Other regions	.0025*	−.0003
West North Central	Region	.0254*	−.0461*
(1809–1988)	Other regions	.0034*	−.0008*
East North Central	Region	.0103*	−.0088*
(1811–1988)	Other regions	.0049*	−.0022*
South Atlantic	Region	.0623*	−.4033*
(1800–1988)	Other regions	.0030*	−.0010*
East South Central	Region	.0235	−.2058
(1858–1988)	Other regions	.0004*	−.0000
West South Central	Region	.1248*	−1.158
(1850–1988)	Other regions	.0023	−.0002
Mountain	Region	.0107	.0467
(1859–1988)	Other regions	−.0001	.0005
Pacific	Region	.0197*	−.0333
(1849–1988)	Other regions	−.0002	−.0009

*$p < .05$ (one-tailed test).

Note: N_t denotes density (in either the region or the rest of the country depending on the specification). N_t^2 is measured in thousands. This analysis uses the log-quadratic model of density dependence (Equation 4.3a). All models contain effects of covariates—see Appendix A. The negative binomial specification with a quadratic relationship between mean and variance is used for all regional populations.

of Carroll and Hannan (1989b) that density has strongest effects on vital rates of local newspaper populations in the largest populations. Replication of this pattern lends credence to the view that the relatively poor performance of the model in explaining the rates in small populations reflects ordinary problems of large sampling errors in studies with few events.

Founding rates of brewing firms in the United States apparently have been sensitive both to regional density and national density, which is not surprising given that regional trajectories of density track the national pattern reasonably closely. Yet, the founding process might have been more sensitive to regional variations than to national ones even though the pattern of signs of effects is the same. Comparison of the estimated effects of regional and nonregional density is a good way to assess this, as nonregional density is defined as national density minus the density of the region being analyzed. The comparison suggests a clear answer: The effects of regional density are stronger in all instances.

The results of our regional analyses are also consistent with the view that competition processes are stronger at the regional level than at the national level. Consider the ratios of effects of regional density to those of nonregional density. In the case of the first-order effect of density, which is associated primarily with the legitimation processes in our theory, this ratio ranges from 2 to 115, with a median of 26. In other words, if we use the median ratio as a summary, the legitimating effect of regional density will be 26 times stronger than the legitimating effect of nonlocal density. For the second-order effect, which is associated with the process of competition, the ratio ranges from 4 to 7720, with a median of 95. Again using the median as a summary, we find that the competitive effect of regional density is 95 times stronger than that of nonlocal density. That is, the competitive process is apparently much stronger at the regional level than is the case for the legitimation process.

Despite the greater strength of effects at the regional level (especially for competition), the consistency of these effects across regions and the persisting strong effects of nonregional density give credence to the national level of analysis. Clearly, little is lost by using the national level and much is gained in terms of parsimony.

Next we consider the same issues as they pertain to organizational mortality. Table 7.2 reports estimates of the effect of regional density on the mortality rates of brewing firms within each of the nine regions. Based on the findings of Chapter 6, we include effects of both contemporaneous density with a log-quadratic form and density at founding in each analysis. The first-order effect of contemporaneous regional density is negative as predicted for seven regions (all but the West South Central and Pacific regions); the effect is significant for five of them. The second-order effect of contemporaneous regional density is positive for five regions. But this effect is significant for only three regions. Finally, the effect of regional density at founding is positive and significant as predicted in all regions.

Somewhat surprisingly, the specification with nonregional density performs about as well as the regional one does. The first-order effect of nonregional contemporaneous density is negative for eight regions; and it is significant for six. The second-order effect is positive for seven regions and significant for three of the seven. The effect of nonregional density at founding is positive and significant for all nine regions.

Again, it is interesting to compare the strength of density effects at the two levels. As with founding rates, we find stronger effects at the regional level. And again we find that this is particularly true for coefficients associated primarily with competition (the second-order effect of density). The ratios of (absolute values of) local and nonlocal estimates of the first order-effect of density range from 2 to 55 with a median of 9, and the ratios of the second-order effect range from 2 to 1146 with a median of 48.

State and City Levels

We now look at density processes in Illinois, Pennsylvania, and Wisconsin separately, as well as those in their largest urban centers, Chicago, Philadelphia, and Milwaukee. Effects of density on founding rates of the brewer populations in these states and cities appear in Table 7.3. For the state level we use two specifications of density: state and national (excluding state). For the city level we use city-level density, and state (excluding city) density. The first-order and second-order effects of state density on the state founding rates have the predicted signs for all three states. All effects are also statistically significant except the second-order effect for Wisconsin. The pattern is the same for the effect of nonstate density. Again all effects agree with the qualitative predictions; and all effects except that of

Table 7.2. Overall rates of mortality of brewing firms by region: ML estimates of effects of contemporaneous and delayed regional and
nonregional density

Region	Specification	N_t	N_t^2	N_{f_i}
Middle Atlantic	Region	−.0033*	.0029*	.0016*
	Other regions	−.0014*	.0005*	.0007*
New England	Region	−.0181	−.0787	.0269*
	Other regions	−.0014*	.0002	.0006*
West North Central	Region	−.0036*	.0033	.0023*
	Other regions	−.0006*	.0002	.0003*
East North Central	Region	−.0031*	.0030*	.0013*
	Other regions	−.0018*	.0009*	.0005*
South Atlantic	Region	−.0111	−.0140	.0126*
	Other regions	−.0004	.0000	.0003*
East South Central	Region	−.1005*	−.1490	.0628*
	Other regions	−.0018*	−.0001	.0009*
West South Central	Region	.0144	.1031	.0359*
	Other regions	−.0016	.0008*	.0006*
Mountain	Region	−.0125*	.0748*	.0057*
	Other regions	−.0010*	.0002	.0005*
Pacific	Region	.0061	−.0107	.0045*
	Other regions	.0022	−.0007	.0006*

*$p < .05$ (one-tailed test).
Note: N_t denotes contemporaneous density (in either the region or the rest
of the country, depending on the specification) and N_{f_i} denotes density (in
either the region or the rest of the nation) at the time of founding. N_t^2
is measured in thousands. This analysis uses the log-quadratic model of
density dependence given in Equation 6.1. All models contain effects of
covariates—see Appendix A. Age dependence has a Weibull form for all
regions.

Table 7.3. Founding rates of brewing firms in states and cities: ML estimates of the effects of density at various levels

Population	Specification	N_t	N_t^2
Illinois	State	.0392*	−.1573*
	Nonstate	.0042*	−.0014*
Chicago	City	.0841*	−.9226*
	State (Noncity)	.0605*	−.4068*
Pennsylvania	State	.0369*	−.0757*
	Nonstate	.0048*	−.0015*
Philadelphia	City	.0681*	−.3406*
	State (Noncity)	.0659*	−.2236*
Wisconsin	State	.0104*	−.0087
	Nonstate	.0014*	−.0003
Milwaukee	City	.0101	.4023*
	State (Noncity)	.0122*	−.0519*

*$p < .05$ (one-tailed test).
Note: N_t denotes density (at city, state, or nonstate levels). N_t^2 is measured in thousands. The log-quadratic model of density dependence is given in Equation 4.3a. All models contain effects of covariates—see Appendix A. The negative binomial specification with a quadratic relationship between mean and variance is used for the state and city levels of analysis.

N^2 for Wisconsin are statistically significant. State density has considerably stronger effects than nonstate density does, suggesting that legitimation and competition did occur as theorized within the state. Again, the competition effect is especially strong at the higher level. That is, local and nonlocal competitive effects differ much more than the comparable legitimation effects. But the continued significant effect of nonstate (national) density demonstrates that these processes were not self-contained or complete.

Estimates of city-level founding rates reveal a similar pattern. Five of the six effects of city density have the predicted signs; four of them also are significant. When state density replaces city density, all six effects continue to have the predicted signs; and all six are significant. Again, the strength of effects varies as a function of level. The city-level effect is stronger then the state (noncity) level. But the strength of effects differs much less than was the case in comparing effects of state and nonstate density on founding rates in state populations. As with the state level analyses, we infer that separate but incomplete processes of legitimation and competition occurred at these lower geographical levels. However, we also conclude that the state population is nearly as relevant as the city population to shaping vital events in city-level populations of brewers.

Estimates of effects of density on state-level mortality rates display a now-familiar pattern. Both specifications of density have significant effects in the predicted directions with magnitudes greater for the smaller geographical area (Table 7.4). That is, the pattern of density dependence at the state level also agrees with the implications of the theory. For the three cities, however, the results fail to support the prediction of nonmonotonic density dependence. Although density at founding has a positive significant effect, as predicted, in several instances, the effects of contemporaneous density are usually not statistically significant, and they often differ in sign from the theory. These estimates give little credence to the notion that intense competition occurred primarily at the local level in the early American brewing industry. The failure to find effects of this kind is surprising given the seemingly widespread view that competition processes are especially strong at the local level. It demonstrates again the importance of distinguishing between indirect and direct forms of competition. These results reveal that the city level is too microscopic for processes of legitimation and competition to be discerned for the population of brewers. Ignoring information on variations in density at the state (or regional or national) level misses variation that turns out to be important to explaining fluctuations in life chances of organizations.

We conclude this section by noting that the evidence suggests some legitimation and competition in the brewing population in the United States at local, state, and regional levels. However, these lower-order processes did not occur in isolation and did not in any

Table 7.4. Overall rates of mortality of brewing firms in states and cities: ML estimates of the effects of contemporaneous density and density at founding at various levels

Population	Specification	N_t	N_t^2	N_{f_i}
Illinois	State	−.0312*	.1354*	.0119*
	Nonstate	−.0018*	.0005*	.0006*
Chicago	City	−.0140	−.1115	.0163
	State (Noncity)	−.0030*	.2091	.0043*
Pennsylvania	State	−.0077*	.0138*	.0037*
	Nonstate	−.0011*	.0003*	.0005*
Philadelphia	City	−.0091	.0368	.0068*
	State (Noncity)	.0005	−.0155	.0038*
Wisconsin	State	−.0119*	.0400*	.0043*
	Nonstate	−.0011*	.0005*	.0003*
Milwaukee	City	.0567	−1.543	.0893*
	State (Noncity)	.0012	−.0006	.0066*

*$p < .05$ (one-tailed test).
Note: N_t denotes density (at either city, state, or nonstate levels) and N_{f_i} denotes density at the time of founding (at each level). N_t^2 is measured in thousands. This analysis uses the log-quadratic model of density dependence is given in Equation 6.1. All models contain effects of covariates—see Appendix A. The negative binomial specification with a quadratic relationship between mean and variance is used for all levels of analysis.

way supersede the larger national processes. Indeed, the most consistent evidence we find is for national processes of legitimation and competition. At a more abstract level, these findings suggest to us that populations that experience transformations in geographical scale may be analyzed meaningfully at the higher levels. We think this is because severe selection occurs when the geographical scale of the population is transformed. Conducting analysis exclusively at the lower levels ignores the organizations responsible for variations in legitimation of an organizational form and for variations in competitive pressure.

Apparent Reversals

We now return to the national level of analysis. Recall that we saw that although the American brewing industry experienced a long-term decline in the number of organizations, recent developments suggest a reversal in the pattern. Whereas in 1880 the United States had 2474 brewing firms operating, by 1980 the number had dropped to 45, and in late 1988 it had climbed to 123. Can the theory of density dependence explain this new upswing? If so, does it require that the legitimation process be (implausibly) invoked again? If not, how can the resurgence in numbers of organizations be accounted for?

Two important facts need to be recognized at the outset. First, market concentration has come hand-in-hand with the decline in density. In 1935, the largest four firms in brewing controlled 11% of the American market. By 1947, their share had risen to 21%, and by 1982 it had swollen to 78%. In order of size, the four largest firms then were Anheuser-Busch, Miller, Stroh, and Heileman.

Second, the recent history of the industry exhibits significant organizational change. Specifically, during the last 15 years or so, two new organizational forms reemerged and proliferated. The first of these, the so-called microbrewery, produces ale and beer by traditional methods for a small but upscale niche in the market. The second form, commonly referred to as the brewpub, sells malt beverages directly to the consumer for immediate consumption at the site of production. Brewpub products resemble those of microbreweries except that they are fresher and are not bottled.

The first microbrewery in the modern age appeared in 1977, and instances of this form now outnumber the larger mass-production brewers.[2] The brewpub has even more recent reappearance. Initially

---

[2] The first American microbrewery since Prohibition is generally identified as Jack McAuliffe's New Albion Brewing Company of Sonoma, California.

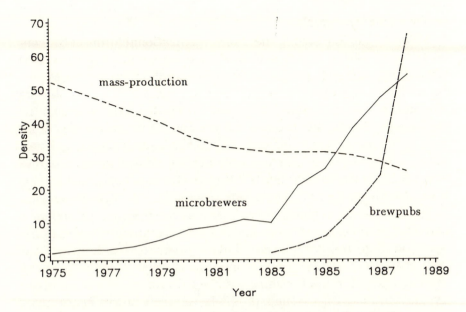

Figure 7.2. Evolution of the densities of mass-production brewers, micro-brewers, and brewpubs, 1977–1988

reappearing in 1982 in California and the state of Washington, it spread very quickly (even though it was still illegal in about half the states in 1989) and shows signs of potentially dwarfing the other two forms in terms of prevalence.[3]

Figure 7.2 disaggregates the recent trends in density by organizational form; it plots the numbers of mass production brewers (declining dashed line), microbreweries (solid line), and brewpubs (rising dashed line). These distinctions have obvious importance. Although the number of mass producers continues to drop for the entire period, the numbers of both microbreweries and brewpubs rise, slowly

---

The operation lasted for five years (from 1977 to 1982). It produced and bottled ale, porter and stout—beverages in short supply on the domestic market initially.

[3] According to the 1987 Microbrewers Resources Handbook and Directory, the first American brewpub is Mendocino Brewing Company's Hopland Brewery, located in Hopland, California. Curiously, the brewery operates with equipment obtained from New Albion Brewing Company, the now defunct first American microbrewery.

at first and then rapidly.

Mobility barriers among the three organizational forms in the contemporary brewing industry have been steep so far. The operation of brewpubs is legally prohibited for the microbrewers and mass producers in many states (although there are signs of a trend allowing the combination of microbreweries and brewpubs). And although the mass producers are monitoring the market for microbrewery products, none has entered this segment of the industry with any real resolve. Its small scale makes this end of the market unattractive to them; there is also sometimes a fear of contaminating hybrid strains of yeast with the more common varieties used by the microbreweries.

Brewery firms of each organizational form also face different strategic challenges. The mass producers compete on a national basis for large market shares. This segment of the industry has been characterized by strong economies of scale, large advertising outlays, and tight relationships with distributors. The microbrewers, by contrast, target their products to small niches in the market. Typically these niches consist of potential consumers who are socioeconomically advantaged and, at least initially, geographically localized. Such markets are sometimes developed by advertising and other promotional activities, but often by the cultivation of elite networks. Gaining and maintaining regular access to such consumers can be problematic, especially given the dominance of distribution networks by the mass producers. Finally, brewpubs face distinctive challenges. It is not clear that they compete with the other two forms so much as they do with local drinking and dining establishments. Potential returns on investment can be quite high, however, as the hefty packaging and distribution costs faced by other brewers are bypassed by firms with this organizational form.

Given these fundamental differences, it is interesting to investigate whether microbreweries and brewpubs constitute distinct organizational forms. If so, then we would expect each to follow similar but separate evolutionary paths based on the organizational form-specific counts of density. That is, microbreweries and brewpubs should each experience separate processes of legitimation and competition governed by the prevalence in numbers of each form. Empirically, however, only the legitimation processes should be detectable at this time, as these forms just recently emerged. This reasoning leads us make the following predictions to test the applicability of our formulation in this context: First, founding rates of microbreweries and brewpubs will increase as the density of each organizational form increases. Second, mortality rates of microbreweries and brewpubs will decline as the density of each organizational form increases. Obviously, empirical backing for these arguments gainsays the need to explain somehow the late rise in density of the composite population of all brewers in terms of density-dependent legitimation and competition.

Another theoretical explanation for the resurgence in breweries takes note of the fact that microbreweries and brewpubs are organizational specialists. In ecological terms, the level of specialism in a population is a matter of *niche width*. When the niche is broadly based and organizational populations can survive on a variety of different resources, the population is composed of generalists. When organizations of a particular form depend on a narrow range of resources, they constitute a specialist population.

Ecological theories of niche width relate environmental conditions to the viability of various degrees of organizational specialism. One theory was developed by Freeman and Hannan (1983). It concerns the extent of variability in different environmental states and the rapidity of change from one state to another. The theory predicts that when environmental conditions are similar from one period to the next, generalist organizational forms will be optimal, regardless of the rapidity of change. By contrast, when environmental states differ radically, the optimal form depends on the speed of change. In this case, rapid environmental change favors specialism whereas slower change (meaning long durations in each state) favors generalism.

A different theory of niche width was advanced by Carroll (1985). This theory, labeled a *resource-partitioning model*, applies to markets characterized by strong economies of scale. Large generalist organizational forms obviously win out in the long run in such markets. The resource-partitioning model, however, focuses on the life chances of specialist organizations at different times in the process. Early on, when the market is crowded, most participants vie for the largest possible resource base. Competition forces them to specialize to some extent, although the overall strategy is clearly generalist in nature. When scale economies dominate, only a few generalists survive and they move toward the center of the market. This lessened crowding of generalists opens up small pockets of resources near the periphery of the market, and it is here that specialist organizational forms often appear and thrive. In terms of the model, the market at this point has been partitioned into generalist and specialist resources. The key predictive variable is the overall level of market concentration. When the market is not highly concentrated, specialist organizational forms will not do as well as they do when it is highly concentrated. That is, increasing market concentration enhances the life chances of specialists.

The resource-partitioning model does not contradict the predictions of the theory of density-dependent legitimation and competition, either in its most general form or as applied to subpopulations of specialists. Yet it does make different predictions in this context. It implies that, as the market becomes increasingly concentrated, the life chances of specialist organizations are enhanced. Generalists move toward the middle of the market and this opens up pockets of resources for specialists. The conditions that might initiate this process in the brewing industry have certainly occurred. Specifically, concentration increased steadily owing to economies of scale in production and advertising. And the increasing number of microbreweries and brewpubs suggests that at least some entrepreneurs believe that new opportunities have been created. The proliferation of these small and specialized microbreweries and brewpubs is consistent with the resource-partitioning model. Whether or not the life chances of organizations with these forms have improved remains an open question. So we test two additional predictions: First, the founding rates of microbreweries and brewpubs increase as the overall market becomes more concentrated; second, the mortality rates of microbreweries and brewpubs decline as the overall market becomes more concentrated. Again, we note that support for these arguments relaxes the need for the basic theory to be reversible.

To test these explanations for the recent increase in breweries, we examine the period from 1975 to late 1988. We thus examine the period that begins shortly before the new organizational forms emerged and continues to the latest date for which information was available when this research was done.

The sample consists of all firms known to have produced beer in the United States during this period. As in other analyses of brewers reported in this book, this delineation excludes companies that sell beer manufactured by other, so-called contract brewers.

The basic sources for the brewing firms are listed in Appendix A. To collect additional data for these analyses, Carroll and his students also interviewed industry participants, both in person and over the telephone.

As in the larger study of (all) breweries over 350 years, for each firm identified we coded basic information on date of founding (when occurring after 1975), date of dissolution or merger (when occurring before the end of our records in late 1988), and type of organizational form (classified as microbrewery or brewpub). We also coded annual production capacity levels for each firm, inferring figures from intervening years when sensible. In addition, we coded the following environmental variables for each year of observation: industry production by organizational form and the "four-firm concentration level" in the overall industry (the fraction of production by the four largest firms).

Although the number of firms with each organizational form is roughly equal, event counts vary dramatically by form. In particular, there were very few mortalities of brewpubs during this period. So this outcome cannot be analyzed for this form—there are simply too few cases.

Table 7.5 presents the estimates of effects on the founding rates for microbreweries (the first three columns) and brewpubs (the last three columns). Microbrewery density has a positive effect on the founding rate in that population (column 1), thereby supporting the subpopulation arguments about density-dependent legitimation. The argument about density-dependent legitimation for subpopulations also receives confirmation for brewpubs (column 4).

The second column in Table 7.5 presents estimates of a specification designed to test the resource-partitioning argument. Industry concentration has a significant positive effect on the microbrewery founding rate, as predicted. Moreover, this effect persists even when the density of microbreweries is included (column 3). Indeed, the effect of microbrewery density is not significant here, suggesting that the resource-partitioning process dominates, but this lack of significance might simply be a result of the small sample. The fifth column in Table 7.5 provides the same simple test of the resource-partitioning argument for brewpubs. As was the case for microbreweries, concentration has a significant positive effect for the founding rate of brewpubs, thereby supporting the hypothesis. However, the

Table 7.5. Estimates of models of the founding rates of microbreweries and brewpubs

	Microbreweries			Brewpubs		
	(1)	(2)	(3)	(4)	(5)	(6)
Constant	.325	−7.86*	−6.84*	.909*	−20.8*	3.15
	(.279)	(1.85)	(2.63)	(.316)	(5.17)	(11.8)
Microbrewery Density	.127*		.024			
	(.026)		(.043)			
Brewpub Density				.092*		.100*
				(.017)		(.044)
Concentration (4-firm ratio)		.140*	.121*		.305*	−.031
		(.027)	(.043)		(.068)	(.164)
Microbrewery production	−.446*	−.106*	−.182			
	(.126)	(.056)	(.152)			
X^2	34.2	41.6	41.9	31.0	25.8	31.0
d.f.	2	2	3	1	1	2

*$p < .05$ (one-tailed test).
Note: Standard errors are given in parentheses. Because of the small number of observed years and events, a constant rate model is assumed and the data are treated as event histories rather than event counts. Most likely these procedures reduce the standard errors of estimates.

sixth column of Table 7.5 shows that including an effect of brewpub density in the model eliminates the effect of concentration, which suggests that the density process is primary.

Taken together, these estimates demonstrate that the founding rates of both forms are density dependent. For microbreweries this is true even when production levels are controlled. In analyses not reported in the Table, we also find that the density of mass producers has a negative, significant effect on the founding rate of microbreweries, a finding consistent with the view that the mass producers compete more with microbreweries than with brewpubs.

Estimates of Weibull models of organizational mortality for the

Table 7.6. Estimates of models of the mortality rates of microbreweries

	(1)	(2)	(3)	(4)
Constant	−1.10*	2.54	6.58*	1.97
	(.511)	(4.99)	(2.83)	(7.03)
Microbrewery density	−.072*	−.102*		−.048
	(.032)	(.045)		(.085)
Mass producer density		−.092		
		(.131)		
Industry concentration (4-firm ratio)			−.131*	−.051
			(.043)	(.121)
Age	−.074	−.020	−.117	−.095
	(.311)	(.333)	(.279)	(.313)

*$p < .05$ (one-tailed test).
Note: Standard errors are given in parentheses. All models specify age dependence with a Weibull form.

microbreweries indicate that the death rate declines with microbrewery density (column 1 in Table 7.6), as predicted. This effect remains strong and significant even when the density of mass producers is controlled (column 2).

These estimates also agree with the resource-partitioning model because industry concentration has a significant negative effect (column 3 in Table 7.6). Neither this effect nor the effect of density remain significant when both are included together (column 4), which we suspect results from the small sample. Therefore, although the evidence supports both the density-dependence and resource-partitioning models, these data are not sufficiently rich to adjudicate between them.

Left-truncated Observation Schemes

Chapters 4 and 6 noted that three earlier studies of density dependence in vital rates of organizational populations report disconfirming or nonsupporting empirical findings. These are Tucker and colleagues' (1988) investigation of voluntary social service organizations in Toronto, Staber's (1989) study of worker cooperatives in Atlantic Canada, and Delacroix, Swaminathan, and Solt's (1989) analysis of California wineries. How can these findings be reconciled with the strongly consistent pattern of nonmonotonic density dependence reported in the foregoing chapters?

The winery study presents the seemingly strongest challenge to the general applicability of the theory of density dependence.[4] Hence we focus on it. Delacroix, Swaminathan, and Solt's (hereafter, DSS) 1989 analysis of mortality of California wineries from 1940 to 1984 finds no consistent effects of density. They conclude that mortality processes for wineries are not density dependent. They explain this result by arguing that commercial business organizations such as wineries do not face legitimacy obstacles of the kind encountered by newspapers and labor unions, which they regard as exceptional.

We maintain that DSS's failure to find effects of density on mortality rates in this analysis has to do with research design rather than type of organization studied. All the "disconfirming" studies use observation schemes that are short compared with other studies and compared with the lifetimes of the populations, 47, 44, and 10 years, respectively for Staber, DSS, and Tucker and colleagues. Each study failed to obtain information on the early history of the population, the time when the effects of increasing legitimation ought to be strongest, according to the theory. For instance, DSS's data begin in 1940, even though the California wine industry developed during the nineteenth century. Indeed there were nearly 400 wineries in the population in 1940, but this number declined steadily over the period of their study.

Features of research design alone may not, however, account for the different findings. For wineries, the history of the population is complicated by the national Prohibition, which effectively closed all wineries from 1920 to 1933. DSS argue that this unprecedented event erased the population's "memory" and destroyed its supporting institutions. At the end of Prohibition, they contend, the population of wineries was effectively a "new" organizational population. If they

---

[4] Tucker and colleagues (1988) report estimates of one specification that actually agree with the theory, as noted in Chapter 6 (see also Tucker, Singh, and Meinard 1990). And Staber (1989) does not appear to have analyzed density as a time-varying covariate.

are correct, the processes of legitimation had to start from scratch; and it may not matter that data on the pre-Prohibition wine industry are not analyzed.

Obviously, the best way to resolve the issue would be to compare results of analyses spanning the Prohibition with those of similar analyses for the post-Prohibition period. Such a comparison would not only bear directly on general issues about the meaning of effects of density on vital rates, but it would also inform about the effects of the Prohibition, a fascinating environmental catastrophe from the population's point of view. Unfortunately, DSS did not collect the data needed to explore these matters.

Our goal here is to move a step closer to resolving this matter. Because the data on brewing firms span the whole history of the industry, we can isolate the effects of Prohibition. In analyses reported in previous chapters, we did so by allowing rates of founding and mortality to shift in the year before the national Prohibition and in years before the relevant state prohibitions (with sets of period effects). Here we mimic DSS and conduct analysis with post-Prohibition data exclusively. We want to learn whether the powerful and systematic effects of density on the vital rates observed in the study of the entire history can be discerned in analysis of the heavily left-truncated data. In other words, this comparison provides a controlled examination of the effect of severe left truncation.

Table 7.7 reports estimates of effects on both founding rates and mortality rates of brewing firms for two periods: the full history of the population (1633–1988) and the period 1940 to 1988. The latter starting time is, of course, the one used by DSS. The left-truncated observation scheme disturbs the pattern of effects completely, making them inconsistent with the theory's predictions. The effects of density on the founding rate now run opposite the predictions of the theory and differ greatly from those for the entire period. So do the effects of density on the mortality rate. The dramatic changes in results due to left truncation strongly suggest that DSS's failure to find the predicted patterns of density dependence with left-truncated data likely results from their research design. Severe left truncation apparently hides density dependence, even in populations such as brewers where it is strong.

In conclusion, we note that we can account for the discrepant findings of DSS as a consequence of poor research design. The patterns

Table 7.7. Effect of left truncation on estimates of density dependence parameters in models of rates of founding and mortality of brewing firms

Covariate	Full Period (1634–1988)	Left Truncation (1940–1988)
A. Founding rates		
Density	.0024* (.0008)	−.0074 (.0056)
Density^2/1000	−.0006* (.0001)	.0159 (.0112)
B. Mortality rates		
Density	−.0010* (.0001)	.0003 (.0007)
Density^2/1000	.00026* (.00003)	.00199* (.0009)
Density at founding	.0005* (.00003)	−.0001 (.0002)

*$p < .05$ (one-tailed test).
Note: Standard errors are given in parentheses. Models for the full period and for the left-truncated period contain effects of the same covariates—see Appendix A.

of density dependence in founding rates and mortality rates differ dramatically depending on which data—the complete data or the left-truncated data—are used. We think that these results undermine DSS's claim that the scope of the theory of density-dependent legitimation and competition is limited to nonbusiness organizations. Results for brewing firms over the full history of the industry show that effects of density on rates of founding and mortality are not limited in the way that DSS assert. At the same time, the findings reported in this section serve to bolster our argument that the implications of the theory hold most clearly when data on the complete histories of organizational populations (including their early histories) are analyzed.

8

Population Trajectories

One of the motivations for the research reported in this book is to understand the empirical regularity of growth in density observed for diverse organizational populations. When examined over long periods of time, counts of the number of organizations in a population initially grow slowly, then grow rapidly for a short time, and finally stabilize (sometimes after declining for some time). In order to analyze these temporal patterns thoroughly, we decomposed the overall population growth rate into its constituent parts, the organizational founding and mortality rates. We found strong and consistent evidence of nonmonotonic density dependence in analyses of these rates with microdata on the context and timing of events. In this chapter, we return to the population level and explore the implications of density dependence in vital rates for population trajectories. We would like to understand the relationship between the various forms of density dependence and the dynamic behavior of population density. Does the model of density dependence produce growth paths of density that resemble the empirical histories of real populations of organizations?

An ideal answer to any question about the relationship between density dependence in vital rates and population trajectories would be analytical. It would provide qualitative results about the implications of specific forms of density dependence (or specific parameter ranges for a given type) for the behavior of the population over time.

The general Lotka–Volterra modeling strategy, which resembles our approach to modeling density dependence, has been examined analytically at length (see, for instance, May 1974; Šiljak 1975).

Close relatives of our models have been used by population biologists and demographers to study density dependence in animal and human populations, and these models have also begun to be understood in analytical terms (see Lee 1974, 1987; Tuljapurkar 1987; Wachter 1988). It might seem only a simple step to conduct such analysis on the models analyzed in Chapters 4 and 6.

Unfortunately, this is not so. The models treated in this book are significantly more complicated in a variety of ways. First, they posit density dependence in both vital rates, whereas most treatments of population dynamics consider only a single overall rate of population growth. Second, the specifications of density dependence in the two vital rates are not constrained to be symmetric in their parameters, an assumption that greatly aids qualitative analysis. Third, we find evidence of two kinds of density dependence, contemporaneous and delayed. Fourth, the nonmonotonic form of contemporaneous density dependence is not a common or readily tractable specification. Fifth, because the two vital rates are specified and estimated at two different levels of analysis (population level for foundings and organizational level for mortality), combining them is not a trivial task. And sixth, the heterogeneity of organizations and environments incorporated explicitly into our models means that the mathematical analyst's critical assumption of homogeneity among units often cannot be invoked.

What should we do? Although we have some confidence that progress can be made in understanding these models analytically, we also believe that it may require a long and arduous effort (see Caswell 1989). We hope that the strength and consistency of our empirical findings will prompt other analysts to work on these important problems. At the moment, however, our goals are more practical and short range. Rather than attempt a thorough and comprehensive analytical examination of our models, we use computer simulation methods to help understand them.

We have two major goals and a variety of minor ones in using the computer to simulate population behavior. The first major goal is learning how well our empirically estimated models can reproduce the observed population trajectories shown in Chapter 1. In other words, we want to assess overall model fit once the two underlying processes of founding and mortality have been coupled. Toward this end, we use predictions based on the complete estimated rate models and their associated values of organizational and environmental covariates.

The second major goal of the simulation studies is to gain insight into the range of population behaviors produced by various dimensions of the underlying processes. More specifically, we are eager to learn how varying forms and strengths of the effects of contemporaneous density and delayed density are exerted on the whole population.

We begin by reviewing briefly our simulation procedures and the assumptions they employ. We then report findings of historical simulations for two populations. Following that, we turn to the simulations exploring the population effects of density dependence, both contemporaneous and delayed for all types of populations studied.

Simulation Methods

Addressing questions about population dynamics requires that both vital rates be considered. In the logistic model, the population growth rate is found by multiplying each (density-dependent) rate by density. However, organizations lack an obvious parallel to the maternity function—foundings occur to the population, as we already noted. And mortality occurs to particular organizations with specific structures and histories. Because founding rates are estimated at the population level and mortality rates at the organizational level, some aggregation or disaggregation rule must be used to compare the two rates and to express them in the same dimension. We express the growth (or decline) in numbers of organizations at any time as the difference between the number of foundings at (near) that time and the number of mortalities at (near) that time. Both the flow of foundings and the flow of mortalities depend on the contemporaneous density. However, the flow of mortalities over time depends on the age structure of the population and on the distribution of density at founding. As a result, the models of population growth and decline are quite complicated.[1]

---

[1] Liu and Cohen (1987) and Caswell (1989) provide detailed discussions of the dynamics of population growth models with both age structure and density delay.

Exploring the dynamic consequences of nonmonotonic density dependence in the rates requires substituting estimates of λ and μ as functions of contemporaneous density, density at founding, age, and possibly other causal factors. The basis for our analyses of these issues is a set of simulation procedures.

This section describes the procedures used in the simulations reported in the section "Simulating Historical Trajectories"; a listing of the computer program, written by David N. Barron, is included as Appendix C. (The "analytic" simulations presented in the last section of this chapter are various simplifications of the models used in the "historical" simulations.) We proceed according to the following steps:

1. Initialize the population and set initial values of covariates for the start of the first year of the simulation. Because we condition on the first observed founding (as discussed in Appendix A), we do not simulate the number of foundings at the start (period 0). Instead, we create a single organization (the "pioneer") at the start. For exposing the pioneer organization to the risk of mortality during its first year, we set density at the start of that year to zero, the number of foundings in previous year to zero, and the number of mortalities in the previous year to zero. By definition, density at founding is zero for the first organization in the population.

2. Construct a predicted mean founding rate for each period (year) after period 0, using an empirically estimated model of founding rates. In the notation of Appendix B, this is

$$\mathrm{E}(Y_t) = \widehat{\phi}_t = \widehat{\varphi}(N_t) \exp\!\left(\widehat{\gamma} N_t^2\right) \exp\!\left(\mathbf{x}'_t \widehat{\pi} + \widehat{\tau}_p\right), \qquad (8.1)$$

where N_t is density at start of year, $\varphi(N_t)$ is the functional form of the legitimation function that fits best for each population (as reported in Chapter 4), $\mathbf{x}'_t \widehat{\pi}$ contains the effects of covariates including previous foundings, and $\widehat{\tau}_p$ is a set of period effects.

3. Use the calculated mean rate from Step 2 along with the estimated overdispersion parameter to define the appropriate negative binomial distribution of counts of foundings per year. (We use the parameterization in Equation B.7.) The first step is to define $k = 1/\widehat{\omega}$ (ω is the overdispersion parameter—see Appendix

B) and $p = k/(k + \hat{\phi}_t)$. Second, choose a realization from a negative binomial distribution given in Equation B.7 with parameters (k, p). This yields the simulated number of foundings for the year.

4. Add newly founded organizations to the base population. Assign the current value of density as the (fixed) density at founding for each.

5. Calculate a hazard of mortality for each organization at risk, including those founded in previous years and newly founded ones, with the model from Chapter 6,

$$\hat{\mu}_i(t, f) = \exp\left(\hat{\theta}_1 N_t + \hat{\theta}_2 N_t^2 + \hat{\theta}_3 N_{f_i}\right) \exp\left(\mathbf{x}'_{it}\hat{\pi} + \hat{\tau}_p\right) a^{\hat{\rho}}, \quad (8.2)$$

where a is the age of the organization and $\hat{\rho}$ is the estimate of the parameter indexing age dependence in mortality rates. Using the estimates from Chapter 6 and the values of density, density at founding, age, and the historically appropriate values of covariates, calculate the predicted rate for each organization for that year. Age (a) is set to its value at the start of the period of risk, either age at the start of year for organizations founded in previous years or 0.1 (because the Weibull model is not defined at zero) for newly founded organizations.

6. Expose each organization to the risk of mortality over the appropriate period of risk. We calculate the organization's predicted probability of mortality over the year (one time unit) using

$$\hat{p} = \widehat{\Pr}\{\text{org } i \text{ fails in year } t\} = 1 - \exp(-\hat{\mu}_{it} \times \text{riskperiod}),$$

where "riskperiod" denotes the length of the period of risk of mortality. This is 1.0 for organizations founded before the year in question. For those founded during the year in question, we assume that the period of risk is half a year (.5). Next, choose a realization from a uniform distribution over $(0, 1)$ and compare it with $\hat{p}$. If the predicted probability of mortality exceeds the random number, then assign a mortality event to the organization; otherwise keep the organization in the population.

7. Define start-of-year density for the next year as density at the start of the current year plus the number of foundings minus the number of mortalities.

8. Set age at start of next year to .5 for organizations founded during the year. Update ages of all other existing organization by one year; update the year by one; define appropriate values of covariates and period effects; and return to the second step (until the appropriate number of years have been simulated).

These procedures yield a count of vital events for each year and a level of density, and they introduce stochastic variation in the construction of both foundings and failures. This variation, compounded through effects of density on vital rates, can cause simulation runs using the same set of parameter estimates to fluctuate in important ways, as we shall demonstrate.

When describing the procedure, we referred to a negative binomial distribution for foundings. Recall that we did not make any distributional assumptions when conducting QL estimation of founding rates. Instead, we specified particular forms of overdispersion and autocorrelation. Although this approach has great appeal in estimation, it does not prove useful in simulation because we need precise specification of the stochastic mechanism in order to generate events appropriately. We rely on the negative binomial specification discussed in Appendix B, estimated by maximum likelihood. This specification contains overdispersion but not autocorrelation because we have not yet learned how to compute ML estimates for the case with autocorrelation. Although the model and estimator differ from Chapter 4, the substantive results do not differ much. The switch probably does not make a substantive difference in the simulation studies. However, this change in estimator does mean that the effects of density used in the simulations (based on ML estimation of models without autocorrelation) are not exactly the same as those in Table 4.1.

One limitation of the procedure used to simulate realizations from a negative binomial distribution is that the overdispersion parameter cannot exceed unity.[2] This constraint is met for all populations except brewers for which the estimate of $\widehat{\omega} = 2.7$. In this case, we set ω to .9. As a result, simulations for this population greatly understate the variability in the timing of initial growth.

---

[2] This constraint arises in the method used to simulate realizations from a beta distribution as an intermediate step—see Appendix C for details.

Simulating Historical Trajectories

We start with the implications of the full models in order to see whether they jointly imply paths of growth in numbers that come close to those observed historically. In particular, we combine effects of density with those of lagged foundings and mortalities, period effects, trends, and environmental covariates in predicting rates of founding and mortality for each year. We call these "historical" predictions of rates because they reflect the historical peculiarities of a population as parameterized in the effects of covariates and periods. We then apply the predicted historical rates over the observed lifetime of a population, beginning with a density of one in the initial year. This procedure yields a path of growth (and possible decline) in numbers by year over the simulated history of a population. We then repeat the procedure numerous times so that we can examine stochastic variation and compare the simulated paths with the observed historical path.

We do not present full details of the results of this procedure for all empirical populations because that would require too many plots of results. Instead, we present some of the details for two populations that illustrate well the range of results: national labor unions and commercial banks.[3] We used the best-fitting models for founding rates, that is the log-quadratic (LQ) model for unions and the generalized-Yule (GY) model for banks. As we noted, the estimates of effects of density are not exactly the same as those in Table 4.1 due to a change in estimation and stochastic specification, especially regarding autocorrelation. The estimated first-order effects of density on founding rates used in this simulation are .043 for unions and .601 for banks. The estimated second-order effects are −.000187 for unions and −.000077 for commercial banks. We used the LQ model for mortality rates for both populations. The effects of contemporaneous density and density at founding on overall rates of mortality used in these simulations are the ones reported in Table 6.1.

Simulations of growth in density of labor unions with the full

---

[3] We consider the subpopulation of commercial banks rather than the whole population because the estimated models of bank mortality contain an effect of organizational form (commercial versus mutual savings) which means that we have predicted rates for each form.

model reveal an interesting instability. In a quarter of the experiments, the population grows in a reasonably close approximation to the historical record. But in roughly three of four runs, the population grows modestly (to a maximum of about 40 unions) and then either stagnates or declines. Figure 8.1 illustrates the pattern with seven simulation results and the observed history (indicated by the dashed line).

Our investigations indicate that the instability is a consequence of the period effects. The paths of runs that grow and those that stagnate tend to diverge shortly after the start of the second period (50 years after the start of the population). The second period has a lower founding rate and a higher mortality rate than does the first period (this can be seen in the full set of estimates reported in Table C.1 in Appendix C). If density has not yet risen beyond a value of roughly 50 when the rates change, density will either stagnate or decline. Because of the structure of the subsequent period effects, the population cannot recover from this decline and density remains low. But, if the population has already grown large before the second period, the changed rates will not have any long-run effect on the evolution of density.

Eliminating the period effects (setting them to zero in Equations 8.1 and 8.2) has a major impact on the simulations. The population grows above or near its observed historic peak in all 50 simulation runs we tried. Density crashed, falling to zero, in only one simulation; and density grew substantially after the crash in this case. Figure 8.2 displays the results of seven simulations without period effects that display typical behavior. Note that one growth path rises substantially above the others and then declines to the neighborhood of the other six growth paths. Such a pattern of overshoot occurred in six of 50 simulation runs.

The shapes of all seven growth paths in Figure 8.2 resemble the historical path reasonably closely in form over the first 130 years or so of the 149 year history. In this sense, the model can reproduce most of the important features of the observed history of growth in density of American labor unions. The model cannot, however, explain the dip in density in the later years. The simulated paths fluctuate in a narrow range considerably above the historical path.

The most interesting variation among growth paths without period effects concerns the timing of the takeoff. Over 50 simulation

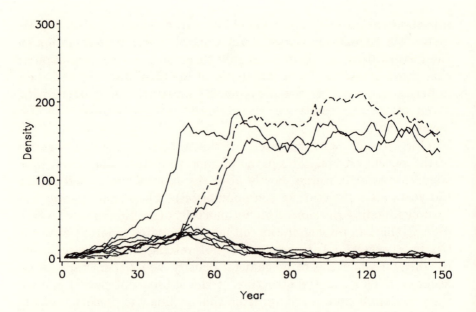

Figure 8.1. Results of seven historical simulations of the growth in density of American labor unions with full model

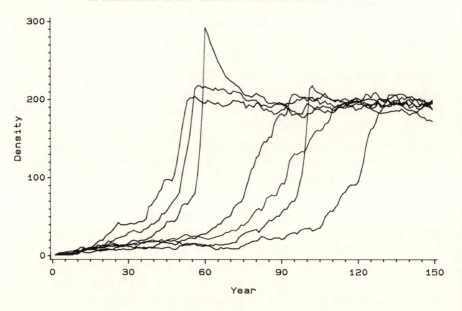

Figure 8.2. Results of seven historical simulations of the growth in density of American labor unions without period effects

runs, the time of takeoff varied by roughly 100 years at the extremes. Thus, stochastic variation in the timing of occurrences of foundings and mortalities can retard the takeoff of density by as much as a century. Such variation in the timing of the takeoff can be partly attributed to overdispersion in the founding process. When we repeat the simulations without overdispersion, there is much less variation in time of takeoff. In this sense, overdispersion makes a real difference in qualitative dynamics.

Several other features of the simulation results in Figure 8.2 deserve comment. First, density dependence of the form we estimated produces an analogue to a carrying capacity. The growth paths of all simulations stabilize within a small range of density. When the number of unions overshoots this range, density rapidly drops back to the range in which other paths are concentrated. None of the paths stays far above the others in these and other simulation results with the model that excludes period effects.

A second interesting feature of the simulated growth paths is hard to see in Figure 8.2 because the paths overlap so much. This is the appearance of a modest cycle in density caused by the effect of density delay. In most cases, density fluctuates by about 10%, but the cycles do not coincide with the historical decline in number of unions over the last 40 years of the observed history. Indeed, few of our simulation results produce a consistent decline in numbers over this period. So, even though there is evidence of cycles, they do not generally reproduce the historical decline in numbers after the peak was reached.

The results for commercial banks provide an interesting contrast with the pattern observed for unions. Whereas the simulated paths of growth in density of unions either rose to the carrying capacity or rose only modestly and then crashed, all of the simulated paths for the subpopulation of commercial banks rose substantially, as can be seen for the path plotted in Figure 8.3 (the solid line is the simulated path and the dashed line again indicates the observed historical path). That is, we did not observe the kind of stalled growth in density that occurred in roughly half of the runs for unions. Another form of instability characterizes the results for banks: In most cases, the population of banks crashed from a high level of density, falling to zero within a couple of years and then surged, crashed, and so on.

A detailed study of the flows of events in the simulation runs

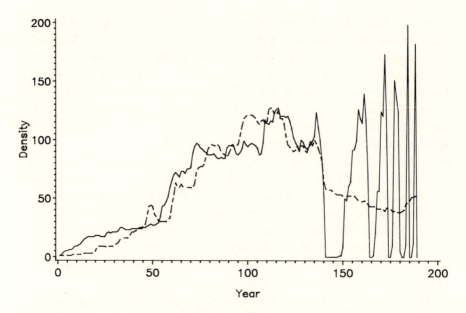

Figure 8.3. Results of a historical simulation of the growth in density of
Manhattan commercial banks

reveals that the crashes were caused by the relatively large positive
feedback effect in the mortality process. The feedback came from the
positive effect of the count of recent mortalities on the mortality rate.
In other words, a shock like an economic depression that increases
the mortality rate can initiate a spiral of increasing mortality rates
that wipes out the population in short order. The feedback effect is
acute here because the effect of lagged mortalities on the mortality
rate is loglinear. In retrospect, it may have been better to have used
a log-quadratic specification that allows a ceiling on the effect.

The estimated effect of density at founding on mortality rates for
banks is about double that for unions (see Table 6.1). As a result,
the cycles in the growth and decline of the density of commercial
banks are quite pronounced, more so than is the case for unions. A
strong effect of density at founding yields cycles in the growth and
decline of density.

Perhaps the most interesting consistency in the simulations for
unions and commercial banks concerns the sources of instability in
the evolution of organizational density. In each case, the source of
population crashes is something extraneous to the model of density

dependence—period effects for unions and effects of lagged mortalities for banks. What does this mean substantively? We think that the pattern means that attention should be focused on the core theory and model of density dependence. Including period effects, effects of lagged events, and effects of other covariates in models that relate density to vital rates in organizational populations serves the important purpose of refining estimates of density dependence. Yet the period effects and covariates appear to pick up the influences of transient events in the histories of populations that affect vital rates in the short run but do not shape the long-run evolution of density.

In particular, period effects and covariates operate on some actual historical path of density that is not necessarily reproduced in any run of the simulation. When we apply the period effects and effects of covariates to time paths of densities for a population that diverge widely from the real history of the population, we may be distorting the effects of the transient influences. More concretely, we impose these effects by using the rule that particular parameters change in specified iterations of the simulation, for example, the 110th turn if the second period is defined as one that began in the year in which the actual historical population was in its 110th year of existence. But we have not ensured that the other conditions that obtained in that year are also met in the simulation, notably we do not constrain density to have the historically correct value, as we are simulating the evolution of density. For this reason, the full historical simulations are less interesting than those that focus on the analytic core of the model of density dependence. But, we are pleased to learn that the estimated models can generally reproduce the observed historical trajectories of organizational density.

Density Dependence

In order to focus on the effects of density we pruned the model radically. We dropped everything in Equations 8.1 and 8.2 except the effects of density (contemporaneous and delayed), the constants, and overdispersion in the founding process. One complication concerned the treatment of the constants. Because the estimated models contain effects of time-varying covariates such as population age and real wages, the constants would change greatly if the covariates were excluded. We prefer to use the estimates of effects of density from

the better specified models that contain the covariates but to simulate growth paths without the effects of covariates. Therefore, we
experimented with choices of constants that yield peak population
sizes in simulations that are similar to those observed historically.[4]

We think that it is interesting to see how the model works for the
full variety of populations we studied. This section reports results
for one of the newspaper populations (San Francisco Bay Area) and
each of the other kinds of populations.

Our simulation studies with the model of density dependence for
the population of labor unions yield a very clear picture. Stripping
away effects of aging, lagged events, periods, time trends, and other
covariates removes virtually all of the instability in paths of growth
and decline in density. Figure 8.4 presents results of seven runs of
the simulation of density dependence for labor unions. In each case
in Figure 8.4 and in numerous other simulations whose results are
not reported, the model generates orderly growth to a carrying capacity. There is little dispersion of growth paths over the early and
late histories of the simulated populations. The only striking variation concerns the timing of the takeoff. The modal pattern is for
density to begin to surge upward at about 80 years into the population history. But one path takes off at about 40 years and another
at about 120 years. It is worth reemphasizing that the variation in
time of takeoff reflects only stochastic variation, as the underlying
rates are the same in all cases.

One feature of the simulated growth paths of density-dependent
processes surprised us. We had reasoned that age dependence inter-
acted with density delay so as to depress the amplitude of cycles of
growth and decline in density. Recall that the Weibull and Gompertz
specifications of age dependence used in our analyses of mortality
rates impose monotonic declines in mortality rates with aging. Thus
the permanent effect of founding at high density (density delay) is
applied to a steadily diminishing baseline mortality rate. Suppose
that organizations founded during times of maximum density have a
permanent doubling of mortality rates compared with some standard
(for example, those founded at half the maximum of density). Dou-

---

[4] Choice of constant affects the degree of overdispersion in the founding
process, because it affects the mean of the process and the level of overdispersion is set proportional to the mean, as Appendix B explains.

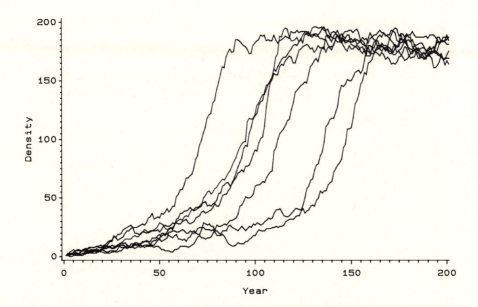

Figure 8.4. Results of seven runs of a simulation of density dependence for the population of American labor unions

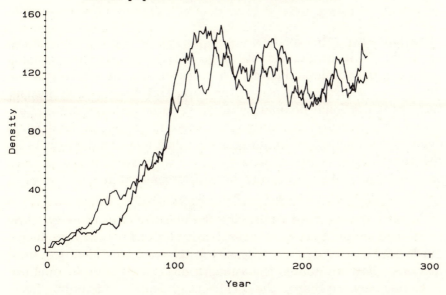

Figure 8.5. Results of two runs of a simulation of density dependence with stronger density delay for the population of American labor unions

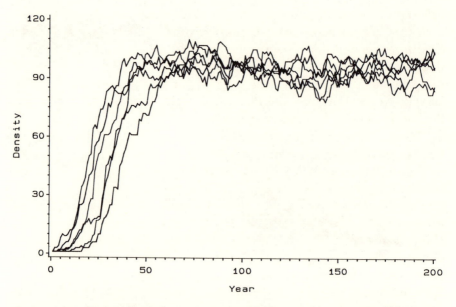

Figure 8.6. Results of six runs of a simulation of density dependence for the population of American life insurance companies

bling mortality rates for new organizations (whose mortality rates are high) produces big absolute gains in the rate. But as organizations age, the absolute differences in rates will decline even if relative differences persist. As a result, the impact of density delay lessens as an organizational population ages. We assumed that turning off the effect of aging on mortality rates, as we have done in the density dependence simulation, would produce much more marked cycles in the growth and decline of density. This turned out not to be the case, however. We can discern little systematic difference between results of simulations with and without age dependence.

What happens if we strengthen the effect of density delay? We already remarked that a stronger density delay for banks produced much more marked cycling of density in the context of historical simulations. Now we double the strength of density delay for unions; more precisely, we change the coefficient of density at founding from .07 to .15 in Equation 8.2. Figure 8.5 shows the result for two runs of the simulation. There are indeed stronger cycles. In addition, a variety of runs not shown in the figure indicate that there is much greater variation in time of takeoff. The exact details of the pattern vary considerably over simulation runs. In many cases, density fluctuates up and down by as much as 40%. Interestingly, a density-dependent process with a stronger density delay than we estimated can produce dynamics of density very much like those actually observed. Notice that one sample path contains a peak with consistent decline in density beyond the peak.

The pattern for life insurance companies (Figure 8.6) is strikingly similar to that for labor unions. All of the simulated paths shown in Figure 8.6 contain brief periods of very rapid growth. Again we see the operation of something like a carrying capacity—after 70 or 80 periods, density remains in the same reasonably narrow range for all growth paths. But there is modest random fluctuation around the carrying capacity for all paths, which reflects mainly the force of density delay. The main difference from the results for labor unions concerns the variation in time of takeoff, which varies by only about 20 years at the extreme for the paths plotted in Figure 8.6.

Simulations for the population of Manhattan commercial banks yield a very stable pattern of almost linear growth and then stabilization (Figure 8.7). The growth paths are clustered about as much as for life insurance companies but are more tightly clustered than was the case for unions (although the difference in time scales between Figures 8.7 and 8.4 exaggerates the difference). As was the case for unions and life insurance companies, there is some apparent cycling in the range in which growth paths are flat; however, the fluctuations are modest in magnitude.

Results for the population of San Francisco Bay Area newspaper publishers resemble those for labor unions and life insurance companies, as can be seen by comparing the results of seven simulations for this population in Figure 8.8 with Figures 8.4 and 8.6. The general pattern of initial growth is roughly exponential as it was for unions. Growth slows abruptly in the range of the apparent carrying capacity and stabilizes. As was the case for unions, there is noticeable fluctuation within the range of aggregate stability in numbers. The most apparent difference between the results for unions and newspaper publishers concerns the times of takeoffs—these are highly variable for unions but not for newspapers.

Perhaps the most interesting results are those for American brewing firms. Density dependence (with overdispersion) produces growth

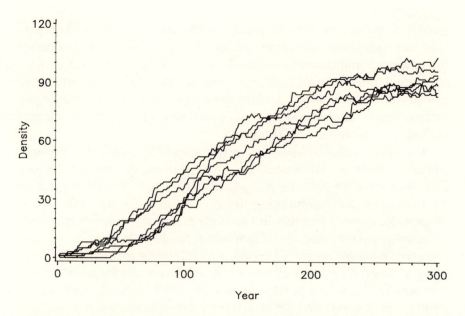

Figure 8.7. Results of seven runs of a simulation of density dependence for the population of Manhattan commercial banks

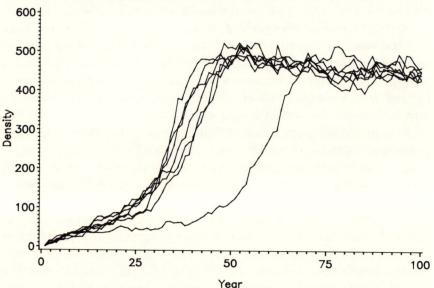

Figure 8.8. Results of seven runs of a simulation of density dependence for the population of San Francisco Bay Area newspaper publishers

paths with huge cycles. This pattern reflects the greater strength of the effect of density delay relative to effects of contemporaneous density for this population (see Table 6.1). The striking consequence of our estimates of density dependence for this population are growth paths that often mimic the boom and bust growth pattern observed historically (see Figure 1.5). The strength of the cycles makes it hard to interpret plots of simulation results with even as many as two growth paths. Figure 8.9 shows two pairs that can be distinguished over the interesting part of the range. Note first that three of the four grow very rapidly. Both growth paths in the top panel contain precipitous drops in density from the initial peaks, in each case dropping from approximately 3000 to about 1600. One path in the bottom panel also drops abruptly, though not as much as in the cases in the top panel. The fourth growth path has a very different shape; it takes about twice as long as the other three to reach a peak. This general pattern occurs in about one seventh of our simulation runs; the rest display rapid growth similar to that for the other three paths in Figure 8.9. The variation in time of takeoff is substantial in that some paths have much slower growth, despite the fact that we reduced the amount of overdispersion by two-thirds to fit the constraints of the simulation program (as we explained earlier).

The fluctuations observed for brewers and other populations presumably reflect the combined effects of density delay and simple random variation in occurrences of events. We explored the effects of turning off the effect of density delay and found that amplitudes of fluctuations (or cycles) were reduced greatly. It is clear that density delay plays the major role in producing large fluctuations in density once the region of the carrying capacity is reached.

Discussion

Although our simulation experiments of population growth were not exhaustive or definitive, we do think that they suggest several important conclusions about the models of density dependence developed in earlier chapters. Foremost among these is that the models can reproduce population trajectories that resemble closely the actual historical trajectories of the populations we study. This means that despite the lack of formal tests of model fit at this level of analysis

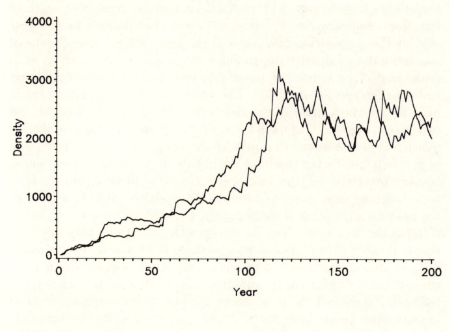

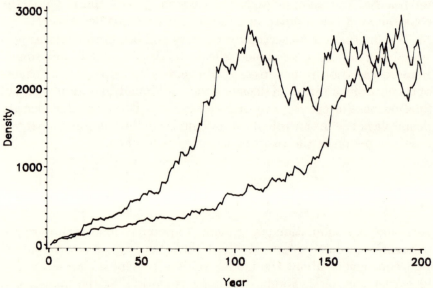

Figure 8.9. Results of four runs of a simulation of density dependence for
the population of American brewing firms

(combining specifications of both vital rates), we have confidence in the predictive power of the model.

The simulations also suggest three general conclusions about the implications of density-dependent processes of legitimation and competition for dynamics of organizational populations. First, the basic processes of contemporaneous density dependence specified by our models yield a fairly stable pattern of S-shaped growth to an approximate ceiling or carrying capacity. Second, the effects of density delay (density at founding) on mortality rates can generate declines and even cycles from the carrying capacity—the stronger the effect is, the bigger the declines and cycles will be. Third, the models imply great stochastic variation in the timing of the explosive growth (or takeoff) period for some populations.

The last point seems to us to have potentially profound substantive significance. When sociologists and other social scientists observe population trajectories such as those we analyzed here, they typically focus on the periods of explosive growth and search for historical or deterministic explanations. That is, they seek to learn what special circumstances held at the exact time of takeoff and attribute causal importance to them. We argued in earlier chapters that focusing on a single organizational form and its idiosyncratic history is too limiting. Now, on the basis of our simulations, it appears that focusing on the actual timing of the growth period and its social and historical context can be misleading as well. At the very least, we know that the same generic sociological processes can produce very different historical realizations of organizational population growth.

9

Implications for Social Organization

We began this book by noting two empirical regularities in the long-term trajectories of growth in numbers in diverse organizational populations. The first pertains to surface resemblances in the shape of paths of growth in numbers from low to high density. The second concerns a deeper resemblance in the causal structures that control the underlying rates of founding and mortality. On the basis of previous theory and research, we proposed that an appropriate formulation of the sociological processes of legitimation and competition and of their effects on vital rates might explain both regularities and thereby provide a general explanation of the sources of population regulation in the world of organizations.

To be more precise, we argued that both legitimation and competition in organizational populations are tied to growth in density, although in very different ways, and that legitimation and competition affect rates of organizational founding and mortality. The theory implies testable qualitative hypotheses about the relationship between contemporaneous density, on the one hand, and rates of organizational founding and mortality, on the other. In particular, it implies that such relationships have specific *nonmonotonic* forms. It also implies that density at founding has a persistent positive effect on mortality rates of organizations. We developed mathematical models of effects of contemporaneous density and density at founding based on this theory and estimated them with data on seven populations of organizations. The results strongly support the theory on these key points. And, simulations based on our estimates show that processes of density-dependent legitimation and competition can account for much, but not all, of the observed regularity in population trajectories.

Much of our book elaborated, refined, and extended the theory and models. Although the theory of density dependence existed previously, its various possible mathematical specifications and their theoretical implications had not been explored in any detail. By examining these issues in depth here, we feel that we have improved our understanding of processes of legitimation and competition. We hope that such elaboration clarifies the status of the theory and the mathematical models and thereby makes them more useful to other researchers.

Chapter 1 highlighted our view that multiple replication has great value in organizational research and has received too little attention. The past two decades have seen a shift in research on organizations from designs that obtain random samples of diverse kinds of organizations to designs involving only a single organizational form, population, or industry (see Freeman 1986). This development has been basically healthy because it allows for much greater detail in specifying processes and better substantive grounding. The strategy suffers the potential disadvantage of producing particularistic (and possibly idiosyncratic) research findings, that is, results that are peculiar to a particular organizational population at a particular time and place. Few sociologists would deem this outcome desirable. One important way to avoid it is by replicating findings across diverse populations and industries, as we have done here.

Few theories in organizational sociology can count as many replications as we have reported here. Without implying universality, we do believe that such an array of findings establishes the general utility of the theory for explaining change in populations of organizations. Our results suggest that future organizational research can rely on the theory and the particular parametric models as baseline specifications for an investigation of substantive questions about environmental selection and long-term evolution of organizational populations. If so, the formulations presented in this book will undergo repeated replication in the course of studies of related problems.

We tried to address the objections and criticisms that have come forward to date. These include matters of logic, modeling, measurement, research design, and statistical inference. Additional matters will undoubtedly arise, and these will have to be dealt with as they emerge. It strikes us that the potentially most interesting challenge will come in the form of alternative theoretical explanations of the robust empirical relationships between density and vital rates. Throughout our work on this project we have claimed that at the very least, identifying these previously unrecognized relationships between density and the vital rates constitutes a new and important contribution. We have encouraged those unconvinced by our theoretical explanation of these empirical associations to advance an alternative explanation. Currently we have yet to see a theory equally capable of explaining these relationships. Once such a rival argument appears, research can be conducted in order to evaluate its merits.

Extending the Theory

In the course of presenting our argument and findings, we described certain concerns as "research problems in their own right" but avoided exploring them in any depth. The reason was that we viewed them as distractions from our primary task, developing and testing the theory. Having accomplished our main goal, we now sketch approaches to addressing several research problems that involve the study of organizational density in one way or another.

Density Dependence and Social Networks

A research problem of this kind with broad sociological significance is to clarify the effects of direct and diffuse competition. Our arguments in this book emphasized diffuse competition, processes that link the life chances of organizations that may or may not interact as direct competitors by, for instance, taking into account each other's actions as rivals. Instead of trying to measure the intensity of diffuse competition, we used arguments about competitive processes to develop implications for the relationship between density and the vital rates of organizational populations.

In Chapter 2 we noted that some social scientists would prefer an exclusive focus on direct competition and on observable social relationships. Measurement of direct competition and rivalry might take a number of forms. The possibilities include measuring (for all pairs of organizations in a population) overlap in market participation, degree of product substitutability, overlap in consumers, advertising rivalry, managerial perception of rivalry, and so forth. In any case, this approach differs from the one used here in that it entails efforts to measure competition by examining observed interconnections.

The obvious question that can readily addressed concerns the extent to which the two conceptualizations overlap or are otherwise related. Does direct competitive behavior generate competitive outcomes? Does diffuse competitive behavior actually benefit rivals by, say, expanding the size of the market or perhaps by excluding new entrants? Are there conditions under which each situation occurs? Empirical investigation of such questions may be, we believe, much more useful than further epistemological debate about the nature of competition.

Clarification of the relationships between direct and diffuse competition would provide a basis for integrating social network analysis and organizational ecology. Direct competition among all pairs of organizations in a population could be readily modeled as a set of ties. Such matrices could be analyzed by the techniques of network analysis to examine network centrality and structural equivalence. These concepts could then be examined further within the context of density-dependent legitimation and competition and their implications for organizational life chances assessed.

Density, Mass, and the Shape of Size Distributions

A second broad problem is distinguishing the effects of density and mass. We focused here single-mindedly on density because we believe that it has theoretical significance and methodological strategic value. Yet density stands as only one of several possible summaries of the scale of an organizational population. Because this specification of scale yields consistent, interpretable results, it would be interesting to consider other possible effects of scale on processes of legitimation and competition. The most obvious alternative specification of scale relies on measures of the *mass* of the population, which can be thought of as density weighted by the sizes of all organizations in the population.

We have begun to address the complaint that effects of density might simply be a by-product of the effect of mass of populations. We did so by showing that the expected pattern of density dependence persists even when organizational mass (individual and population) has been controlled. This research strategy was dictated by our focus on density and by the limitations of our data rather than by a lack of interest in mass dependence.[1] Much more work remains to be done on this point.

The question of interest now concerns the relationship between mass dependence and density dependence. Whereas density declines late in the development of the populations studied here, population mass presumably continues to grow. Can a model be built to integrate these two important features of organizational evolution?

In the hope of sparking theoretical and empirical work on this question, we pose a series of questions about the relations between density and mass, on the one hand, and legitimation and competition, on the other. In the case of legitimation, we argued that growing density in an organizational population conveys a sense of taken-for-grantedness. Does growth in mass produce similar increases in taken-for-grantedness as does growth in density? In order to sharpen the question, compare the situation in which (1) a population contains only one single organization whose mass grows large with (2) one in which growth in mass comes about through the proliferation of small organizations. Do the two growth paths yield similar growth in legitimation of the organizational form?

This question raises interesting issues that have not yet been studied. Presumably the answer depends on the locations of the organization(s) in the social structure and on the form of the social structure. For instance, the legitimating effect of growth in a population of small organizations presumably depends on the distribution of the organizations over space and over other dimensions that structure interaction. The more concentrated the set is, the more it will resemble a single large organization in terms of conveying information about the form and creating a sense of its taken-for-grantedness.

There are strong reasons for expecting differences in the effects of growth in density and of growth in mass in the case of competition. The main reason has to do with complexity and its implications for strategic action. If density increases with mass held constant, the strategic problems facing each existing organization will become

---

[1] Indeed, we have elsewhere (Carroll 1981; Nielsen and Hannan 1977; Tuma and Hannan 1984, chap. 14) developed and used models of mass dependence to study organizational evolution.

more difficult, as the actions of many more potential competitors must be taken into account. Virtually all accounts of industrial organization agree that the likelihood of successful collusion to weaken competitive pressures falls rapidly as the number of independent organizations in the population (or industry) rises. This is the reason for formulating special theories of oligopolistic industrial organization. And, it must be emphasized, problems of oligopoly concern density, not mass.

Both density and mass are scalar descriptions of the magnitude of an organizational population. Perhaps it also makes sense to consider *distributions* of numbers and size. We suspect that organizational size distributions may be more important than mass in shaping the dynamics and evolution of organizational populations.

Consider, for example, the implications of size-localized competition. Hannan and Freeman (1977, p. 945) argued that organizations of very different sizes typically employ different strategies and structures and therefore "competition between pairs of organizations in an activity will be a decreasing function of the distance separating them on the size gradient." They proposed further that the competitive balance among organizations of different sizes changes as the size distribution evolves. In particular, the emergence of very large organizations diminishes the life chances of those of medium size so that the center of the size distribution shrinks relative to that of commonly used baseline distributions.

Hannan and Ranger-Moore (1990) conducted simulation experiments in which growth rates of organizations are depressed by competitive pressures in tightly packed regions of the size axis. They found that strongly localized competition does tend to produce the predicted qualitative pattern of gaps toward the center of the size distribution. Hannan, Ranger-Moore, and Banaszak-Holl (1990) compared simulation results with sequences of empirical size distributions calculated at ten year intervals over 150 years for the populations of banks and life insurance companies. Size distributions of both empirical populations evolve toward a pattern that agrees with the argument, beginning with lognormal distributions. That is, size-localized competition creates gaps in size distributions.

More important to our purposes, we now have empirical evidence (from the real world) that size-localized competition affects life chances of organizations. Ranger-Moore (1990) found that location in a densely packed region of the size distribution increased mortality rates and depressed growth rates of life insurance companies located in New York State between 1870 and 1980, even when the effects of firm size and population mass are taken into account. We think it likely that much more insight into population dynamics will result from incorporating effects of size distribution into models of density dependence than from incorporating mass. In other words, it is more profitable to add distributional information than to proliferate scalar summaries of the magnitude of populations.

Issues of Microfoundations

The theory of density-dependent legitimation and competition can also be developed further by investigating its possible microfoundations. This means attempting to derive the macropropositions and models from assumptions about microbehavior and rules of aggregation. Indeed, such an effort constitutes the natural next step in the view of many with whom we discussed these issues.

Action in Multilevel Systems

Interest in developing models of social structure as implications of processes of rational choice and the aggregation of individual actions is currently widespread in the social sciences. In keeping with the ecological tradition (Hawley 1950, 1986), our formulation is silent on the role, if any, of individual action. In the interests of making connections with other lines of theory and research, it may be useful to discuss the relations between individual action and organizational ecology, especially in regard to density-dependent legitimation and competition. Most sociological theories operate at two (or more) levels—there are actors and macrostructures, which are sometimes regarded as "systems of action." It is common to treat human persons as the actors and organizations, communities, markets, or nations as the macrostructures. Organizational ecology, as we develop it, has two kinds of actors, depending on the problem. In the case of founding processes, the actors are the social units that can create organizations. For mortality and structural change, the actors are organizations. In either case, the macrosystems are populations of organizations (or systems of populations, that is, communities of organizations). What difference, if any, does the specification of the actor have for the role of theories of action, including theories of rational action, in organizational ecology?

Most social science work on multilevel systems assumes the desirability of a tight fit between levels. That is, it is commonplace to assume that good theoretical strategies contain close correspondences between microbehavioral assumptions and macroprocesses. If levels of analysis are linked tightly, then changing the details of microassumptions will alter the specifications of macroprocesses.

Robustness of Macrotheories

Although the idea of building tight links across levels of analysis has broad support, this strategy of theory building does not necessarily yield useful macrotheories. Indeed, the general ecological-evolutionary approach provides an interesting example: A major source of the power of Darwin's theory of evolution by means of natural selection lies in its extreme decoupling of the form of macroprocesses from the precise specification of the relevant microprocesses: genetic mixing and transmission. As is well known, Darwin assumed what turned out to be the wrong model of genetic transition—blending inheritance rather than particulate (Mendelian) inheritance. Yet, he got the macroprocess right in the sense that his theory continues to serve as the main unifying framework in virtually all modern biology. Consider what would have happened had he built tight links between his macroevolutionary theory and his genetics—the macrotheory would have become obsolete with the victory of Mendelian genetics.

We do not mean to diminish the importance of specifying the genetic mechanisms underlying a process of biotic evolution. This task surely is important and completing it has been the major preoccupation of modern evolutionary population biology. But the example of Darwin makes clear that one can arrive at the correct macroformulation with incorrect microfoundations *if the macrotheory is made sufficiently robust.* To us, this example suggests that robustness with respect to changes in microfoundations is an important goal in developing macrotheories. This strategy makes sense given considerable uncertainty about the precise forms of the microprocesses, as in the social sciences.

The concrete strategic issues in considering microfoundations for theories of organizational change require deciding how much flexibility and foresight to attribute to social units at the different levels of analysis. The reason is that isomorphism between organizational forms and environmental conditions can arise through two very different kinds of processes. In one, successful planned adaptations are initiated by prescient actors who found appropriate organizations at appropriate times and in appropriate places and who redesign existing organizations appropriately as conditions change. In the second, isomorphism arises through processes of differential selection operating on random action at lower levels or on the purposeful action of highly inflexible actors.

Some theorists assume that both individuals and organizations are flexible and purposive (even maximizing) adapters to changeable external conditions. This seems to be the main point of view in contemporary economics, which regards both the entrepreneurs who found organizations (or the principals who possess rights to organizations) and the organizations they build to be flexible optimizers over a broad range of external conditions. Coleman (1990) also adopts this point of view when considering multilevel systems of action. That is, he advocates treating both individuals and organizations as subject to the axioms of rational choice.

Other theorists treat the individual actors as flexible and substantively rational in pursuing their interests but assume that the organizations resulting from their joint self-seeking behavior are highly inflexible and limited in substantive rationality. Selznick (1948) proposed the imagery of organizations as "recalcitrant tools." Much recalcitrance and inflexibility reflects the operation of organizational culture in which precedent takes on a moral character and of organizational politics, especially processes of coalition formation (Hannan 1986b).[2]

Some sociological work makes the opposite assumption, namely, that individual actors cannot conduct their affairs rationally but

[2] Consider, for instance, Arrow's (1951) impossibility theorem: collective decisions that follow from the rational choices of individuals cannot satisfy the axioms of rational choice if the decisions are unconstrained. If organizations operate as committee decision structures, it follows that their preferences deviate from the axioms of rational choice even when each member has preferences that do agree with these axioms.

that organizations can and do. Stinchcombe, for example, espouses this position and attributes it to Weber (see Swedberg 1990, pp. 288–289). He argues that organizations develop special expertise in gathering information and making decisions that allow it to overcome the limitations on individual capacities.

Meyer (1983) disagrees with both of these views and contends instead that total rationality in social systems is approximately a constant. For him, the more that rationality is invested in individuals, the less rational will be the set of organizations they build and occupy, and vice versa. In this view, either individuals or corporate actors might behave rationally, but not both.

Illustration with Founding Processes

There is no consensus about how best to conceptualize rationality in processes of organizational change. What difference do choices in this matter have for the development of theories like ours? This question arises in a potentially interesting way when considering processes of organizational founding. We specified the population as the unit at risk for founding, as we explained in Chapter 4 and Appendix B. The organization observed to be founded cannot be the unit, as "nonevents" (the absence of foundings in some period) are as important as are observed foundings for testing theories about founding rates (for further discussion see Carroll and Hannan 1989c; Delacroix and Carroll 1983; Hannan 1991; Hannan and Freeman 1987). So we treat foundings as a realization of a point process for the organizational population.

Zucker (1989) rejects this reasoning and suggests that theoretical attention must focus on the potential founder. In the simplest case, all the potential founders are just "natural" persons. Then the risk set (the set of all actors who might found an organization) consists of all persons in the relevant social system. Narrowing the set further can create selection bias. Following this proposal in the cases we studied would require collecting information on the millions of Argentines, Irish, and Americans who did and did not start newspapers, on the set of all possible bank founders in Manhattan, and so forth. Furthermore, attempting to specify the set of actors at risk of founding a newspaper would require considering itinerant printers who can and do migrate to a city or nation and begin a newspaper; specifying the set of actors who might begin a banking organization in a city must include all foreign banks that might decide to do so. The latter example makes clear that not all potential founders are natural persons because partnerships and collectives start firms. An analyst taking this approach must consider all pairs, triplets, and so forth. Because the size of the risk set, so defined, quickly becomes impractically large, studies of arrival processes generally take the population as the unit of action.

Fortunately, these difficulties raise problems only in attempts to study theories that specify the individual, collective, and corporate-actor sources of organizational foundings. As long as attention focuses on the types of macrosociological questions we treat, nothing is lost by considering the population to be the relevant social unit. It is a strategic mistake to attempt to specify empirical founding processes at the level of the potential founder because it is so unlikely that relevant information on all potential founders can be found. Nonetheless, assessing the theoretical implications of possible relationships between action at the level of potential entrepreneurs and events at the population level can clarify processes of macroorganizational change.

The theory of density-dependent legitimation and competition seems fairly robust with respect to variations in assumptions about individual action of entrepreneurs. Rational utility maximization by entrepreneurs is one possibility. When legitimation of an organizational form increases, potential founders may come to believe that there are gains to be made from starting such an organization. That is, legitimation may affect the formation of beliefs about possibilities for profitable investment and thereby affect efforts at founding organizations. When competition intensifies, potential founders postpone or cancel efforts to found organizations. Both responses would be rational for profit-seeking actors with some understanding of the market and industry.

What other models of individual action are compatible with the theory's predictions? For our purposes, it suffices to demonstrate that the theory is consistent with cases of apparently nonrational behavior rather than to develop fully some alternative models of individual action. To see this, it is important to recognize that environments affect rates of organizational founding in two general ways: First, changing environmental conditions affect the *number of attempts at organizing* around a particular activity, using a particular organizational form. Second, environments affect flows of foundings by altering the *odds of success of organizing attempts*. By success we mean only that attempts at founding organizations succeed, not that the resulting organizations perform well once begun.

Images of rationality in organization building seem to focus on the first element in the process, the causes of attempts to start organizations. Resources sometimes become available and opportunities are identified in a manner consistent with our image of rational entrepreneurship. At other times, the exact causes of attempts to start organizations can vary enormously from person to person (or group to group) in a way that can be well described as random. For instance, studies of attempts at entrepreneurship reveal that individuals can be prompted to try to start a business (or some other kind of organization) by many other kinds of environmental events such as a spell of involuntary unemployment, forced retirement, or a change in working conditions (see Cooper, Woo, and Dunkelberg 1989; Evans and Leighton 1989; Mayer and Goldstein 1961). These attempts at organizing can be as little as an idea or planning but might go so far as the acquisition of capital and material resources.

Every organizing effort must pass through these initial steps but many efforts fail before a functioning organization results. Hannan and Freeman (1989, chap. 4) emphasize the importance of such processes of selection during periods of "gestation." In some kinds of environments, entrepreneurs typically make many attempts to organize but with little success, whereas under other conditions, the success rate of those attempting to organize may be high in that most of them actually get an enterprise off the ground and begin operations. The types of factors likely to induce success in opening a "business" include low capital requirements, little regulation, no real tacit knowledge, and the like. These factors probably differ in impact from those responsible for the rate of organizing attempts.

An empirically estimated organizational founding rate reflects both types of selection processes, and these may work at cross-purposes. High rates of founding attempts can be coupled with low rates of success in organizing, and vice versa. The same observed level of founding may be the result of very different environmental forces. Moreover, rationality may characterize only one of the two portions of the founding process. That is, the apparent rationality of a founding process may reflect the rationality of selection operating on random founding attempts.

Such possibilities further confound the interpretation of entrepreneurial action, even at the collective level. When a high observed founding rate reflects the actions of large numbers of entrepreneurs attempting to enter a market and experiencing a high success rate in doing so, their behavior may well be rational. But, when a high observed founding rate reflects massive numbers of attempts and many failures, making the case for rationality at the level of individual founders proves more difficult.

Clearly there are many opportunities for experimenting with microfoundations of organizational ecology, including processes of density-dependent legitimation and competition. The analytic issues involved are complex. Moreover, efforts to build microfoundations and assess their relevance are sure to be hampered by a general lack of data on the crucial preorganizing processes because we lack data on the rate of attempts to build organizations and thus on selection processes that operate at this point in the general process of founding. Given the complexity of the analytic issues and the absence of necessary data, we continue to favor the strategy of building robust macrotheories and models.

Applications to Other Types of Problems

Strategic Groups

We now shift gears and discuss some other research areas that might benefit from adopting the general modeling framework developed here. The density framework can be applied straightforwardly and, we think, profitably to research on "strategic groups" of firms in a single industry. Conventional organizational research on strategic groups has reached something of an impasse. After the persuasive theoretical formulation of Caves and Porter (1977) and some popularity among strategy theorists (see McGee and Thomas 1986), the value of the strategic group concept has been called into question by recent empirical research. This recent work suggests that, although strategic groups can usually be identified within an industry, membership in strategic groups has few or no systematic consequences for organizational performance (Cool and Schendel 1987, 1988). Such a conclusion represents a significant retreat from the original promise of the strategic group research program.

It may be premature to retract the proposition that strategic groups differ systematically in performance. We suspect that the current impasse can be overcome by redirecting theoretical attention back to the formulation of Caves and Porter (1977) and by borrowing models and methods from organizational ecology. Specifically, we advocate a return to using evidence on mobility barriers to define groups, the use of mortality as a performance measure, and the examination of interdependencies among groups with models of density dependence in vital rates.

The research reported in Chapter 7 on the contemporary American brewing industry illustrates the potential of such an approach (see also Carroll and Swaminathan 1991b). When defined by relatively immutable organizational forms, the modern brewing industry can be seen to contain three strategic groups: mass producers, microbrewers, and brewpubs. Mortality rates of brewing firms in the different groups depend on different factors, thus demonstrating a fundamental relationship between group membership and performance. Founding rates also vary across groups defined in this way. And for both foundings and deaths, interdependencies appear within and across groups. These findings suggest to us that there may be great value in applying the density framework to study strategic groups in many other industries.

Professions

A quite different substantive research area that may profit from using the density framework is the study of occupations and professions. Consider the professions. Traditionally, social scientists studied professions as single social entities that evolve from loosely defined jobs to highly exclusive occupations. Wilensky's (1964) famous article outlines the stages in the development of a profession including emergence of an association, state sponsored licensing, establishment of examinations, foundings of educational programs and schools, and the formalization of codes and journals. Wilensky also suggests that in modern society an increasing number of occupations are being professionalized.

The growth and decline of professions (and other occupations) can be analyzed within the theoretical perspective we have developed.

For instance, Abbott (1988) advocates that professions be studied as a system of interdependent occupations rather than as isolated social entities. Professions continually engage in jurisdictional battles and other forms of competition with one another. Abbott gives numerous insightful examples from a wide variety of occupations and industries, but he does not put forth any models of the process of expansion and contraction of the professions. Although we are persuaded that shifting to the ecological community level of analysis has value for clarifying the dynamics of professions, we think that it is possible, and indeed advisable, to do so in a more systematic way. Specifically, competition and other forms of interdependence among different professions might be usefully modeled as involving density-dependent legitimation and competition using either counts of individual professionals or their associated organizations. Following the logic used for direct and diffuse organizational competition, we believe that such application of the density framework might lead to different insights into interprofessional competition than does one (such as Abbott's) that examines only the direct competition of jurisdictional battles. In any case, processes of density-dependent legitimation and competition would provide a more systematic and readily comparative way to study expansion and contraction of professions.

Social Movements, Collective Action, and Organizational Change

A very different type of research problem is suggested by the finding that mutualism (positive density dependence) characterizes population interactions in affecting rates of foundings and mortality at low density early in the history of some organizational populations. Specifically, we are intrigued by notion that cooperative behavior apparently characterizes the beginnings of many industries and organizational populations. We are also impressed by the amount of noncompetitive organizing that occurs at these times in the form of clubs and pre-industry associations of various kinds.

It might be revealing to study industry origins in much the same way that sociologists study social movements (see, for example, Tilly 1978). The task should be made easier by the fact that some researchers, most notably Carroll and Huo (1988), McCarthy and colleagues (1988), and Olzak (1989, 1992), have used the tools of organizational ecology to study social movements.

The interactions between social movements and dynamics of organizational populations are fundamental to processes of large-scale social change. Although such interactions have received little attention, the conditions appear to be ripe for a serious effort to understand them. Potential contributions come from both social movement research and organizational research (see Olzak and West 1991). The most sustained theoretical development in the study of social movements and collective action has centered on the role of organizations in creating and sustaining movements and collective actions. Theory on such matters has become known as resource mobilization theory.[3] Organizational ecology theory provides an analytic structure for explaining patterns of change in organizational populations, including those in the social movements of groups contending for power.

We sketch an approach to integrating our ecological theory of organizational change into treatments of macrostructural change in the hope of stimulating new work. Many, if not most, interesting features of processes of macrochange can be characterized as consisting of bursts of collective actions and changes in the composition of corporate actors and their interrelations. Tilly (1978) suggested that typical processes of change include at least three kinds of actions. First, new corporate actors take form and construct organizations, such as labor unions, political parties, and guerrilla armies. Second, the contending organizations attempt to mobilize broader populations and create waves of collective actions such as demonstrations, strikes, and riots. Third, defenders of opposing interests take collective action in response. Often these opposing actions are taken by organizations of the state, such as the police and the army. But opposing actions can also be taken by private organizations such as business associations or private armies. Depending on the conditions, the interactions of these processes can have diverse outcomes. Challenges can be put down, succeed, or persist for long periods. Depending on the scope of the challenge, success can mean either that a new corporate actor gains legitimated rights over certain actions or that major elements of the social structure are replaced, as in the case of social and political revolution.

The basic data needed to represent such a process of change con-

---

[3] For a review of this approach, see McAdam, McCarthy, and Zald (1988).

sist of two kinds of histories, those of the set of corporate actors and of their organizations, including times of founding and times and causes of ending, and those of collective actions. What is needed are models in which (1) the flow of collective events affects the rates of organizational founding and failure and (2) the rates of collective action depend on the changing roster of collective actors and their organizations.

Theory and research on organizational ecology have identified a set of general processes that promise to prove useful in attempts at developing such models of macrochange (see Hannan 1989b). First, ecological studies emphasize the effects of external conditions on the rates of the rise and fall of collective actors and on the rates of collective action. Economic, social, and political conditions and changes have been shown to have strong effects on the various rates. Second, research on organizational ecology finds that the rates of organizational founding and mortality vary with time (the waiting time between events in the case of foundings and age in the case of mortality). Time dependence also plays a role in shaping the flow of events of collective action. Olzak (1989) showed that it often makes sense to conceptualize such time dependence in terms of processes of contagion, in which the occurrence of an event increases the rate of occurrence. Such a process can help explain why social change often has a *punctuational* character, with collective events occurring in bursts.

More germane to the theme of this book, processes of legitimation and competition also can be framed so as to apply broadly to processes of social change. Because the possibilities for collective action depend on the distribution of collective actors in a system, it is important to incorporate processes of density dependence and frequency dependence. Density dependence means that rates of certain kinds of actions depend on the density of various kinds of *corporate actors* in the system. Frequency dependence means that a rate depends on the number of *actions* of various kinds. Coleman (1964, 1990) developed models in which the rates of various kinds of actions depends on the number of times that such actions have occurred.

We argued that processes of density dependence reflect the operation of opposing processes of legitimation and competition. Studies of various kinds of organizational populations agree with the claim as it applies to change in organizational populations. However, these

processes are not somehow idiosyncratic to organizational populations. They can also be applied usefully to studies of the rise and
demise of all kinds of corporate and collective actors, such as social
movements, interest groups, and political parties.

Although the possibility has not yet been considered, similar
structures may well characterize processes of frequency dependence.
Indeed, a special form of frequency dependence has been studied by organizational ecologists. Carroll and Delacroix (1982) and
Delacroix and Carroll (1983) found that the rates of founding and
demise of organizations (newspaper firms) vary with the number
of recent events of the type and that the dependence is nonmonotonic. For example, the founding rate increases with the number
of recent foundings at a decreasing rate. The empirical analyses
that we reported specify such effects, although we did not emphasize
them. The analytic importance of frequency dependence comes from
the strong form of path dependence that it imparts on processes of
change. Random events that trigger a few actions of a type raise the
rate of occurrence of such actions, perhaps leading to the persistence
of the form of action in the system. But systems that do not experience the random events may never come to "adopt" the practice.
Such *path dependence* of processes of social change deserves considerably more attention than it has received from sociologists.[4] We saw
the power of such path dependence in the simulation studies reported
in Chapter 8.

Models that consider links among social aggregates or collective
actors can be built along the lines of those used in our analyses of
subpopulations and in other recent studies of organizational ecology.
These models treat the effects of the density of each population in
a system on rates of founding and demise of other populations. It
is worth exploring whether the density of social actors other than
organizations (or the frequency of various kinds of collective actions)
can be linked in this fashion. If so, these models provide a powerful
tool for analyzing change in social structures.

Finally in concluding the book, we mention a set of research problems that we discussed previously in other publications. We think

---

[4] The idea of path dependence is at least as old as Darwinian evolutionary
theory. David (1985) and Arthur, Ermoliev, and Kaniovski (1987) discuss
economic examples of such processes.

that organizational ecology to date has done a good job of identifying and studying the sources of organizational diversity and associated processes such as density dependence. However, it is important to continue down the causal chain and to examine the sociological *consequences* of diversity as well. At various times, we suggested that innovation, inequality and even job satisfaction all may be affected by organizational diversity (Carroll, Haveman, and Swaminathan 1990; Hannan 1986b, 1988c). Demonstration of strong links to any of these important social outcomes would constitute a major discovery for organizational ecology and would provide great policy motivation for the research agenda of organizational ecology.

Appendix A: Designs of Empirical Studies

This appendix provides information about the organizational populations studied and the sources of data used. It provides a brief sketch of the history of each population, identifies sources of data, defines key variables, and discusses the sets of covariates and temporal effects used in the analyses that yield the results presented in Chapters 4 through 7.

Our emphasis on the specific features of individual studies should not obscure the fact that they all use the same basic design. Each study records the time of founding of each member of the population and collects information on the subsequent history of each organization. Each study uses the same definition of density: the count of the number of organizations in the population at the beginning of the year. The studies differ in selection of environmental covariates and treatment of time variation in the processes of interest. Some of the studies specify period effects with dummy variables to represent the most important environmental variations; others use a functionally specified time trend, namely, the age of the population.

A critical issue when designing research on any organizational population is delineating its boundaries (Freeman 1978). For organizations with a geographical dimension, the issue becomes one of level of analysis, as the various boundaries are often nested. Newspapers, for instance, might be studied at the level of metropolitan area. Each metropolitan area contains several cities, and each of these in turn contains numerous neighborhoods. A researcher's choice of boundaries for the population of newspapers sets the level of analysis. Such choices therefore have major consequences for the problem we study because the decision determines the number of organizations to be counted. How should the decision be made?

We believe that the level of analysis should be set so as to include within a single unit most of the competitive activity occurring among like organizations. Although this unit might not be readily identifiable at first, it can be eventually determined on empirical grounds (see Barnett and Carroll 1987). Correct specification implies that the density of external populations will not have as strong an impact as will the density of the population itself. Populations specified properly should be roughly comparable, whatever the chosen geographical unit. Similarly, neighboring populations should evolve relatively independently if the level of analysis has been specified correctly.

The research reported in this book implements this type of thinking. Some populations, such as labor unions, we study strictly at the national level because we think that unions competed most intensively for resources at this level. We analyze banks at the city level, because for most of their history this was the domain of competition, especially in the case of savings banks. Indeed, banking in the United States was restricted legally to single states and even cities and counties for most of the period of interest.

When analyzing populations of newspapers, we vary the level of analysis depending on the national context. In the case of Argentina and Ireland, we use the nation-state as the unit, as the press has been national in orientation. By contrast, the press in the United States has been primarily local in nature, and so we use the metropolitan area as the unit (Bagdikian 1971).

For brewing, we experiment with different levels because the scale of competition apparently changes across history. Many brewers today operate on a national scale but this was not the case in the seventeenth, eighteenth, and nineteenth centuries, when the industry was predominantly organized at the city level. Consequently, in Chapter 7 we attempt an empirical assessment of the appropriate level of analysis.

Thinking about level of analysis in this way reveals that organizational density also often includes a geographical basis in much the same way that ordinary language usage does. For instance, density of newspaper publishers in a metropolitan area as we define it is a count of such publishers in a defined spatial unit. It is a kind of per unit count. Likewise, defining organizational density on a national scale assumes that it makes sense to standardize on this level of social organization, with its attendant spatial limits. If there were no reference to the scale of the system in which counts are taken, it would make no sense to compare counts across systems. The point is that the counts are standardized on the basis of substantive understandings of the appropriate scales of social organization (which usually means a geographical boundary).

Recent empirical research by Rumelt (1989) suggests strongly that the level of analysis implied by an ecological perspective also goes some way towards accounting for rates of return of business organizations. When analyzing the Federal Trade Commission's Line of Business data for the four years 1974 through 1977, Rumelt partitioned the total variance in rates of return into industry factors, corporate "parent" factors, and business-specific (or intraindustry) factors. He found that the most important source of variation in rates of return were business specific, that industry and corporate factors were far less important. Rumelt (1989, p. 28) concluded that "theoretical and statistical work seeking to explain an important portion of the observed dispersion in ... profit rates ... must focus on sources of heterogeneity within industries other than relative size." The model of density dependence clearly fits the order, as does most research in organizational ecology.

Labor Unions

Analyzing the effect of density on vital rates of national labor unions has interest for ecological theorists for two main reasons. First, these are a pure case of "nonmarket" (or "nonbusiness") organizations. The other populations we study are composed of firms. In assessing the generality of the processes of density-dependent legitimation and competition, it is especially important to include instances of both types. Second, the archival record contains information on numerous small unions with short lifetimes (often less than a year). The richness of the record reflects the adversarial and often radical nature of many new unions. The formation of national labor unions, no matter how small, appears to have been mentioned in the press. In addition, labor historians and the older schools of institutional economists (especially the Wisconsin school under John Commons) made a sustained effort to reconstruct the historical record. These scholars created a record that paints the broad picture of the evolution of unions and points to many of the relevant primary sources. For these reasons, the study of national labor unions can avoid the problem of bias due to endogenous sampling.

Collective action directed at affecting wages, conditions of work, control over jobs, and other more fundamental changes in the organization of work has taken many forms. Sometimes it was episodic, consisting of bursts of spontaneous collective action by workers and their families. Some episodes of collective action were directed narrowly at employers at the work site, as in strikes and boycotts. Other episodes were directed at other corporate actors such as legislative and judicial bodies, as in general strikes and political demonstrations.

At various times each kind of collective action by workers became embodied in formal organization. Organizations of workers directed at the work relation are usually called labor unions. Those that take on a broader political agenda are usually called worker political movements or political parties. Following Hannan (1988a) and Hannan and Freeman (1989), we define a labor union as a permanent organization of workers with the ostensible goal of affecting the conditions of work by threatening the collective withholding of labor. The restriction to (intendedly) permanent organization distinguishes a union from a prolonged strike or boycott. The restriction to the goal of affecting conditions of work distinguishes a union from broader political movements of workers, such as socialist parties, and from utopian movements, such as the Owenite community movement of the nineteenth century. The restriction to the device of threatening to withhold labor distinguishes a union from company sponsored unions, mutual benefit associations of workers, and organizations of workers that try to affect working conditions by other means, such as terrorist organizations like the Molly McGuires.

The most obvious difference among American labor unions concerns the scope of organizing. Unions have varied widely in the breadth of types of workers (crafts and occupations) and types of industries they tried to organize. Several organizational forms served as precursors of national unions. The earliest permanent labor organizations in the United States, called trade societies, organized journeymen in a single craft in a single city. The first of these was the Federal Society of Journeymen Cordwainers founded in Philadelphia in 1794. The trade society form was dominant until the Panic of 1837, which destroyed most of the unions. Next, federations of trade societies within cities were formed. The first of these, the Mechanics Union of Trade Associations established in Philadelphia in 1827, initially included carpenters, painters, bricklayers, and glaziers.

During the year before the Panic of 1837, the first *national* unions were founded: the Society of Cordwainers, the Society of Journeymen House Carpenters, and the National Typographic Society. Each of these unions adopted what is known as the *craft form* of organization, which defines jurisdictions on the basis of the boundaries of crafts or occupations. Each of these unions was disbanded in the aftermath of the panic. The craft form, however, became the dominant form of union organizing until the 1930s.

As industrialization increased in scope, it became apparent that many craft unions had organized too narrowly. A number of mergers took place in the late nineteenth century among unions whose members had shared fates by virtue of working at the same site (meaning that a strike by one union would stop work for the others), working with substitutable processes or materials (for example, painters and wallpaperers), or working along a vertical flow of work (for example, warehousemen and stevedores). For example, the Bricklayers' International Union (1865–1985) absorbed the Stonemasons' Union in 1883. The resulting form is called the "compound-craft" (Ulman 1955).

Craft unionism—even the compound-craft variant—did not always match well with the changing nature of industrial organization in later periods. Semiskilled and unskilled workers played an increasingly important role, as technical innovations replaced some kinds of skilled workers and the scale of enterprise grew; and technical change kept reshuffling the roster of identifiable jobs. What came to be known as the *industrial form* used a different organizing principle. Instead of defining its jurisdiction in terms of a set of crafts or occupations, industrial unions attempted to organize all production workers in a set of industries, regardless of job title or skill level. The first unambiguous industrial union in the United States was the American Miners' Association (1861–1867), which attempted to organize all workers "in and around the mines."

The difference between craft and industrial forms coincided fairly well with a crucial difference in political orientation. Craft unions were inclined by and large to engage in "business unionism" whereas industrial unions were much more likely to propose radical transformations of the organization of work. Most historical accounts of the American union movement conclude that these two forms of organization were indeed different. Earlier ecological research by Hannan and Freeman (1989) corroborates this view. We concentrate on this difference in the research reported in this book.

Historians of the American labor movement provide ample illustration of processes of legitimation and competition operating strongly in the case of national unions. The union movement fought long, hard battles for recognition by workers, employers, and the state. High mortality rates of early American unions have often been attributed to factors that can reasonably be viewed as implications of a low level of legitimation (see Hannan and Freeman 1989, chap. 11).

Labor historians have also stressed the role of direct competition, sometimes called interunion rivalry, as a cause of decline and eventual disbanding or merger (Galenson 1940, 1960). Indeed, it was common for two or more unions to attempt to organize the same set of workers. Such rivalry was sometimes prompted by the expansion of unions that had begun in different sections of the country. For example, the Western Federation of Miners (1893–1982) competed with the (mainly eastern) United Mine Workers (1890–) before merging with the United Steelworkers. Sometimes the rivalry reflected disagreements over politics or tactics, as in the case of the conservative Journeymen Tailors' Union (1883–1914) and the mainly socialist Tailors' National Progressive Union (1885–1889). At other times a national federation created an affiliated union to compete with an independent union. For example, the American Federation of Labor (AFL), a federation of craft unions, created the American Federation of Musicians (1896–) to compete with the National League of Musicians (1886–1904) after it refused repeatedly to affiliate with the AFL. Much rival unionism led to competition between national federations promoting different forms of unionization. The most important example was the competition of the Congress of Industrial Organizations (CIO), a federation of industrial unions, with the AFL. After the founding of the CIO within the AFL in 1936 and its expulsion in 1938, the CIO was instrumental in founding industrial unions to compete with the AFL unions (Galenson 1940, 1960). For example, the CIO created the United Paperworkers' International Union (1944–1957) to compete with the AFL-affiliated Brotherhood of Paper Makers (1902–1957).

Sources

Hannan and collaborators collected data on *national* labor unions, unions that organized in more than one state (Hannan 1980, 1988b). They tried to collect information about every national labor union that has existed, however briefly, in the United States. The first step was to compile the lists of names (with starting dates) contained in reports published in various years that claimed exhaustive coverage of the population of unions. The following listings served as the initial screen: New Jersey Bureau of Labor Statistics (1898), Finance (1894), Industrial Commission (1901, Volume 17), U. S. Bureau of Labor Statistics (1926), Stewart (1936), Peterson (1944), National Industrial Conference Board (1956), Troy (1965), Fink (1977), and Gifford (1985). These publications, supplemented by annual reports of the Department of Labor from 1932 through 1985, yielded an initial master list of unions. The master list was extended in the course of consulting standard histories of the labor movement, which were especially useful for the period between 1830 and 1870, including Commons and colleagues (1927), Foner (1947), and Fink (1977).

This procedure produced data on 633 unions. Although there is no way to tell exactly what fraction of all national unions this number represents, Hannan and Freeman (1989) suggest that most members of the population have been identified. However, 12 of these unions, members of the Trade Union Unity League (TUUL), disbanded on the same day at the order of the Comintern. As these were obviously not independent events, we follow Hannan and Freeman (1988a, 1989) and exclude these 12 unions in our analysis of mortality.

A *founding* is defined as the formation of a national union by the joint decision of several locals or by some unorganized group of workers; of the 633 unions, 479 (76%) began with a founding. The ending event of most interest in the analyses reported in this book is *disbanding*. A total of 191 of the 621 non–TUUL unions (31%) disbanded; 140 of them were absorbed by merger to a dominant union; and 130 merged with one or more "equal-status partners." We distinguish disbandings from the two kinds of mergers because Hannan (1989a) found that the pattern of density dependence was quite different for the different types of mortality. The remaining 60 unions were still in existence in 1985 and are treated as having been censored on the right at the time of last observation.

Covariates Used in the Empirical Analyses

As is the case for each of the studies, the long period of study means that only a few measures of environmental conditions are available for the full period. Hannan and Freeman (1987, 1988a) explored the effects of numerous measures of general economic conditions, such as an index that identifies years of economic crisis and depression, the real wage of common laborers, business failures, gross national product per capita, and so forth. They used data on immigration and dummy variables that distinguish years of "employer offensives" and wars. Most of these variables failed to have any systematic or sizable effect on the union founding rate and mortality rate when period effects and the measures discussed next are included in the model.

Based on previous research, we include only one measure of economic conditions—economic depression—in the analyses reported in Chapters 4 through 6. In addition, the models whose estimates appear in those chapters allow rates of founding and mortality to vary among five historic periods. The first begins in 1836, the start of national unionization, and ends in 1886, the year in which the American Federation of Labor (AFL) was founded. The second period begins in 1887 and ends in 1931. The third period begins in 1932 with the New Deal. This third period ends in 1947, when the Taft–Hartley Act retracted some New Deal protections for union organizing. The fifth period begins in 1955, the year of the merger of the AFL and Congress of Industrial Organization (CIO), and extends to 1985.

Mortality analyses include a Weibull specification of age dependence and the union's type of starting event (founding, secession, or merger). Some analyses also include size (membership) at founding. In many cases, this means membership at the time of the convention at which the national union was initiated. (Comparable data on membership size over union lifetimes are not available for many unions whose initial sizes are known.) In some cases, this refers to membership after roughly a year of operation. Data on membership were coded from Troy (1965), records of individual unions, and various other archival sources.

Estimates of the full models of founding rates (including effects of covariates and periods) can be found in Hannan (1991) and Barron and Hannan (1991); estimates of full mortality models can be found in Carroll and Hannan (1989a).

Newspapers and Newspaper Publishers

An ecological analysis of newspaper publishing firms has great appeal because good data on even small and short-lived firms are available over long historical periods. Such data are available because newspaper publication leaves dated material products of direct interest to historians who catalogued their publishing histories. In addition, directories used by advertisers have been published yearly for almost 120 years.

An analysis of populations of newspaper publishers is also attractive for the study of density-dependent processes of legitimation and competition because historical research on these industries suggests that processes of legitimation and competition played important roles in shaping them. In order to place our analysis in institutional context, we briefly review what is known about such processes in the case of the American industry.

The earliest American papers had trouble staying open unless they received the explicit blessing of authorities. The first known newspaper, *Publick Occurrences Both Foreign and Domestick,* published only one issue in 1690 before its owner was jailed for printing "the truth as he saw it" (Emery and Emery 1984). The next paper, John Campbell's *Newsletter,* began publishing in 1704 under the condition that all copy be approved by the governor. Later postmasters continued publishing newspapers, noting that they were circulated "by authority." In 1721 James Franklin's *New England Courant* challenged the notion of official sponsorship. Although his efforts landed him in jail, his paper lasted for five years and had a profound influence on the development of an independent press. By 1785, all 13 colonies had witnessed the emergence of a newspaper, most of which were private enterprises.

Failure rates of the early newspapers were extremely high. Of the more than 2100 papers founded before 1820, more than half are estimated to have closed within two years (Emery and Emery 1984). Although financial difficulties accounted for most of the failures, indicating a lack of full consumer acceptance, there were also legal, political and civil difficulties. In particular, charges of libel could result in jail sentences or bankruptcy. Not until at least 1805 did legislation allow the introduction of evidence as to the truth of an alleged libel as legitimate defense (Mott 1962). Previously the courts had not usually allowed such evidence and recognized the principle "the greater the truth, the greater the libel" (Emery and Emery 1984).

Until 1830, American newspapers had two forms of organization. Mercantile papers reported commercial news; and partisan papers printed political news and opinions and usually received funding from political parties and candidates. Both kinds of enterprises were typically one-person operations. The emergence of the "penny press" (named after its retail price) in the 1830s marked the beginning of independent, mass-based newspapers. The sales and advertising income that accrued from their broad social base (or niche) allowed these papers to gain independence from political parties. In editorial policy, the penny papers were conscientiously nonjudgmental—accounts of trials and the like were often published verbatim from the official records. Although such actions were called sensational by the established press of the day, at least one scholar credits the penny press with inventing the concept of "news" (Schudson 1978). By the late nineteenth century, newspaper reporting had become a profession, and press clubs were started in many cities. The informational component of journalism increasingly stressed fairness, objectivity, and dispassion (Schudson 1978).

Each of these developments led to increased acceptance of the newspaper, its taken-for-granted right of existence, and its value as a source of information. Yet the process by which this occurred was slow and gradual, with fits and starts. For instance, duels between publishers and their editorial targets were not uncommon until at least the mid-nineteenth century (Mott 1962). Challenges to a free press during later periods were more common in the newly settled areas of the South and the West. Although national events set the stage for legitimation, the battle was fought afresh in localities on the expanding frontier.

Journalism history of the nineteenth century abounds with accounts of bitter newspaper rivalries. Yet from the perspective of organizational mortality, competition intensified in the twentieth century. The best aggregate data on competition and consolidation in the newspaper industry concern English-language, general-circulation dailies (Emery and Emery 1984; Rosse, Owen, and Dertouzos 1975). The number of these newspapers grew from 850 in 1880 to a peak of 2200 immediately before World War I and then declined to about 1750 between World Wars I and II. It has remained roughly stable since then, with periodic small fluctuations. This national trend masks an underlying process of severe local competition. Within cities, there has been a steady downward trend toward a single daily. Among all cities with dailies, the percentage with two or more competing dailies has fallen from 61% in 1880, to 57% in 1910, to 20% in 1930, to 1.9% in 1981. The usual explanation for the "evolution of one newspaper cities" focuses on daily newspapers and relies on arguments about economies of scale (Bogart 1981; Høyer 1975; Rosse 1978, 1980). Once a newspaper achieves a size advantage over its local rivals (for whatever reason), it becomes extraordinarily difficult for the smaller competing general-circulation dailies to survive. In the long run, the equilibrium outcome of the process triggered by this condition is a local monopoly. Exceptions to this rule usually occur in only the largest markets or where the competitors manage to differentiate by serving different markets or developing special appeal to certain submarkets. Although the daily markets have consolidated, there has been a concomitant upswing in the viability of specialized newspapers (Carroll 1987; Emery and Emery 1984). Density-dependent competitive processes appear to operate both within overall markets and within submarkets.

Sources

Carroll and collaborators conducted studies that attempted to define and enumerate the complete historical populations of newspapers in Argentina, Ireland, and seven metropolitan areas in the United States. Most countries, including Argentina and Ireland, have had newspaper industries that are essentially *national* in scope (Bagdikian 1971). By contrast, American newspapers depended primarily on local markets, usually consisting of a metropolitan area. Therefore these researchers used different geographical units to define populations. For Argentina and Ireland, they used the nation-state and its political boundaries. But for the United States they used the *metropolitan area* level, more precisely the standard metropolitan statistical area (SMSA). Carroll (1987) studied seven SMSAs: San Francisco–Oakland–San Jose, California; Little Rock, Arkansas; Springfield, Missouri; Shreveport, Louisiana; Elmira, New York; Lubbock, Texas; and Lafayette, Louisiana. Here we concentrate only on the largest of them: the San Francisco Bay Area (that is, San Francisco–Oakland–San Jose). Results for the other areas can be found in Carroll and Hannan (1989b).

We follow Carroll (1987) in defining a newspaper as a periodical printed by mechanical means, that appeals to those with common literacy, whose contents consist of timely information and whose publication is directed to a geographically delimited markets of consumers and advertisers. This definition of a newspaper has the advantage that it makes sense for the full historical period. Moreover, it distinguishes early newspapers from newsletters, pamphlets, and corantos and later newspapers from journals and magazines.

The unit of observation in Argentina and Ireland is a newspaper; and in the San Francisco Bay Area it is a newspaper publishing firm. The founding of a newspaper is defined in terms of the beginning of publication; its mortality is defined as the ending of publication. In the case of publishing firms, founding means the start of the first publication; mortality means the ending of the last publication.

For each locality, archival sources were used to code records on complete historical populations of newspapers. The cornerstones of this effort were compilations of library newspaper holdings prepared by councils of librarians (Brigham 1947; British Library 1975; British Museum 1905; Gregory 1937; Lathem 1972) and annual directories of advertising agencies (Ayer, various years; Rowell, various years). Area-specific sources were also used when available (Daggett 1939; Fernandez 1943; Galvan-Moreno 1944; Wheeler 1973). A more complete discussion of these sources and their quality can be found in Carroll (1987).

These sources provide extraordinary coverage. In most instances, a fairly complete historical population has been assembled, with the exception of Argentina, where the sources found cover only the nineteenth century. The coding procedures recorded every newspaper leaving a trace in the historical records. When available, the exact dates of a founding and demise were coded. In other cases, a paper's appearance and disappearance in a periodical directory were used to infer the approximate, usually annual, dates of founding and closure.

The sources contain histories of 1453 Argentinean newspapers between 1800 and 1900. Of this number, 108 were still in operation in 1900 when the record ends. For Ireland, these sources cover 996 newspapers between 1800 and 1975; 107 were still in operation in 1975. Finally, there are 2169 newspaper publishing organizations in the record for the San Francisco Bay Area between 1845 and 1975; 189 of these were still in business at the end of 1975.

Covariates Used in the Empirical Analyses

Carroll and collaborators coded the history of political turmoil in Argentina, Ireland, and San Francisco. They found that political turmoil coincides with increased foundings and that papers founded in turmoil-ridden periods have higher mortality rates (Carroll 1987). Based on these findings, we incorporated effects of "political turmoil" in all our analyses of vital rates in populations of newspapers.

Analyses of both vital rates for newspaper organizations include the effects of population age (the time in years elapsed from the date of its first recorded newspaper to the beginning of the spell). Although it is somewhat crude, this variable is used to control for the possible historical obsolescence of the newspaper organizational form (Høyer 1975 makes a similar argument).

Analyses of mortality rates also include an effect of organizational age. When analyzing age dependence in mortality rates, we used an exponential specification (commonly called a Gompertz model— see Equation B.7) which fits better for these populations than the Weibull model that we used for all other populations. Both sets of analyses also include the effects of the count of foundings in the previous year and its square and of the count of mortalities in the previous year and its square. We also included the real wage of common laborers, an index of depression years, and a dummy variable indicating war years in the model for founding rates in the San Francisco Bay Area.

Brewing Firms

Beer brewing is one of the oldest production activities on earth yet it remains an important industry in modern economies. The first American breweries were begun in Albany and in New Amsterdam in 1633. For the next 200 years, American brewing remained a small craft-based industry. Expansion of individual breweries was severely limited by the technology of the time, especially the lack of refrigeration other than by the use of ice. As the human population grew in size and moved westward, new breweries sprang up. By 1840, there were 97 brewing firms in the territorial United States.

The second half of the nineteenth century was a period of vast and dramatic change for the industry. On the one hand, numerous factors accelerated rapidly the foundings of breweries and the size of the market for beer. These included the country's growing population, steadily increasing affluence, abundance of locally produced grain, continued large-scale immigration of Germans, the development of a national system of transportation, and technical refinements in the processes of production. On the other hand, American ambivalence about alcohol led to numerous crusades and occasional state-level prohibitions of the production and sale of beer. The first state to enact a prohibition was Maine in 1846. Maine's prohibition was repealed in 1856 and then imposed again from 1858 to 1933.

The technological and other developments that spurred the market also greatly expanded the potential size of brewing firms. Electricity, in particular, seems to have freed breweries from the need for proximity to icehouses. This allowed breweries to grow larger and meant that many existing firms began to compete with broader circles of brewing firms.

The history of American brewing in the twentieth century is most remarkable for that great national experiment, the federal Prohibition. From 1920 to 1933 the production and sale of alcohol were for practical purposes forbidden by law. Most breweries closed early in this period, although some remained in operation by developing other lines of business (such as soft drink or yeast production). Repeal of the prohibition led to many new and renewed entrants in the brewing industry.

The other important transformation of the modern industry was economically driven. Except for the hiatus caused by Prohibition, the number of firms in the industry shows a steady and precipitous decline for the hundred years beginning around 1880. Our data indicate that 2474 breweries were operating at that time. By 1980, the number had dropped to 45, with much of the loss occurring through acquisition and merger (Tremblay and Tremblay 1988). Concentration increased as well. Today the American brewing industry—as well as many others around the world—is a fairly concentrated one, in which strong economies of scale in production and advertising are thought to favor the largest firms. Yet, as we discuss at length in Chapter 7, a recent countertrend has appeared. The number of breweries rose rapidly during the 1980s, reflecting the reemergence of two new organizational forms: microbreweries and brewpubs (see also Carroll and Swaminathan 1991b).

Sources

Carroll and Swaminathan (1989) collected data on the foundings of beer producers from 1633 through 1988 and on the life spans of all firms active in the industry over this period. The primary source for data is Bull, Friedrich, and Gottschalk (1984), a compilation that strove for comprehensive coverage (excluding data on contract breweries, firms that market beer produced by others). Bull and collaborators relied on numerous private and brewing industry sources. Because the listings in their volume pertain to plants rather than to firms, Carroll and collaborators aggregated the histories for all plants operated by each identifiable corporate organization. This task was accomplished with the aid of the *Modern Brewery Age Bluebooks* (various years) and Tremblay and Tremblay (1988). This coding effort produced data on 7709 firms. Of these, 122 were still operating at the end of the period of observation in late 1988; these are treated as right censored in the analysis of mortality.

These data allow distinctions among three ending events: dissolution, acquisition, and suspension of operations[1] (during a prohibition). Of the 7587 ending events coded, the vast majority (5773) are dissolutions. Suspensions are the next most prevalent with 1606 events. Acquisitions totaled 208. In Chapters 6 and 7, we analyzed

---

[1] A brewing firm was coded as suspended when a known prohibition was in effect in its locale. The Bull and colleagues volume is inconsistent in its coding of suspensions.

the combined mortality process as well as the separate kinds of mortality. For particular periods we were also able to introduce controls for organizational size and organizational form. The organizational size data measure annual production in barrels of beer—a barrel of beer contains approximately 31 gallons. For the years 1878 and 1879, these data are available in Salem (1880). For 1977 to 1988, they come from the *Modern Brewery Age Bluebooks* and the *Microbrewery Resource Handbooks*. Organizational form was defined as mass production, microbrewery, or brewpub (see Chapter 7). Information on form was coded from the *Microbrewery Resource Handbook*, and it was supplemented by consulting industry experts at the Institute for Fermentation and Brewery Studies in Boulder, Colorado. The measure of total mass of the population, used in Chapter 6, refers to production in the industry, namely, the total tax-paid withdrawals of malt beverages in millions of gallons. This variable was recorded from the various issues of the *Brewers Almanac* and is available for the period between 1863 and 1984.

More than 1200 foundings (almost a sixth of the total) were reported for 1874. This clumping is apparently an artifact in the original sources used by Bull, Friedrich, and Gottschalk (Gottschalk, personal communication; Friedrich, personal communication). This peculiarity of the data has implications for analyzing both mortality rates and founding rates. In the case of foundings, the problem is that the events recorded for 1874 appear to reflect a cumulation of events over the previous decade. An examination of the yearly counts of foundings suggests that foundings were likely to be undercounted for the years 1865 through 1873 and that the undercount is probably included in the number for 1874.

We adjusted for this defect in the data by assuming that the founding rate was constant over the ten-year period ending in 1874 and by using the total count of foundings over this period to estimate the constant rate. We then drew ten realizations from a Poisson process with the estimated rate, one for each of the ten years, and adjusted the revised counts of foundings by a fraction that equates the number of foundings over the ten-year period to the observed total. This strategy requires that density and counts of lagged foundings also be recalculated. We reported estimates of models of founding rates with these revised data in Chapter 4. Comparison with the results of Carroll and Swaminathan's (1991a) analysis, which used the unadjusted counts reported by Bull, Friedrich, and Gottschalk (1984), reveals that making these drastic changes in the counts does not change the basic qualitative pattern of density dependence.

Covariates Used in the Empirical Analyses

The constraints on covariates are even more severe in this study than in the others since the record begins in 1633. There are virtually no systematic data on economic or social conditions that extend that far back into American history. Carroll and Swaminathan (1991a) reported two kinds of analyses. The first uses the entire period; the second considers only periods beginning at various points in the nineteenth century. Restricting the period of observation to begin in 1801, for instance, allows the use of measures of size of human population and urbanization. Figures on aggregate industry production are available for the period beginning in 1864 and so forth. It turns out that the qualitative pattern of density dependence in rates of founding and mortality within the American brewing population is highly robust with respect to limitations on the period of study and to inclusion of covariates, as long as the study period begins before the 1880s when the density of brewing firms reached a peak.[2]

Because the findings are robust and we wanted to analyze the full histories of populations whenever possible, we reported findings from analyses of the entire period, 1633 to 1988. This means that these analyses do not contain controls for environmental economic and social conditions other than the occurrence of prohibitions. However, Carroll and Swaminathan (1991a) reported that the qualitative patterns we found using this simple specification over the complete historical period also hold for models that contain effects of economic covariates analyzed over the nineteenth and twentieth centuries. Analyses of both founding and mortality control for the effects of the federal Prohibition. Analyses of mortality also control for state prohibitions (as the state in which each observed brewer has operated is known).

Analyses of mortality use a Weibull specification of age dependence. Because some of the breweries opening after Prohibition did

---

[2] Chapter 7 showed that restricting attention to the period after the national Prohibition (in the style of Delacroix, Swaminathan, and Solt 1989) destroys the pattern of density dependence that comes through clearly over longer periods, as expected.

not have permits, we included a dummy variable that distinguishes firms operating without a permit. Finally, as we noted, an unusually large number of foundings was reported for 1874. In the case of mortality analyses, the problem is that the firms appearing first in the records in 1874 may have been several years old. We distinguish firms that are coded as beginning in 1874 and introduced a dummy variable for this distinction into models for mortality rates.

Banks

An analysis of banks broadens the range of variation in organizational forms and relevant environments. We think that the study of financial institutions provides useful information about the applicability of the model to populations of "market" organizations as well as informative contrasts with previous studies. Banks and insurance companies (described next) differ from unions, newspapers, and brewing firms both in the kinds of resources they seek to exploit and in the kinds of institutional constraints they face (mainly in the form of governmental regulation).

Accurate records of vital events begin in the eighteenth century and records of major changes in government regulation over this long period are also available. We regard the opportunity to study density dependence over 300 years as highly desirable. Beginning in the eighteenth century allows us to compare rates in periods in which the organizational forms were virtually unknown to those in which they have become so commonplace as to appear natural.

We defined the population of banks at a *local* level, the borough of Manhattan in New York City, because banking was restricted to local markets for most of the period we studied. Banking operations were limited to the state and even more local city levels by government regulations restricting the number of branches a bank can have and the location of those branches. Rose (1987) reports that 92% of American banks did not have branches at the close of the World War II and that in New York State, banks have been allowed to operate branches outside the township or city in which their central offices are located only since 1976 (Rose 1987).[3] Consequently, for

[3] Although banks have been restricted geographically, they have always

all but the last decades of the 200 year history, the local economy appears to be the relevant unit within which to define a population of banks in New York. The design that produced these data reflects this understanding.

Because New York State led the way in banking and state regulation of banking, Ranger-Moore, Banaszak-Holl and Hannan (1989, 1991) decided to focus on its main city: New York City. They collected data on banks in its eventual five boroughs, which were separate municipalities until the early twentieth century. They began by pooling data on foundings in the first and second most important cities/boroughs from the perspective of banking, Manhattan and Brooklyn. This produced much worse fits than analyzing them separately did. In other words, these exploratory analyses indicated that the early evolution of bank population in Manhattan and Brooklyn were reasonably separate. Therefore, we concentrate in this book on the borough of Manhattan, which led the way. The Manhattan bank population includes the nation's second bank, the Bank of New York, which was chartered by the legislature in 1791.

Sources

Information on the founding dates for banks was coded from the reports of Dillisten (1946), the *Annual Reports of the Superintendent of the Bank Department of New York State* (1830–1980), the *An-*

---

been active to some extent in national and international markets. In the national market, bank holding companies have not only offered banking services but also credit cards, the handling of realty and investments, and occasionally manufacturing. Bank-holding companies can offer this wide array of services because they are not legally considered banks, even though they control banking interests. These holding companies were not common before the Second World War, and the 53 largest bank holding companies held only 8% of U. S. bank deposits and owned only 7% of all banking offices by the mid 1960s (Rose, 1987). Even in the current period, the core banks dominate the holding companies. For instance, among the five largest holding companies headquartered in Manhattan in 1989, the fraction of holding company assets deriving from the core bank ranged from 81% (Citicorp and Citibank) to 94% (J. P. Morgan & Company and Morgan Guaranty and Trust; Bankers Trust New York Corporation and Bankers Trust Company) (Rand McNally 1989, pp. 98, 289).

nual *Reports of the Comptroller of Currency of the United States* (1864–1980), *Moody's Bank and Finance Manual* (1900–1980), and a number of historical sources. When available, we used the date of government chartering or incorporation as the time of founding. In some cases, the date of incorporation/chartering was not available and the earliest known date of business was used. Banks received new charters not only when they started, but also when a bank company succeeded a private banking business or when two incorporated banks merged.

On the basis of historical accounts of the industry, we distinguished between commercial banks and savings banks, as we pointed out in Chapter 5. In defining the population of commercial banks, we included trust companies that offer banking services because they provided the same services for most of the history of the industry and have been subject to the same types of regulations. Because management of personal estates requires such banking services as investing and holding deposits, the government has allowed trust companies to conduct banking services from the beginning. Commercial banks have also offered trust services since late in the nineteenth century.

The year of founding was available for 495 commercial and savings banks and trust companies. We excluded two firms from our analysis because their dates of founding are not recorded. The first banks in Manhattan were commercial banks. This form has always been more numerous than the savings bank, as we noted in Chapter 1. The second bank in the United States, the Bank of New York, was chartered in Manhattan in 1791 as a commercial bank. The first savings bank in Manhattan was founded in 1819. Of the 495 banks, 165 went bankrupt, 210 were absorbed by other banks, and 53 entered into equal-status mergers between 1791 and 1980. At the end of 1980, 67 banks were still in operation as autonomous firms.

Covariates Used in the Empirical Analyses

The analyses of both founding rates and mortality rates presented in Chapters 4 through 7 allowed rates to vary among five periods. The initial period, the excluded baseline in our analyses, starts in 1792. The second period begins in 1839, the year following passage of New York's Free Banking Act. Before this legislation, obtaining a charter for a bank required an act of the state legislature. According to Olmstead (1976), legislators had an extremely low regard for banks at this time and frequently defeated attempts to obtain charters. The Free Banking Act eliminated the requirement of legislative approval for the establishment of banks. Historical accounts suggest that the Free Banking Act greatly increased the founding rate of banks. The third period begins in 1864, the year following passage of the National Bank Act, which allowed banks to receive a national charter, placed nationally chartered banks under federal supervision, and created the office of Comptroller of the Currency to supervise them. In other words, this federal legislation created a new kind of link between the state and banking, which may have changed the institutional standing of the entire population of banks. The fourth period begins in 1914, following the creation of the Federal Reserve System, which placed further restraints on the actions of banks of all types. The fifth period, starting in 1934, marks the creation of the Federal Deposit Insurance Corporation and a great increase in federal government intervention. During this last period, the government responded to the bank failures of the Depression and took a more active role in restricting bank foundings and preventing bank failures, which undoubtedly affected both founding rates and mortality rates.

The estimated models for both rates also include the effects of controls for changes in the level of resources available to the institutions. Although exact measures of economic prosperity and depression in the country and in Manhattan would have been ideal for analyzing how changes in the economy affect the populations of financial institutions studied, such data were usually not available for the broad range of years studied, 1791 through 1980. We used the real wages of common laborers[4] and an index of years of depression and economic crisis. We also controlled for wartime conditions with a dummy variable that indicates years of war.

In our analyses of founding rates (in Chapters 4 and 5), we also included the effects of foundings in the previous year and the square of foundings in the previous year. When analyzing the founding rates of savings banks, we included a loglinear time trend (age of the population), but this trend did not contribute significantly to the fit of the model for the total population of banks or of the subpopulation

---

[4] The series ends with 1974; we assigned the 1974 value to the years 1975 to 1980.

of commercial banks.

In our analysis of mortality, we used the same covariates with two exceptions. First, instead of lagged foundings and its square, we used lagged ending events and the square of lagged ending events. In our analyses of overall mortality, this meant the counts of all forms of mortality; in our analyses of the event-specific forms of mortality, these were counts of the particular type. We also included a multiplicative effect of organizational form (commercial versus savings). Finally, we used a Weibull specification of age dependence.

Life Insurance Companies

A study of the population of life insurance companies has an appeal similar to that of banks. Moreover, comparing results for banks and life insurance companies provides interesting information about levels of analyses of processes of legitimation and competition—the relevant boundaries differ for the two kinds of organizations.

As was noted in the previous section, in the United States, government regulation has restricted most banking activities to a fairly local level. In the case of life insurance companies, the relevant system is *national.* During the eighteenth century, limitations on transportation and communication constrained American life insurance companies to operate in local markets. Then, however, they rapidly moved into national markets with the economic expansion of the nineteenth century. During that time, some companies restricted their business to one or a few states, some conducted business in all states, and some did substantial overseas business. Thus, any localization of business on the part of a company reflects the outcome of strategic choices or life chances, rather than any limitation inherent to the population. For this reason, we analyzed data on the entire national population for life insurance companies.

Sources

We coded the information on foundings of life insurance companies from the most extensive known compilation (Stalson 1942) of historical statistics on the national population over an extended period. This source reports yearly counts of density and number of foundings for the entire national population of life insurance companies for the period 1759 through 1937. Because Stalson did not report event histories for each firm, our analyses of mortality use the data provided by Pritchett (1977) who also compiled the national population, but only for the years between 1759 and 1900 (see Banaszak-Holl, Ranger-Moore, and Hannan 1990). Because of the different coverage of the two sources, we analyzed mortality processes over a shorter period. Pritchett's data contain records for 185 firms. Of these, 105 had gone bankrupt and 60 were absorbed by 1900. The remaining 20 firms were still operating as independent firms.

We defined the founding date as the date of incorporation whenever that date was available. When incorporation dates were not available, we used the starting date as the date on which life insurance underwriting business commenced. Starting dates of either type were not available for 23 firms whose existence is noted and whose ending dates were recorded. Stalson assumed that the entry of such firms occurred four years before the date of exit, a value that is both the modal life span of all terminated companies and the median life span for all companies surviving for 10 years or less. The results reported here reflect the adoption of that assumption.[5]

The main distinction between organizational forms in this industry appears to be stock company versus mutual company, as we observed in Chapter 5. The first two companies, founded in 1759 and 1769, were mutuals. The first stock company was founded in 1878. Of a total of 1065 life insurance companies founded before 1938, form (stock versus mutual) was reported for all but 76 companies. We excluded from our analysis the foundings of these firms (7.2% of the total), and we also excluded three other companies because their dates of starting and ending had not been reported. These exclusions left 986 foundings to be analyzed.[6]

Some life insurance companies are known to have switched from

[5] The analysis was replicated several times with the random replacement of life spans based on the distribution of actual life spans of the remaining 963 firms. Assigning entry dates in such fashion to the 23 firms of unknown starting date yielded essentially identical results.

[6] The results for the total population of life insurance companies reported here excludes the 76 firms of unknown type, for the sake of consistency. However, our analysis of the total population including those 76 firms yielded nearly identical results.

mutual to stock or vice versa. Although Stalson's counts of density did not take account of such transitions, he provided an exhaustive list of all such switches occurring during the lifetimes of firms still in existence in 1937. We did not treat these transitions as foundings per se, but we did use them to correct the population densities recorded in Stalson (1942).

Covariates Used in the Empirical Analyses

The results reported in Chapters 4 through 7 are estimates of parameters of models that allow founding rates and mortality rates to vary among three historical periods. The first period begins with the first founding in 1759. The second period begins in 1849, with the first attempts to regulate the industry in the form of a legal reserve requirement of $100,000 for life insurance companies to do business in the state.[7] It has been suggested that this legislation damaged the life chances of mutual companies and enhanced the success of stock companies because of the greater ease of raising such a large capital sum through selling of stock (Keller 1963). The third period begins in 1859 when New York State created the office of Commissioner of Insurance to regulate the insurance industry. Massachusetts followed suit in 1860. The great majority of life insurance companies were either based or conducting business in one or both of these two states.

The environmental covariates we used in the analyses of both founding rates and mortality rates include some of those noted in discussing the study of Manhattan banks: economic depression, and war. In addition, earlier analyses revealed that size of the (human) population affected the life chances of the national population of life insurance companies (Banaszak-Holl, Ranger-Moore, and Hannan 1990). We included an effect of log-size of urban and rural populations when analyzing the mortality of life insurance firms. Before

[7] Legislative changes in New York State are important to the national population of life insurance companies as a whole, for two reasons. Up to the beginning of the twentieth century, the majority of life insurance companies did business in New York State and were thus subject to its regulations. Second, regulation of the life insurance industry has never occurred at the federal level, and other states frequently looked to New York State as a source for innovations in life insurance regulation. Changes in New York State law tended to diffuse to many other states in this fashion.

the middle of the nineteenth century, the life insurance salesman as an agent active in soliciting business did not exist as a significant force (Pritchett 1985; Stalson 1942). This means that life insurance companies could not solicit business far from their urban locations. Even after their life insurance salesmen became common, the greater concentration of potential clients in urban areas (especially for the large companies that promoted industrial insurance at the workplace) should have facilitated the task of solicitation. The estimates reported for this population in Chapters 4 through 7 come from models that also contain an effect of the number of cities of population greater than 10,000, an indicator of the number of potential markets available to life insurance companies. In addition to these covariates, analyses of founding rates specify effects of lagged foundings.[8]

The analyses of mortality rates used somewhat simpler models because many of the covariates used in analyzing founding rates did not appear to have affected mortality rates. The results in Chapter 6 come from models that include only the effects of density, age (with a Weibull specification), and lagged numbers of mortality events of the kind under analysis and its square. Full details and estimates can be found in Banaszak-Holl, Ranger-Moore, and Hannan (1990); see also Banaszak-Holl (1991). We also used a measure of total mass of the population in analyses reported in Table 6.5. This measure is based on the series of total assets of all life insurance companies compiled by Pritchett (1977) for 1842 to 1900, converted to constant (1860) dollars. We extrapolated this series back to 1759 using estimates of an exponential regression model.[9] It turned out that the same qualitative pattern as that reported in Table 6.5 obtained when analysis was restricted to the period for which Stalson was able to measure total assets, that is between 1842 and 1900.

[8] The square of foundings in the previous year does not add significantly to the fit of any of the models reported.

[9] The R^2 of the regression of real assets on time for the years 1842 to 1900 is .98.

Appendix B: Methods of Analysis

This appendix explains how we embed density dependence in stochastic models of the vital rates and how we estimate the effects of density on the vital rates. We discuss both founding rates and mortality rates. However, because the methods we use to analyze founding rates are relatively new and those we use to analyze mortality rates are standard ones, we give a more detailed account of the former.

Event Data and Stochastic Models of Vital Rates

Different social processes usually control the rates of entry and rates of mortality in organizational populations. If so, working with the growth trajectories alone by focusing on the overall growth rates of populations can obscure more than it enlightens. Until we know much more about the dynamics of organizational populations, modeling and analyzing each rate separately makes sense.

Focusing on the vital rates has broad consequences for modeling. The most important concerns the choice between deterministic and stochastic models. Virtually all defensible models of vital rates of organizational populations are *stochastic*. Therefore we develop and estimate stochastic models for rates of organizational founding and mortality. Using stochastic models of vital rates means that we operate in the general realm of stochastic birth-death processes. For example, we consider the stationary Markov birth-death process. This process describes the dynamics of the size of the population, $N(t)$. The stochastic process $N = \{N(t) \mid t \geq 0\}$ is defined on the state space $\{0, 1, 2, \dots\}$. The stationarity assumption in this context means that $P_{ij}(t) = \Pr\{N(t+s) = j \mid N(s) = i\}$ depends on t but not on s. Let $\mathbf{P}(t)$ denote the matrix of transition probabilities. Then the dynamics of this stochastic process can be described by the backward Kolmogorov equations[1]

$$\frac{d\,\mathbf{P}(t)}{dt} = \mathbf{A}\mathbf{P}(t)\,,$$

where

$$\mathbf{A} = \begin{pmatrix} -\lambda_0 & \lambda_0 & 0 & 0\ldots \\ \mu_1 & -(\lambda_1 + \mu_1) & \lambda_1 & 0\ldots \\ 0 & \mu_2 & -(\lambda_2 + \mu_2) & \lambda_2\ldots \\ 0 & 0 & \mu_3 & -(\lambda_3 + \mu_3)\ldots \\ \vdots & \vdots & \vdots & \vdots \end{pmatrix}.$$

The matrix $\mathbf{A}$ is called the infinitesimal generator of this process.

Notice that this process involves a high degree of simplification in that it invokes the Markov property and assumes that the transition rates do not vary over time. At the same time, it allows the most general form of density dependence—each population size has its own (possibly distinct) birth rate and death rate. In particular, the process as just specified contains as many birth rates and death rates as there are states in the state space (each rate is subscripted by the relevant value of the state space). In cases like the ones we study, in which the number of states is large, it is neither tractable nor substantively useful to assume that each state has a distinct founding rate and mortality rate. Rather than pursue models of this form, we relax the assumption of time dependence and introduce simplifications into the specification of density dependence. In particular, we replace the huge set of birth rates and death rates with a relatively small number of parameters. That is, we parameterize density dependence. In doing so, we concentrate on each vital rate separately. Once we have a pair of provisional models that make sociological sense and fit the observed data, we combine the subprocesses into an overall stochastic process of population growth.

[1] These equations are derived in standard texts on stochastic process theory. See, for instance, Çinlar (1975, chap. 8) and Karlin and Taylor (1975, chap. 4).

Before turning to substantive matters, we discuss briefly the relationship between two seemingly different forms of analysis of stochastic processes. The data we analyze contain event histories of foundings and failures of organizations. Expositions of event-history analysis consider the issues in studying *state transitions,* changes between structurally different states (Blossfeld, Hamerle, and Mayer 1989; Coleman 1981; Tuma and Hannan 1984). But state transitions are not the only kind of process of interest. Many event histories tell the times of *event recurrences,* repetitions of the same kind of event to a social unit (Coleman 1981; Hannan 1989b).

One difference between the two kinds of processes concerns the lengths of typical durations in states. With state transitions, states have nontrivial expected durations. But for event recurrences, durations of the events themselves are infinitesimal relative to the waiting times between events. A typical founding event (for example, a national convention to establish a labor union or the granting of a state charter for a bank) lasts one or a few days whereas the time between foundings of unions is on the order of months or years—the founding event can be considered a point in a process.

A second difference is the size of the state spaces. For state transitions, the size of the state space is typically small, and each state is substantively interesting. For example, our analysis of mortality in several populations distinguishes several "forces" of mortality (destination states): "disbanding," "absorption," "equal-status merger," and "suspension." Because the implications of these outcomes may differ greatly for an organization and for the social structure, organizational analysts often want to treat them separately within the limits of the data. The situation for typical event recurrences differs considerably, as is the case for foundings. Because the number of recurrences can become very large and each value of the counter of events is a distinct state, the state space is large. As a result, no specific state (for instance, the state of having had exactly y foundings in a population) has particular interest. Instead the overall rate of occurrence—rather than the rates of particular transitions—has most direct substantive interest.

Processes of state transition and event recurrence are often represented differently as stochastic processes. With state transitions, analysts identify a small number of states as the state space and attempt to model transitions among the various states. Researchers commonly allow transitions among all states, with the exception of absorbing states (those that terminate a process). In the case of event recurrences, analysts usually think of the outcomes in terms of a point process—a timed counter of events, with the set of integers representing the state space of the process. In this case, transitions can move only from a count y to $y + 1$, and no value of the state space is regarded as absorbing.

Although these differences should be accommodated when representing the processes, they do not mean that different models and methods of estimation must be used for the two cases (Hannan 1989b). In each case, the basic data consist of information on durations between events, along with information about the nature of the events that begin and end the waiting time. Empirical study of instances of either kind of process can be built on methods for analyzing waiting times or durations.[2]

When analyzing mortality, we do use durations between events because the available data provide reasonable accuracy in measuring durations of lifetimes. However, most of data we analyze here do not record exact times of foundings, which means that we cannot determine waiting times between foundings with much precision. For this reason, we use different methods for analyzing founding rates and mortality rates.

Analysis of Organizational Founding Rates

For understandable reasons, organizational analysts customarily take the individual organization as the unit of observation and analysis in research. But in an analysis of organizational foundings, the unit of observation must be something other than the set of individual organizations whose appearances are recorded. The most telling argument regarding the appropriate unit of analysis in this case is that "nonevents," the conditions under which the founding rate falls and no new organizations appear, figure just as importantly in understanding the process of founding as do observed foundings. Because

---

[2] For a treatment of the theory of point processes, see Cox and Isham (1980). Amburgey and Carroll (1984) and Amburgey (1986) provide useful reviews of the social scientific applicability of the theory.

nonevents cannot be associated with particular organizations, it follows that the unit of analysis cannot be the individual organization. Rather the *organizational population* itself experiences the foundings. Detailed information on foundings tell the times at which increments to the population take place.

An organizational founding process can usefully be considered as an instance of an *arrival process* for the population. An arrival process is a type of point process that characterizes the stochastic behavior of the flow of arrivals to some system, such as a queue or a population. We denote the cumulative number of foundings by time t with the random variable $Y(t)$ and the time of the ith founding by T_i. The stochastic process of interest, the founding process, is $\{Y(t) \mid t \geq 0\}$, with state space equal to $\{0, 1, 2, \ldots\}$. The *founding rate*, the rate of arriving at state $y + 1$ at (just after) time t, can be defined as

$$\lambda_y(t) = \lim_{\Delta t \downarrow 0} \frac{\Pr\{Y(t + \Delta t) - Y(t) = 1 \mid Y(t) = y\}}{\Delta t}.$$

An equivalent definition of the founding rate uses the distribution of interarrival times. Let U_y denote a random variable that tells the *interarrival time*, the waiting time between the yth and $(y + 1)$th founding: $U_y = T_{y+1} - T_y$. The density of interarrival times is given by

$$f(u_y) = \lim_{\Delta u \downarrow 0} \frac{\Pr\{U_y \leq u_y + \Delta u \mid u_y > U_y\}}{\Delta u}.$$

The survivor function, $G(u)$ gives the probability that an interarrival time exceeds any chosen value

$$G(u) = \Pr\{U > u\}.$$

Using the definition of conditional probability, the founding rate can be defined as the ratio of the density to the survivor function:

$$\lambda_y(u) = \lim_{\Delta u \downarrow 0} \frac{\Pr\{U_y \leq u_y + \Delta u \mid U_y > u_y\}}{\Pr\{U_y > u_y\} \Delta u} = \frac{f(u_y)}{G(u_y)}.$$

Poisson Regression

The Poisson process serves as a natural baseline model for arrival processes. In a Poisson process, the rate of arrival does not depend on the history of previous arrivals, including the number of previous arrivals and time of the last arrival. If the rate at which organizations enter a population follows a Poisson process, the rate of arriving at state $y+1$ at (just after) time t is a constant. That is, $\lambda_y(t) = \lambda$ under the assumptions of a Poisson process. A basic result for Poisson processes is that the distribution of interarrival times is exponential,

$$f(u) = \lambda e^{-\lambda u} ,$$

and

$$G(u) = e^{-\lambda u} .$$

Most of our sources of data record times of foundings only to the year. Therefore, we use yearly counts of foundings to estimate the parameters of continuous-time Poisson processes, treating the outcomes as grouped in time (to the year).

The arguments of Chapters 2 and 3 imply that founding rates are not constant but instead depend on contemporaneous density (N_t). In order to take account of changing social, economic, and political conditions, we also specify that the founding rate depends on a vector of time-varying covariates, x_t, possibly including time trends or period effects. We concentrate on a process whose rate has the general form

$$\lambda(t) = \lambda(N_t, x_t) = \varphi(N_t) \exp(x_t'\pi) ,$$

where $\varphi(N_t)$ is one of the four specifications of density dependence discussed in Chapter 3: the generalized-Yule (GY), log-quadratic (LQ), logistic, and Gompertz models. This specification of the rate assumes that the time variation in the founding rate reflects only time variation in the vector of covariates. The fact that we dropped the subscript y from the rate signals that we assume that we represented the dependence of the rate on y with the specification on the right-hand side. In other words, we assume that the founding rate does not depend on the cumulative number of foundings (y), net of the effects of density and the covariates.

If the flow of arrivals follows a Poisson process, then the number of arrivals in any interval of constant width is governed by the probability law

$$\Pr(Y_t = y_t) = \frac{e^{-\lambda(N_t, \mathbf{x}_t)} \lambda(N_t, \mathbf{x}_t)^{y_t}}{y_t!}. \tag{B.1}$$

Well-known implications of the Poisson process are that the expected number of events in a unit interval equals the rate, $\lambda(N_t, \mathbf{x}_t)$, and that the variance of the number of events also equals $\lambda(N_t, \mathbf{x}_t)$.

Given that the data on foundings in the populations under study provide yearly counts, we treat a year as the unit interval and use the probability law in Equation B.1 to analyze the flow of foundings over years. When estimating models from yearly counts of foundings, we do not include the observation for a population's first year. The first observation has a peculiar status. By definition, it is the first positive value of the count of yearly foundings. In other words, the first year of a population's history is constrained to have a count of foundings greater than zero. No subsequent year is so constrained. That is, each subsequent year can have zero foundings or some positive number. The first year's count cannot be assumed to be a realization of the same probability mechanism as counts for subsequent years. For this reason, we condition on the appearance of a population in a particular year by beginning the record in that year and analyzing the flow of foundings in all subsequent years.

A related issue arises in analyses of interactions between subpopulations. Because the subpopulations do not start at the same time, the question is how to treat the years before the first founding in the later-developing subpopulation in each pair. In the case of Manhattan banks (whose subpopulations are savings banks and commercial banks), the first savings bank was founded 28 years after the first commercial bank. One possibility is to begin both subpopulations at the same time and treat the 28 consecutive counts of zero foundings per year as valid outcomes. The alternative begins each subpopulation with its first founding. We adopted the latter alternative because we wanted to treat subpopulations in the same ways as we do the complete populations. We reasoned that the subpopulations might be so distinct as to comprise bounded populations with little interaction over the boundary. In this case, we would treat the date of initiation of each as the starting time. Because we did not want to prejudice the issue of independence of subpopulations by design, we started the record on each with the first observed event in each subpopulation.

Negative Binomial Regression

Biostatisticians have long questioned the applicability of Poisson processes to the flow of events because empirical research seldom finds that the mean equals the variance, even approximately, as the Poisson process implies. Instead, it has been common to find the variance of event counts exceeds the mean, often by a considerable margin. This condition, commonly called *overdispersion*, can arise for a number of different reasons, including unobserved heterogeneity and time dependence.

It has often proven useful in prior research to regard the Poisson model as a special case of a negative binomial model. The seemingly most common representation, begun by Greenwood and Yule (1920), assumes that a Poisson process operates but is disturbed by a multiplicative error process,

$$\lambda(t) = f(N_t) \exp(\mathbf{x}_t'\boldsymbol{\pi}) \, \epsilon_t \, , \tag{B.2}$$

where ϵ_t is uncorrelated over units at risk (time periods, regions, and so forth, depending on the application). The probability law for the event counts is then a mixture of Poisson processes. That is,

$$\Pr\left(Y_t = y_t\right) = \int \frac{e^{\lambda(t)} \lambda(t)^{y_t}}{y_t!} g(\epsilon) \, d\epsilon \, , \tag{B.3}$$

where $\lambda(t)$ has the form indicated in Equation B.2. The negative binomial model follows from the assumption that the unobservable has a gamma distribution. That is, $g(\epsilon_t) \sim \Gamma(\phi_t, \nu_t)$.[3] In this case,

---

[3] The parameterization used here assumes following "index" parameterization of the gamma function

$$\Gamma(\phi_t, \nu_t) = \frac{1}{\Gamma(\nu_t)} \left(\frac{\nu_t \lambda(t)}{\phi_t} \right)^{\nu_t} \exp\left(\frac{-\nu_t \lambda(t)}{\phi_t} \right) \frac{1}{\lambda(t)}.$$

$E[\lambda(t)] = \phi_t$ and $Var[\lambda(t)] = \phi_t^2/\nu_t$. As is usual in such a setup, one "integrates out" the unobservable in Equation B.3 to obtain an estimable model. In the present case, this procedure yields a version of the negative binomial model,

$$\Pr(Y_t = y_t) = \frac{\Gamma(y_t + \nu_t)}{\Gamma(y_t + 1)\Gamma(\nu_t)} \left(\frac{\nu_t}{\nu_t + \phi_t}\right)^{\nu_t} \left(\frac{\phi_t}{\nu_t + \phi_t}\right)^{y_t}, \quad \text{(B.4)}$$

with

$$E(Y_t) = \phi_t \quad \text{and} \quad Var(Y_t) = \phi_t + \frac{1}{\nu_t}\phi_t^2.$$

In order to maintain the parallel with the Poisson regression model, we again specify that the mean of the process is a loglinear function of the covariates:

$$E(Y_t) = \phi_t = f(N_t)\exp(x_t'\pi).$$

Unlike the case of the Poisson process, the variance does not necessarily equal the mean; this model can accommodate overdispersion.

In empirical analysis, we tried two different relationships between the mean and variance (two choices of ν). Each is a special case of a general framework

$$\nu_t = \frac{1}{\omega}\left(f(N_t)\exp[x_t'\pi]\right)^c = \frac{1}{\omega}E^c(Y_t),$$

where c is an arbitrary constant and ω is an overdispersion parameter. Following McCullagh and Nelder (1989) (see also Cameron and Trivedi 1986), we chose two values of c. The first, $c = 1$, causes the variance of the expected count to be proportional to the expected count

$$Var(Y_t) = (1 + \omega)E(Y_t). \quad \text{(B.5)}$$

In other words, this specification assumes a constant coefficient of variation (ratio of the variance to the mean). The second, $c = 0$, results in quadratic dependence

$$Var(Y_t) = E(Y_t)\left(1 + \omega E[Y_t]\right). \quad \text{(B.6)}$$

This specification assumes that the coefficient of variation increases linearly with the mean. In either case, setting $\omega = 0$ reduces the model to a Poisson process. Thus one can form likelihood ratio tests of the Poisson process versus the negative binomial.[4]

An alternative derivation assumes "contagion" in the process over time within the intervals chosen (within years in the case of our research). This means that the occurrence of an event affects the rate of subsequent occurrences, meaning that the occurrences are not independent within time intervals. Positive contagion leads to overdispersion.[5]

Either interpretation fits our applications, as we explained in Chapter 4. There is reason for suspecting that founding rates fluctuate randomly over time, net of the effects of covariates, due to unmeasured changes in environments. And it is likely that contagion operates *within* years, such that the occurrence of one or more foundings early in a year increases the rate for the rest of the year. This would be an instance of unobserved contagion in the process. Our data did not permit us to choose between alternative sources of overdispersion. We simply controlled for overdispersion with the pair of specifications of the negative binomial regression model so that our estimated standard errors were not understated.

When simulating founding processes in Chapter 8, we used an alternative but equivalent parameterization of the negative binomial probability law which is more convenient in the simulation context. Replace ν in Equation B.4 with k and ϕ with k/λ to obtain

$$\Pr\left(Y = y\right) = \frac{\Gamma(y + k)}{\Gamma(y + 1)\Gamma(k)} \left(\frac{\lambda}{1 + \lambda}\right)^{k} \left(\frac{1}{1 + \lambda}\right)^{y}.$$

This representation can be simplified to yield the standard representation of the negative binomial probability law as producing the

[4] A procedure for maximum-likelihood (ML) estimation of the specification in Equation B.5 is included in the negative binomial routines distributed in the GAUSS (Aptech Systems 1991) "applications package" for counted data (written by Gary King 1988, 1990). A procedure for ML estimation of the specification in Equation B.6 is included in LIMDEP (Greene 1986) and has also been programmed in GAUSS by David Barron.

[5] More precisely, the negative binomial can be derived as a limiting distribution of an Eggenberger-Pólya urn scheme in which the probability of an event depends on the previous number of events (see Johnson and Kotz 1969, pp. 124–125).

number of failures until k successes occur in a binomial process with probability of success of p by setting λ to p/q where $q = 1 - p$. This gives

$$\Pr(Y = y) = \frac{\Gamma(y + k)}{\Gamma(y + 1)\Gamma(k)} p^k q^y. \tag{B.7}$$

We refer to this parameterization in Appendix C in describing the simulation procedures. The relation between the parameterization used in estimation (Equation B.4) and the one used in simulation (Equation B.7) is

$$p = \frac{\nu}{\nu + \phi}; \quad k = \nu. \tag{B.8}$$

Introducing Autocorrelation

Chapter 4 pointed out that yearly counts of foundings are unlikely to be independent from year to year, as is assumed implicitly in conventional ML estimation of either Poisson regression or negative binomial regression.[6] We address this potential problem by specifying that the unobservable in Equation B.2 is autocorrelated. This change in the model has major implications for estimation, even when one assumes a very simple structure of autocorrelation. In particular, the task of deriving the likelihood functions for such structures has not yet been accomplished. The most feasible approach at this point is to shift from the more common ML estimation to quasi-likelihood (QL) estimation, as we describe next.

Quasi-likelihood Estimation

Quasi-likelihood estimation finds solutions to the system of equations

$$\frac{\partial \boldsymbol{\lambda}'}{\partial \mathbf{b}} \mathbf{V}^{-1} (\mathbf{y} - \boldsymbol{\lambda}) = 0,$$

where $\boldsymbol{\beta}$ is a $(k \times 1)$ vector of parameters to be estimated, $\mathbf{V} = \mathrm{Var}(\mathbf{y})$, and $\boldsymbol{\lambda} = \mathrm{E}(\mathbf{y}) = f(\mathbf{x}, \boldsymbol{\beta})$. This technique differs from ML estimation in that it is based only on assumptions about the mean and variance of $\mathbf{y}$; no assumptions are made about the underlying probability

---

[6] This issue is not, however, restricted to time-series analysis. Data on a cross section of actors are subject to spatial autocorrelation or network autocorrelation, in which case the same issues would arise.

distribution. McCullagh (1983) demonstrated that this estimator is consistent, asymptotically Gaussian, and robust in the sense that consistent estimates of effects can be obtained given only that the mean is specified correctly. Moreover, the quasi-likelihood function and the maximum-likelihood function are equivalent in the case of Poisson regression. Indeed, the two estimators are equivalent for all members of the linear exponential family (McCullagh and Nelder 1989).

In applications of QL estimation V has generally been assumed to be a diagonal matrix; that is, observations have been assumed to be independent (McCullagh 1983; Wedderburn 1974). However, Zeger (1988) proposed a generalization of this method that allows the off-diagonal elements of V to be nonzero.[7] We consider the case of generalized quasi-likelihood (GQL) estimation in which the stochastic disturbance, ϵ_t, is a stationary latent process. If $\text{Cov}(\epsilon_t, \epsilon_{t+\tau}) = \omega \rho_\epsilon(\tau)$, $\text{E}(\epsilon_t) = 1$, and $\text{E}(y_t \mid \epsilon_t) = \text{Var}(y_t \mid \epsilon_t) = \exp(x_t' b)\epsilon_t$, then it follows that V will have nonzero off-diagonal elements that depend on $\rho_\epsilon(\tau)$.

Chapter 4 reported estimates of models in which autocorrelation has a first-order autoregressive form. In this case, there is a single autoregression parameter, which we denoted as ρ. Estimates of the effects of density and of covariates can then be found by means of iteratively reweighted least squares, with $\widehat{\omega}$ and $\widehat{\rho}$ being evaluated by the method of moments.[8] The GQL method has the two-fold advantage of allowing for overdispersion *and* autocorrelation, in contrast with ML estimation of Poisson and negative binomial regression models. We compared two sets of estimates. The first set imposes the constraint $\rho = 0$; the observations are thus assumed to be independent. However, overdispersion is controlled by allowing ω to be nonzero.[9] The second relaxes the constraint on ρ, and thus allows the observations to be stochastically dependent.

[7] Barron (1990, 1992) provides a detailed discussion of this approach and of its potential value to social science research.

[8] Details of this method can be found in Zeger (1988) and Barron (1990, 1992).

[9] A drawback of the QL approach is that the range of possible variance–mean relationships is more restricted than in the case of ML estimation. The specification we used implies the quadratic relationship between the variance and the mean, which is shown in Equation B.6.

Analysis of Rates of Organizational Mortality

An analysis of mortality rates differs in two important ways from that of founding rates. First, events of mortality occur to identifiable individual organizations (not to the population), meaning that one can use organizational characteristics when analyzing mortality rates. Second, the meaningful analytic structure involves state transitions rather than event recurrences, because by definition mortality events do not recur for individual organizations. The observable data include the lifetimes and the destination state (mortality or censoring in the simplest case).

Our analysis of mortality rates uses standard methods of event history analysis (Tuma and Hannan 1984). We analyzed information on the lifetimes of individual organizations rather than interarrival times. Let T_i denote a random variable that records the time of the end of an organization's observed lifetime (possibly due to right censoring). Then the mortality rate characterizes the distribution of T, for times after the founding of the organization in question. We denoted the time of founding as T_{f_i}. The mortality rate of the ith organization in a population was defined as

$$\mu_i(t) = \lim_{\Delta t \downarrow 0} \frac{\Pr\{T_i \leq t + \Delta t \mid T_i > t\}}{\Pr\{T_i > t\}\,\Delta t} = \frac{f_i(t)}{G_i(t)}, \qquad T_i > T_{f_i}$$

where $f_i(t)$ and $G_i(t)$ are again the density and survivor functions. In order to represent the arguments of Chapters 2 and 3, we expressed both of these functions as depending on contemporaneous density (N_t), density at the time of an organization's founding (N_{f_i}), and a vector of covariates.

We relied on ML estimation. The relevant likelihoods have the following general form:

$$\mathcal{L} = \prod_{i=1}^{I} f_i(t)^{\delta_i}\, G_i(t)^{(1-\delta_i)},$$

where δ_i equals one if time of mortality of the ith organization is observed (that is, is uncensored); and it equals zero otherwise. We replaced $f_i(t)$ and $G_i(t)$ by parametric functions of age, the two density terms, and the covariates and maximize the log-likelihood function directly.

When only overall mortality is considered, knowledge of the hazard alone suffices to describe the process. But when multiple types of mortality are possible, one needs to know both the overall hazard of mortality and the relative odds of each type or the set of instantaneous transition rates (or cause-specific hazards). We relied on a formulation based on the latter. Consider the joint distribution of a random variable (T, Y), where T_i still denotes time of mortality or right censoring, and Y_i denotes the type of mortality observed to occur to the ith organization. The *cause-specific mortality rate* (for cause k) is defined as

$$\mu_{ik}(t) = \lim_{\Delta t \downarrow 0} \frac{\Pr\{t < T_i < t + \Delta t, Y_i(T_i) = k \mid T_i \geq t\}}{\Delta t}.$$

Given a sufficient number of observations on cause-specific waiting times, the joint distribution can be estimated arbitrarily closely without the assumption of latent waiting times and independence of competing risks, which allows estimation of parameters of structural models for cause-specific mortality rates. Kalbfleisch and Prentice (1980, pp. 168–172) demonstrated that this approach leads to the same ML estimators as does the assumption of independence of competing risks. One simply treats the waiting times that end with an event other than the one under study as having been censored on the right at the time of the event. Kalbfleisch and Prentice (1980), Cox and Oakes (1984), and Tuma and Hannan (1984) all explained in detail how estimates of parameters of models of transition rates (including cause-specific mortality rates) can be obtained from event history data using maximum likelihood. We used this approach in Chapter 6.

Once again, the Poisson process serves as a useful baseline in a hierarchy of models. As we have already seen, this process assumes that the rate (of mortality, in this case) is a time-independent constant: $\mu_i(t) = \mu$. By obvious analogy to a Poisson founding rate, an ML estimate of the Poisson mortality rate in a population is the number of observed mortalities divided by the total of the observed lifetimes (up to mortality or censoring) for all members of the population.

A Gompertz Model of Age Dependence

We have strong reasons for expecting that the rate of organizational mortality varies with age. An organization's age is defined in our notation as $A_i = T - T_{f_i}$ for $T > T_{f_i}$. Organizations appear to experience a liability of newness—the mortality rate starts high and drops steeply with age (Carroll 1983; Freeman, Carroll, and Hannan 1983; Hannan 1989a). Most of the empirical literature on organizational mortality has used the Gompertz model of age dependence and its extension, the Makeham model, in representing age dependence. The Gompertz model of age dependence in mortality rates, which is *not* the same as the Gompertz model used in analyzing density-dependent legitimation, assumes that the rate declines exponentially with age. This model with effects of covariates has the form

$$\mu_i(t) = f(N_t, N_{f_i}) e^{-\rho a} \exp(\mathbf{x}'_{it}\boldsymbol{\pi}) . \tag{B.9}$$

This model, like the deterministic model of nonlinear population growth discussed in the section on "Classical Models of Population Growth" in Chapter 3, is called a Gompertz model.

When analyzing the Gompertz model (and the Weibull model discussed next) we used step-function approximations in age in order to be able to represent the effects of time-varying density. This approximation uses an organization's age at the beginning of each year as a covariate in the loglinear model. We broke each organization's history into P_i periods, where P_i is the completed age of the organization in years, and we updated the organization's age (and all time-varying covariates) at the beginning of each year. Let p denote an organization's age at the beginning of each of these spells. Then we approximated the Gompertz model of age dependence with

$$\exp(\rho a) \approx \exp(-\phi p), \qquad p = 1, \ldots, P_i.$$

A Weibull Model of Age Dependence

Some recent research (Hannan 1989a; Hannan and Freeman 1989) revealed that the Gompertz model does not always fit data on organizational mortality as well as the Weibull model does. According to the Weibull model, the rate changes as a power function of time (age in this case),

$$\mu(a) = \rho\theta(\theta a)^{\rho-1} .$$

This rate is a monotonic decreasing function of duration if $\rho < 1$, a monotonic increasing function of duration for $\rho > 1$, and equals the exponential (or Poisson) model when $\rho = 1$. We generalized the Weibull to include the effects of measured covariates with the assumption

$$\mu_i(t) = f\left(N_t, N_{f_i}\right) \rho(\theta a)^{\rho-1} \exp\left(\mathbf{x}'_{it}\boldsymbol{\pi}\right) . \qquad \text{(B.10)}$$

We used the approach of "spell splitting" to handle temporal changes in density and other covariates, and we used the following step-function approximation to the Weibull model:

$$a^{\rho-1} \approx p^{\phi}, \qquad p = 1, \ldots, P_i .$$

Because our method of approximating age dependence by a step function assumes that the rates are constant within years, we could use standard "constant rate" procedures to obtain ML estimates of effects of density, age (at start of year), and covariates. We used Tuma's (1980) RATE program (with the "constant-rate model"), the SAS Institute's (1985) PROC LIFEREG (with the "exponential model"), and Petersen's (1986) BMDP programs to obtain the estimates reported in Chapters 6 and 7.

Appendix C: Simulation Program

The following is the GAUSS computer program used to conduct the simulations reported in Chapter 8. The program was written by David N. Barron. For information about GAUSS, see Aptech Systems (1991).

The listing is for the "historical simulation" for American labor unions. It uses the estimates of effects on rates of founding and mortality found in Table C.1. This version of the program produces five simulations of the evolution of density over 149 periods (years).

A Version of The Simulation Program: SIMNB.PF

```
/**********************************************************
** A GAUSS PROGRAM TO SIMULATE DENSITY DEPENDENT
** GROWTH OF ORGANIZATIONAL POPULATIONS OVER TIME
** WRITTEN BY DAVID N. BARRON, DEPARTMENT OF
** SOCIOLOGY, CORNELL UNIVERSITY.
** LAST REVISED 1/16/91.
**
**********************************************************/

/* DEFINITION OF VARIABLES

   maxtrial :  NUMBER OF TIMES SIMULATION IS RUN
   maxper :  NUMBER OF PERIODS PER SIMULATION
   trial :  COUNTER OF NUMBER OF TRIALS
   period :  COUNTER OF PERIOD (YEAR)
```

```
maxden :  MAX SIZE OF THE POPULATION
phi :  MEAN FOUNDING RATE
founds :  NUMBER OF FOUNDINGS IN THE PERIOD
founded :  VECTOR OF ONES WITH LENGTH EQUAL TO THE NUMBER
            OF FOUNDS
mu :  HAZARD OF MORTALITY
risktime :  DURATION OF RISK OF MORTALITY DURING PERIOD
dprob :  PROBABILITY OF MORTALITY DURING PERIOD OF RISK
uni :  VECTOR OF UNIFORM RANDOM NUMBERS
age :  ORGANIZATION'S AGE AT START OF PERIOD
density :  NUMBER OF ORGANIZATIONS AT START OF PERIOD
fdens :  DENSITY AT FOUNDING
tempnf :  VECTOR TO HOLD FOUNDING DENSITY
lagf :  FOUNDINGS IN PREVIOUS PERIOD
depyr :  DUMMY VARIABLE CODING OF DEPRESSION YEARS
per :  PERIOD EFFECTS
k :  Overdispersion PARAMETER (SEE APPENDIX B)
l :  PARAMETER OF THE NEGATIVE BINOMIAL DIST
founded :  LOGICAL VARIABLE TELLS WHETHER AN ORG
            WAS FOUNDED DURING CURRENT PERIOD
dead :  LOGICAL VECTOR TO TELL IF ORG HAS FAILED
            DURING THE CURRENT PERIOD
status :  LOGICAL VECTOR TO TELL WHETHER AN ORG IS STILL
            ALIVE DURING CURRENT PERIOD
deaths :  NUMBER OF MORTALITIES DURING THE PERIOD
*/

clearg lagf,density,age,fdens,status,maxden,trial,period;
clearg maxtrial,maxper,deaths,founds,mu,phi,founded;

cls;locate 10,20;"SIMULATING....";locate 11,20;
"Please don't switch me off.";

/* WRITE THE OUTPUT ON A FILE CALLED SIMNB.OUT */

opf="\\gauss\\simnb.out";
output file=^opf reset;
output off;

load depyr; /* LOADS DEPYR FROM AN EXTERNAL FILE */
```

```
/* SET PARAMETERS OF THE SIMULATION */

maxtrial=5;
maxper=149;
maxden=800;

/****************** MAIN LOOP STARTS ********************/

trial=1;
do until trial > maxtrial;
/* CALL SUBROUTINE TO INITIALIZE VARS--SEE BELOW */

  gosub init;

/***************** SIMULATION LOOP STARTS ****************/

  period=1;
  do until period > maxper;
/* FOUNDING PROC NOT CALLED IN FIRST PERIOD BECAUSE
ESTIMATED RATES ARE CONDITIONAL ON FIRST FOUNDING */

    if period > 1;
/* CALL TO FOUNDING PROC */

      call found();
    endif;

/* CALL TO MORTALITY PROC */
    call death();

/* CALL TO OUTPUT PROC */

    call op();

    period=period+1;
  endo;

  trial=trial+1;
endo;

output off;
screen on;
print "\ g";
```

```
end;
```

/****************** END OF MAIN PROGRAM ******************/

/*********** START OF INITIALIZATION SUBROUTINE **********/

/* INITIAL CONDITIONS: A SINGLE ORG IS FOUNDED AT THE
MIDPOINT OF THE FIRST PERIOD AND WILL BE EXPOSED TO THE
RISK OF MORTALITY DURING ITS FIRST HALF YEAR. FOR
SIMULATING MORTALITY OF THE PIONEER ORG DURING THE FIRST
PERIOD, DENSITY (AT START OF YEAR) IS SET TO ZERO AND
DENSITY AT FOUNDING TO ZERO. ALL FOUNDINGS ARE ASSUMED TO
OCCUR AT MIDYEAR; THUS THE PERIOD OF RISK OF MORTALITY
DURING AN ORGANIZATION'S FIRST YEAR IS SET TO .5 AND AGE
AT START OF THE NEXT PERIOD IS SET TO .5. AS THE HAZARD
IS NOT DEFINED AT AGE ZERO FOR THE WEIBULL MODEL, AGE AT
START OF PERIOD OF RISK DURING AN ORGANIZATION'S FIRST
YEAR IS SET TO .1 */

```
init:
    age=zeros(maxden,1)+.1; /* AGE INITIALIZED TO .1 */
    fdens=zeros(maxden,1); /* CREATES VECTOR */
    status=zeros(maxden,1); /* CREATES VECTOR */
    founded=zeros(maxden,1); /* CREATES VECTOR */
    risktime=zeros(maxden,1); /* CREATES VECTOR */
    density=0; /* DENSITY IS ZERO AT START */
    lagf=0; /* NO FOUNDINGS PRIOR TO START */
    founded[1]=1; /* FIRST ORG FOUNDED IN FIRST YEAR */
    founds=1; /* NEEDED FOR FIRST PERIOD */
    risktime[1]=.5; /* PIONEER AT RISK OF MORTALITY FOR
                ONLY HALF OF ITS FIRST YEAR */
return;
```

/********** END OF INITIALIZATION SUB ROUTINE **********/

/******** START OF PROC TO GENERATE FOUNDINGS **********/

```
proc (0)=found();

    local per,omega,k,p,tempnf;
```

```
    founds=0;
    founded=zeros(maxden,1);
```

/* CALCULATE PERIOD EFFECTS */

```
    if period > 50; per=exp(-.297);
    elseif period> 95; per=exp(-.297+.651);
    elseif period> 111; per=exp(-.297+.651+.219);
    elseif period> 118; per= exp(-.297+.651+.219-1.60);
    else; per=1;
    endif;
```

/* CALCULATE THE MEAN FOUNDING RATE */

```
    phi=exp(-.454).*exp(.043*density).*
      exp(- (.000187*(density^2))).*
      exp(.056*lagf).*exp(.117*depyr[period]).*per;

    if phi > 200; /* REQUIRED TO PREVENT OVERFLOW */
      phi = 200;
      print "** phi set to 200 **";
    endif;

    lagf=0;
```

/* DEFINE PARAMETERS OF THE NEGATIVE BINOMIAL DIST IN
TERMS OF THE ESTIMATED Overdispersion PARAMETER (omega) AND
THE MEAN FOUNDING RATE (phi) */

```
    omega=.192
    k=1./omega;
    p=k./(k+phi);
```

/* CREATE A REALIZATION OF THE NEGATIVE BINOMIAL RANDOM
VARIABLE AS THE NUMBER OF FOUNDINGS IN THE PERIOD.
CALLS A SUBROUTINE, RNEGBIN, LISTED BELOW */

```
    founds=rnegbin(k,p); /* CALL TO RANDOM NUMBER GENERATOR */

    if founds > 0; /* IF NO FOUNDS THIS PERIOD, PROC IS EXITED;
ELSE THE FOLLOWING STATEMENTS ARE EXECUTED */

    founded=ones(founds,1);

    tempnf=seqa(density,1,founds);
```

/* STATEMENTS TO PRODUCE FOUNDED AND TEMPNF VECTORS

```
OF CORRECT ORDER AND WITH CELLS CORRESPONDING
TO ORGS FOUNDED THIS PERIOD IN THE CORRECT PLACES */

if sumc(status) == 0; /* BLOCK FOR DENSITY=0 AT START OF
  PERIOD */

  founded=founded|zeros(maxden-founds,1); /* NEW CELLS AT
  TOP OF VECTOR */

  tempnf=tempnf|zeros(maxden-founds,1);
else; /* BLOCK FOR DENSITY > 0 */

/* NEW CELLS PLACED UNDER VECTOR OF ZEROS WITH LENGTH
EQUAL TO DENSITY AT START OF PERIOD */

  founded=zeros(sumc(status),1)|founded;
  tempnf=zeros(sumc(status),1)|tempnf;
  if rows(founded) < maxden; /* VECTOR PADDED WITH
    ZEROS IF NEEDED */

    founded=founded|zeros(maxden-founds-sumc(status),1);
    tempnf=tempnf|zeros(maxden-founds-sumc(status),1);
  endif;
endif;

/* FOUNDING DENSITY OF NEW ORGS ADDED TO PERMANENT
VECTOR OF FOUNDING DENSITIES */

fdens=substute(fdens,founded,tempnf);

/* RISKTIME SET TO .5 FOR NEWLY FOUNDED ORGANIZATIONS */

  risktime=substute(risktime,founded,.5);

endif; /* END OF BLOCK CARRIED OUT ONLY IF FOUNDS > 0 */

  lagf=founds; /* LAGF SET READY FOR NEXT LOOP */

endp;

/******** END OF FOUNDING PROCEDURE. NO RETURNS ********/

/******** START OF PROC TO GENERATE MORTALITIES ********/

proc (0)=death();

local dead,lagf,per,mu,dprob,uni;
```

```
mu=zeros(maxden,1); /* VECTOR OF HAZARDS INITIALIZED */
deaths=0; /* VARIABLE INITIALIZED */
```

/* CALCULATE PERIOD EFFECTS */

```
if period> 50; per=exp(.830);
elseif period> 95; per=exp(.830-.418);
elseif period> 111; per=exp(.830-.418-.100);
elseif period> 118; per=exp(.830-.418-.100+.150);
else; per=1;
endif;
```

/* CALCULATE VECTOR OF HAZARDS OF MORTALITY */

```
mu=mu+(exp(-2.93+.293).*exp(-.023*density)).*
  (exp(.0000562*density^2)).*exp(.02*fdens).*
  (age^(-.109)).*exp(.283*depyr[period]).*per;
```

/* CALCULATE MORTALITY PROBS FOR PERIOD OF RISK */
```
  dprob=1-exp(-mu.*risktime);
```

/* EXPOSE EACH ORGANIZATION TO PROBABILITY OF MORTALITY */

/* CREATE A VECTOR OF UNIFORM RANDOM NUMBERS USING
THE PROCEDURE rndu AS IMPLEMENTED IN GAUSS 2.0 */
```
  uni=rndu(maxden,1);

  dead=dprob .> uni; /* IF DPROB > UNI, ORG FAILS,
    AND DEAD SET TO 1 */
```

/* CALCULATE NUMBER OF MORTALITIES DURING THE PERIOD */
```
  deaths=sumc(dead);
```

/* UPDATE DENSITY TO REFLECT NEW FOUNDINGS FROM PREVIOUS
PASS THROUGH FOUNDING PROCEDURE AND NEW MORTALITIES */
```
  density=density+founds-deaths;
```

/* INCREASE AGE OF SURVIVING ORGANIZATIONS BY 1 */
```
  age=substute(age,status,age+1);
```

/* SET AGE OF NEW ORGS SURVIVING PERIOD FOR NEXT LOOP */
```
  age=substute(age,founded,.5);
```

/* UPDATE STATUS VECTOR TO REFLECT NEW FOUNDINGS */
```
  status=status+founded;
```

```
/* DELETE DEAD ORGS FROM STATUS, AGE, AND FDENS VECTORS */

if density > 0;
  if deaths > 0;

    status=delif(status,dead);
    age=delif(age,dead);
    fdens=delif(fdens,dead);
    status=status|zeros(deaths,1);
    age=age|(zeros(deaths,1)+.1);
    fdens=fdens|zeros(deaths,1);

  endif;
else;

/* BRANCH SETS VECTORS TO ZEROS IF DENSITY IS ZERO */

  status=zeros(maxden,1);
  age=(zeros(maxden,1)+.1);
  fdens=zeros(maxden,1);
endif;

/* SET RISK PERIOD TO 1 FOR ALL ORGS SURVIVING PERIOD */
  risktime=status;

endp;

/***************** END OF MORTALITY PROC ***************/

/************** START OF OUTPUT PROCEDURE ****************/

/* THIS PROC WRITES THE RESULTS OF EACH PERIOD TO THE FILE
NAMED AT THE TOP OF THE PROGRAM. ONE LINE OF OUTPUT PER
PERIOD. 6 VARIABLES PER LINE. THESE ARE (IN THE ORDER IN
WHICH THEY ARE WRITTEN:
  var1 :  NUMBER OF THE SIMULATION
  var2 :  NUMBER OF THE PERIOD
  var3 :  PREDICTED FOUNDING RATE IN THE PERIOD
  var4 :  ACTUAL NUMBER OF FOUNDINGS IN THE PERIOD
  var5 :  ACTUAL NUMBER OF MORTALITIES IN THE PERIOD
  var6 :  DENSITY AT END OF PERIOD
*/

proc (0)=op();
```

```
    output on;
    screen off;

    format /m1 /ld 6,0;

print trial~period~phi~founds~deaths~density;
endp;

/***************** END OF OUTPUT PROC *****************/

/********************** PROC RNEGBIN *********************
**
** THIS PROCEDURE RETURNS A RANDOM NUMBER FROM A NEGATIVE
** BINOMIAL DISTRIBUTION WITH PARAMETERS k and p.
** THE PDF ON WHICH IT IS BASED IS
**   f(x) = Gamma(k+x)/[Gamma(x+1)*Gamma(k)]*(p^k)*(q^k),
**     where q=1-p.
**   E(x)=phi=(k*q)/p and Var(x)=(k*q)/(p^2).
**
** SOURCE: BRATLEY, FOX, AND SCHRAGE (1983, PP. 173--4).
**
*********************************************************/

proc rnegbin(k,p);
  local theta,l;
  if p == 1;
    l=0;
  else;
    l=p./(1-p);
  endif;
  theta=rgamma(k,l);
  retp(rpoisson(theta));
endp;

/******************** PROC RGAMMA **********************
**
** THIS PROCEDURE RETURNS A RANDOM NUMBER FROM A
** GAMMA DISTRIBUTION WITH PARAMETERS k AND l.
** THE PDF ON WHICH IT IS BASED IS
```

```
**   f(x) = l*exp(-l*x) (l*x)^(k-1) / Gamma(k-1)
**      for 0 <= x.
** USAGE:
**   x = rgamma(k,l);
**   E(x) = k/l, Var(x) = k/(l^2).
**
*********************************************************

proc rgamma(k,l);
  local m,q,z,w,y;
  m=floor(k);
  q=k-m;
  z=rndu(m,1);
  z=prodc(z);
  z=-ln(z);
  w=rbeta(q,(1-q));
  y=rndu(1,1);
  y=-ln(y);
  if l >0;
    retp((z+(w*y))./l);
  else;
    retp(0);
  endif;
endp;

/********************** PROC RBETA *********************
**
** THIS PROCEDURE RETURNS A RANDOM NUMBER DRAWN
** FROM A BETA DISTRIBUTION WITH PARAMETERS a AND b.
** THE PDF ON WHICH IT IS BASED IS:
** f(x) = [x^(a-1) * (1-x)^(b-1)] / BETA(a,b),
** WHERE BETA(a,b) IS THE BETA FUNCTION.
** USAGE:
**   x = RBETA(a,b);
**   E(x) = a/(a+b), Var(x) = ab/(a+b+1)(a+b)^2.
**
*********************************************************/
```

```
proc rbeta(a,b);
  local alpha,beta,gam,u1,u2,w,v;
  alpha=a+b;
  if minc(a|b) <= 1;
    beta=1./minc(a|b);
    else;
    beta=sqrt((alpha-2)./((2*a*b)-alpha));
  endif;

  gam=a+(1./beta);
lab:
  u1=rndu(1,1);
  u2=rndu(1,1);
  v=beta*ln(u1./(1-u1));
  w=a*exp(v);
  if (alpha*ln(alpha./(b+w)))+(gam*v)-ln(4) <ln(u1*u1*u2);
  goto lab;
  endif;
  retp(w./(b+w));
endp;


/********************** PROC RPOISSON ********************
**
** THIS PROCEDURE RETURNS A RANDOM NUMBER DRAWN
** FROM A POISSON DISTRIBUTION WITH PARAMETER = theta.
** USAGE:
**    x = rpoisson(theta);
**    E(x) = Var(x) = theta.
**
*******************************************************/

proc rpoisson(theta);
quad local p,plim,fi,count;
  count=0;
  plim=exp(-theta);
  p=rndu(1,1);
  do while p >plim;
    fi=rndu(1,1);
```

```
    p=p*fi;
    count=count+1;
  endo;
  retp(count);
endp:
```

/********************* END OF FILE *******************/

Table C.1. ML estimates of models of rates of founding and overall mortality of labor unions used in historical simulations

	Founding	Mortality
Constant	−.454	−2.93
Density	.043	−.024
Density^2/1000	−.187	.056
Density at founding		.007
Lagged foundings	.056	
Period 2 (1886–1985)	−.297	.830
Period 3 (1932–1985)	.651	−.418
Period 4 (1947–1985)	.219	.100
Period 5 (1955–1985)	−1.60	.150
Depression year	.117	.283
Log of age		−.109
Start by founding		.293
Start by secession		.455
Overdispersion (ω)	.192	

Note: The model for the founding rate uses a log-quadratic specification of density dependence and negative binomial specification with a quadratic relationship between the variance and the mean of the rate (the specification that underlies the results reported for union foundings in Table 4.1, which however reports QL estimates rather than ML estimates). The specification of density dependence in the rate of overall mortality is log-quadratic (the specification that underlies the results reported in Table 6.1).

References

Abbott, Andrew. 1988. *The System of Professions: An Essay on the Expert Division of Labor*. Chicago: University of Chicago Press.

Aldrich, Howard E., and Peter V. Marsden. 1988. "Environments and Organizations." Pp. 361–392 in *Handbook of Sociology*, edited by Neil J. Smelser. Newbury Park, Calif.: Sage.

Aldrich, Howard E., Udo Staber, Catherine Zimmer, and John J. Beggs. 1990. "Minimalism and Mortality: Patterns of Disbandings Among American Trade Associations in the 20th Century." Pp. 21–52 in *Organizational Evolution: New Directions*, edited by Jitendra V. Singh. Newbury Park, Calif.: Sage.

Allee, W. C. 1931. *Animal Aggregations*. Chicago: University of Chicago Press.

Amburgey, Terry L. 1986. "Multivariate Point Processes in Social Research." *Social Science Research* **15**: 190–207.

Amburgey, Terry L., and Glenn R. Carroll. 1984. "Time Series Models for Event Counts." *Social Science Research* **13**: 38–54.

Anderson, Philip C. 1988. "On the Nature of Technological Progress and Industrial Dynamics." Ph.D. dissertation, Columbia University.

Aptech Systems, Inc. 1991. *The GAUSS System Version 2.1*. Kent, Wash.

Arrow, Kenneth J. 1951. *Social Choice and Individual Values*. Cowles Commission Monograph 12. New York: Wiley.

Arthur, W. Brian, Y. M. Ermoliev, and Y. M. Kaniovski. 1987. "Path-dependent Processes and the Emergence of Macro-structure." *European Journal of Operational Research* **30**: 294–303.

Ayer, N. W. Various years. *American Newspaper Directory Annual.* Philadelphia: Ayer Press.

Bagdikian, Ben. 1971. *The Information Machines.* New York: Harper & Row.

Banaszak-Holl, Jane. 1989. "Evidence for Competition and Legitimation Within Organizational Populations: Banks in Manhattan, 1791–1975." M.A. thesis, Cornell University.

_____ 1991. "Incorporating Organizational Growth into Models of Organizational Dynamics: Manhattan Banks, 1791–1980." Ph.D. dissertation, Cornell University.

Banaszak-Holl, Jane, James Ranger-Moore, and Michael T. Hannan. 1990. "Density Dependence in the Mortality Processes of Financial Institutions: American Life Insurance Companies and Manhattan Banks." Technical Report 90–1, Department of Sociology, Cornell University.

Barnett, William P. 1990. "The Organizational Ecology of a Technological System." *Administrative Science Quarterly* **35**: 31–60.

Barnett, William P., and Terry L. Amburgey. 1990. "Do Larger Organizations Generate Stronger Competition?" Pp. 78–102 in *Organizational Evolution: New Directions,* edited by Jitendra V. Singh. Newbury Park, Calif.: Sage.

Barnett, William P., and Glenn R. Carroll. 1987. "Competition and Mutualism Among Early Telephone Companies." *Administrative Science Quarterly* **30**: 400–421.

Barron, David N. 1990. "Analysis of Event Counts: Over-dispersion and Autocorrelation." M.A. thesis, Cornell University.

_____ 1992. "The Analysis of Count Data: Over-dispersion and Autocorrelation." In *Sociological Methodology 1992,* edited by Peter V. Marsden. Oxford: Basil Blackwell, forthcoming.

Barron, David N., and Michael T. Hannan. 1991. "Assessing Autocorrelation in Models of Organizational Founding Rates: Quasi-likelihood Estimation." *Sociological Methods and Research,* in press.

Blossfeld, Hans-Peter, Alfred Hamerle, and Karl Ulrich Mayer. 1989. *Event History Analysis.* Hillsdale, N.J.: Erlbaum.

Bogart, Leo. 1981. *Press and Public.* Hillsdale, N.J.: Erlbaum.

Bratley, Paul, Bennet L. Fox, and Linus E. Schrage. 1983. *A Guide to Simulation.* New York: Springer–Verlag.

Brigham, Clarence S. 1947. *History and Bibliography of American Newspapers 1690–1820.* Worcester, Mass.: American Antiquarian Society.

British Library. 1975. *Catalogue of the Newspaper Library (Ireland).* London: British Library.

British Museum. 1905. *Catalogue of Printed Books Supplement—Newspapers Published in Great Britain and Ireland 1801–1900.* London: William Clowes.

Bull, Donald, Manfred Friedrich, and Robert Gottschalk. 1984. *American Breweries.* Trumball, Conn.: Bullworks.

Burt, Ronald S. 1983. *Corporate Profits and Cooptation.* New York: Academic Press.

Cameron, A. Colin, and Pravin K. Trivedi. 1986. "Econometric Models Based on Count Data." *Journal of Applied Econometrics* **1**: 29–53.

Carroll, Glenn R. 1981. "Dynamics of Organizational Expansion in National Systems of Education," *American Sociological Review* **46**: 585–599.

——— 1983. "A Stochastic Model of Organizational Mortality: Review and Reanalysis." *Social Science Research* **12**: 303–329.

——— 1984. "Organizational Ecology." *Annual Review of Sociology* **10**: 71–93.

——— 1985. "Concentration and Specialization: Dynamics of Niche Width in Populations of Organizations." *American Journal of Sociology* **90**: 1262–1283.

——— 1987. *Publish and Perish: The Organizational Ecology of Newspaper Industries.* Greenwich, Conn.: JAI Press.

Carroll, Glenn R., and Jacques Delacroix. 1982. "Organizational Mortality in the Newspaper Industries of Argentina and Ireland: An Ecological Approach." *Administrative Science Quarterly* **27**: 169–198.

Carroll, Glenn R., Jacques Delacroix, and Jerry Goodstein. 1988. "The Political Environments of Organizations: An Ecological View." Pp. 359–392 in *Research in Organizational Behavior, Volume 10*, edited by Barry Staw and Lawrence Cummings. Greenwich, Conn.: JAI Press.

Carroll, Glenn R., and Michael T. Hannan. 1989a. "Density Delay in the Evolution of Organizational Populations: A Model and Five Empirical Tests." *Administrative Science Quarterly* **34**: 411–430.

_____ 1989b. "Density Dependence in the Evolution of Newspaper Populations." *American Sociological Review* **54**: 524–541.

_____ 1989c. "On Using Institutional Theory in Studying Organizational Populations (Reply to Zucker)." *American Sociological Review* **54**: 545–548.

Carroll, Glenn R., Heather A. Haveman, and Anand Swaminathan. 1990. "Karrieren in Organizationen: Eine ökologische Perspektive." *Kölner Zeitschrift für Soziologie und Sozialpsychologie Sonderheft* **31**: 146–178.

Carroll, Glenn R., and Yanchung Paul Huo. 1986. "Organizational Task and Institutional Environments in Evolutionary Perspective: Findings From the Local Newspaper Industry." *American Journal of Sociology* **91**: 838–873.

_____ 1988. "Organizational and Electoral Paradoxes of the Knights of Labor." Pp. 175–194 in *Ecological Models of Organizations*, edited by Glenn R. Carroll. Cambridge, Mass.: Ballinger.

Carroll, Glenn R., Peter Preisendorfer, Anand Swaminathan, and Gabriele Wiedenmayer. 1989. "Brewery und Brauerei: The Comparative Organizational Ecology of American and German Brewing Industries." Technical Report OBIR–34, Center for Research in Management, University of California at Berkeley.

_____ 1992. "Brewery and Brauerei: The Organizational Ecology of Brewing." *Organization Studies*, forthcoming.

Carroll, Glenn R., and Anand Swaminathan. 1989. "Documentation for Public-Use Data Set on American Brewers." Technical Report OBIR–37, Center for Research in Management, University of California at Berkeley.

_____ 1991a. "Density Dependent Evolution in the American Brewing Industry from 1633 to 1988." *Acta Sociologica*, in press.

—— 1991b. "The Organizational Ecology of Strategic Groups in the American Brewing Industry from 1975 to 1990." *Industrial and Corporate Change* 1, in press.

Carroll, Glenn R., and James B. Wade. 1991. "Density Dependence in the Organizational Evolution of the American Brewing Industry Across Levels of Analysis." *Social Science Research*, in press.

Caswell, Hal. 1989. *Matrix Population Models*. Sunderland, Mass.: Sinaeur.

Caves, Richard E., and Michael E. Porter. 1977. "From Entry Barriers to Mobility Barriers." *Quarterly Journal of Economics* 91: 241–262.

Çinlar, Erhan. 1975. *Introduction to Stochastic Processes*. Englewood Cliffs, N.J.: Prentice Hall.

Coleman, James S. 1964. *Introduction to Mathematical Sociology*. New York: Free Press.

—— 1974. *Power and the Structure of Society*. Syracuse: Syracuse University Press.

—— 1981. *Longitudinal Data Analysis*. New York: Basic Books.

—— 1990. *Foundations of Social Theory*. Cambridge, Mass.: Harvard University Press.

Commons, John R., and colleagues. 1927. *History of Labor in the United States*. 4 vols. New York: Macmillian.

Comptroller of Currency of the United States. 1865–1988. *Annual Report*. Washington D.C.

Cool, Karel O., and Dan Schendel. 1987. "Strategic Group Formation and Performance: The Case of the U. S. Pharmaceutical Industry, 1963–1982." *Management Science* 33: 1102–1124.

—— 1988. "Performance Differences Among Strategic Group Members." *Strategic Management Journal* 9: 207–223.

Cooper, Arnold C., Carolyn Y. Woo, and William C. Dunkelberg. 1989. "Entrepreneurship and the Initial Size of Firms." *Journal of Business Venturing* 4: 289–332.

Cox, D. R., and V. Isham. 1980. *Point Processes*. London: Chapman & Hall.

Cox, D. R., and D. Oakes. 1984. *Analysis of Survival Data*. London: Chapman & Hall.

Cushing, J. M. 1977. *Integrodifferential Equations and Delay Models in Population Dynamics*. Berlin: Springer–Verlag.

Daggett, Emerson (supervisor). 1939. *History of Journalism in San Francisco*. Vols. 1–6. San Francisco: Works Project Administration Project 10008, O. P. 665–08–3–12.

David, Paul. 1985. "Clio and the Econometrics of QWERTY." *American Economic Review* **75**: 332–337.

Delacroix, Jacques, and Glenn R. Carroll. 1983. "Organizational Foundings: An Ecological Study of the Newspaper Industries of Argentina and Ireland." *Administrative Science Quarterly* **28**: 274–291.

Delacroix, Jacques, Anand Swaminathan, and Michael E. Solt. 1989. "Density Dependence Versus Population Dynamics: An Ecological Study of Failings in the California Wine Industry." *American Sociological Review* **54**: 245–262.

Dillisten, William H. 1946. *Historical Directory of the Banks in the State of New York*. New York: New York State Bankers Association.

DiMaggio, Paul J., and Walter W. Powell. 1983. "The Iron Cage Revisited: Institutional Isomorphism and Collective Rationality in Organizational Fields." *American Sociological Review* **48**: 147–160.

Elzinga, Kenneth G. 1986. "The Beer Industry." Pp. 203–238 in *The Structure of American Industry*, edited by Walter Adams. 7th ed. New York: Macmillan.

Emery, Edwin, and Michael Emery. 1984. *The Press and America*. 5th ed. Englewood Cliffs, N.J.: Prentice–Hall.

Evans, David, and Linda Leighton. 1989. "Some Empirical Aspects of Entrepreneurship." *American Economic Review* **79**: 519–535.

Fernandez, J. R. 1943. *Historia del periodismo argentino*. Buenos Aires: Perlado.

Finance, Maurice. 1894. *Les Syndicates ouvriers au Etats-Unis*. Paris: Imprimerie Nationale.

Fink, Gary, ed. 1977. *National Labor Unions*. Greenwood, Ala.: Greenwood Press.

Fisher, Franklin. 1989. "Games Economists Play: A Noncooperative View." *RAND Journal of Economics* **20**: 113–124.

Foner, Philip. 1947–1975. *History of the Labor Movement in the United States*. Vol. 1, 1947; Vol., 2, 2nd ed., 1975; Vol. 3, 1964; Vol. 4, 1972. New York: International Publishers.

Freeman, John. 1978. "The Unit of Analysis in Organizational Research," Pp. 335–351 in *Environments and Organizations*, edited by Marshall Meyer and colleagues. San Francisco: Jossey–Bass.

———. 1986. "Data Quality and the Development of Organizational Science." *Administrative Science Quarterly* **31**: 298–303.

Freeman, John, Glenn R. Carroll, and Michael T. Hannan. 1983. "The Liability of Newness: Age Dependence in Organizational Death Rates." *American Sociological Review* **48**: 692–710.

Freeman, John, and Michael T. Hannan. 1983. "Niche Width and the Dynamics of Organizational Populations." *American Journal of Sociology* **88**: 1116–1145.

———. 1989. "Setting the Record Straight on Organizational Ecology: Rebuttal to Young." *American Journal of Sociology* **95**: 425–439.

———. 1990. "Technical Change, Inertia, and Organizational Failure." Technical Report 90–4, Department of Sociology, Cornell University.

Friedman, Milton. 1953. *Essays in Positive Economics*. Chicago: University of Chicago Press.

Galenson, Walter. 1940. *Rival Unionism in the United States*. New York: American Council on Public Affairs.

———. 1960. *The CIO Challenge to the AFL: A History of the American Labor Movement 1935–1941*. Cambridge, Mass.: Harvard University Press.

Galvan-Moreno, C. 1944. *El Periodismo argentino, Ampila y documentada historia desde sus origenes hasta el presente*. Buenos Aires: Editorial Clavidad.

Gifford, Courtney D. 1985. *Directory of United States Labor Organizations 1984–85*. Washington, D.C.: Bureau of National Affairs.

Granovetter, Mark. 1985. "Economic Action and Social Structure: The Problem of Embeddedness." *American Journal of Sociology* **91**: 481–510.

Greene, William. 1986. "LIMDEP Manual." Unpublished mimeo, New York University.

Greenwood, Maurice, and G. Udny Yule. 1920. "An Enquiry into the Nature of Frequency Distributions of Multiple Happenings, with Particular References to the Occurrence of Multiple Attacks of Disease or Repeated Accidents." *Journal of the Royal Statistical Society* Series A **83**: 255–279.

Gregory, Winifred, ed. 1937. *American Newspapers 1821–1936.* New York: H. W. Wilson.

Hannan, Michael T. 1980. "The Ecology of National Labor Unions: Theory and Research Design." Technical Report 1, Organization Studies Section, Institute for Mathematical Studies in the Social Sciences, Stanford University.

———— 1986a. "Competitive and Institutional Processes in Organizational Ecology." Technical Report 86–13, Department of Sociology, Cornell University.

———— 1986b. "Uncertainty, Diversity and Organizational Change." Pp. 73–94 in *Social and Behavioral Sciences: Discoveries over Fifty Years,* edited by Neil Smelser and Dean Gerstein. Washington, D.C.: National Academy Press.

———— 1988a. Documentation of Public-Use Data Set: Ecology of Labor Unions Study." Technical Report 88–2, Department of Sociology, Cornell University.

———— 1988b. "Organizational Population Dynamics and Social Change." *European Sociological Review* **4**: 1–15.

———— 1988c. "Social Change, Organizational Diversity, and Individual Careers." Pp. 161–174 in *Social Structures and Human Lives,* edited by Matilda White Riley. Newbury Park, Calif.: Sage and the American Sociological Association.

———— 1989a. "Age Dependence in the Mortality of National Labor Unions: Comparisons of Parametric Models." *Journal of Mathematical Sociology* **15**: 1–30.

_____ 1989b. "Macrosociological Applications of Event-History Analysis: State Transitions and Event Recurrences." *Quantity and Quality* **23**: 351–383.

_____ 1989c. "Competitive and Institutional Processes in Organizational Ecology." Pp. 388–402 in *Sociological Theories in Progress: New Formulations,* edited by Joseph Berger, Morris Zelditch, Jr., and Bo Andersen. Newbury Park, Calif.: Sage.

_____ 1991. "Theoretical and Methodological Issues in the Analysis of Density-dependent Legitimation in Organizational Evolution." Pp. 1–42 in *Sociological Methodology 1991,* edited by Peter V. Marsden. Oxford: Basil Blackwell.

Hannan, Michael T., David N. Barron, and Glenn R. Carroll. 1991. "On the Interpretation of Density Dependence in Rates of Organizational Mortality: A Reply to Petersen and Koput." *American Sociological Review* **56**: 410–415.

Hannan, Michael T., and John Freeman. 1977. "The Population Ecology of Organizations." *American Journal of Sociology* **82**: 929–964.

_____ 1984. "Structural Inertia and Organizational Change." *American Sociological Review* **49**: 149–164.

_____ 1986. "Where Do Organizational Forms Come From?" *Sociological Forum* **1**: 50–72.

_____ 1987. "The Ecology of Organizational Founding: American Labor Unions, 1836–1985." *American Journal of Sociology* **92**: 910–943.

_____ 1988a. "The Ecology of Organizational Mortality: American Labor Unions, 1836–1985." *American Journal of Sociology* **94**: 25–52.

_____ 1988b. "Density Dependence in the Growth of Organizational Populations." Pp. 7–32 in *Ecological Models of Organizations,* edited by Glenn R. Carroll. Cambridge, Mass.: Ballinger.

_____ 1989. *Organizational Ecology.* Cambridge, Mass.: Harvard University Press.

Hannan, Michael T., and James Ranger-Moore. 1990. "The Ecology of Organizational Size Distributions: A Microsimulation Approach." *Journal of Mathematical Sociology* **15**: 67–90.

Hannan, Michael T., James Ranger-Moore, and Jane Banaszak-Holl. 1990. "Competition and the Evolution of Organizational Size Distributions." Pp. 246–268 in *Organizational Evolution: New Directions*, edited by Jitendra V. Singh. Newbury Park, Calif.: Sage.

Haveman, Heather A. 1990. "Between a Rock and a Hard Place: Organizational Change and Failure Under Conditions of Fundamental Environmental Transformation." Unpublished manuscript, Duke University.

Hawley, Amos H. 1950. *Human Ecology: A Theory of Community Structure*. New York: Ronald.

———— 1986. *Human Ecology: A Theoretical Essay*. Chicago: University of Chicago Press.

Høyer, S. 1975. "Temporal Patterns and Political Factors in the Diffusion of Newspaper Publishing: The Case of Norway." *Scandinavian Political Studies* **10**: 157–171.

Hutchinson, G. Evelyn. 1957. "Concluding Remarks," *Cold Spring Harbor Symposium on Quantitative Biology* **22**: 415–427.

———— 1959. "Homage to Santa Rosalia, or Why Are There So Many Kinds of Animals?" *American Naturalist* **93**: 145–159.

———— 1978. *An Introduction to Population Ecology*. New Haven, Conn.: Yale University Press.

Industrial Commission. 1901. *Report*. Washington, D.C.: U. S. Government Printing Office.

Institute of Fermentation and Brewing Studies. Various years. *Microbrewers Resource Handbook*. Boulder, Colo.: Institute of Fermentation and Brewing Studies.

Jacquemin, Alexis. 1987. *The New Industrial Organization: Market Forces and Strategic Behavior*. Cambridge, Mass.: MIT Press.

Johnson, Norman L., and Samuel Kotz. 1969. *Distributions in Statistics: Discrete Distributions*. Boston: Houghton Mifflin.

———— 1970. *Distributions in Statistics: Continuous Univariate Distributions*. Volume 2. Boston: Houghton Mifflin.

Kalbfleisch, John D., and Ross L. Prentice. 1980. *Statistical Analysis of Failure Time Data*. New York: Wiley.

Karlin, Samuel, and Howard M. Taylor. 1975. *A First Course in Stochastic Processes.* 2nd ed. New York: Academic Press.

Keller, Morton. 1963. *The Life Insurance Enterprise.* Cambridge, Mass.: Harvard University Press.

King, Gary. 1988. "Statistical Models for Political Science Event Counts: Bias in Conventional Procedures and Evidence for the Exponential Poisson Regression Model." *American Journal of Political Science* **32**: 838–863.

—— 1990. "COUNT: A Program for Estimating Event Count and Duration Regressions." Department of Government, Harvard University.

Kingsland, Sharon E. 1985. *Modeling Nature: Episodes in the History of Population Biology.* Chicago: University of Chicago Press.

Koopmans, Tjalling. 1957. *Three Essays on the State of Economic Science.* New York: McGraw–Hill.

Lathem, E. C. 1972. *Chronological Tables of American Newspapers 1690–1920.* Barre, Mass.: American Antiquarian Society.

Lee, Ronald D. 1974. "The Formal Dynamics of Controlled Populations and the Echo, the Boom and the Bust." *Demography* **11**: 563–585.

—— 1987. "Population Regulation in Humans and Other Animals." *Demography* **24**: 443–465.

Lehrman, William G. 1986. "Competing Organizational Forms in the Emergent American Life Insurance Industry: An Ecological Perspective." Paper presented at the annual meetings of the American Sociological Association, Washington, D.C.

Leslie, P. H. 1959. "The Properties of a Certain Lag Type of Population Growth and the Influence of an External Random Factor on the Number of Such Populations." *Physiological Zoölogy* **3**: 151–159.

Liu, L., and J. E. Cohen. 1987. "Equilibrium and Local Stability in a Logistic Matrix Model for Age-structured Populations." *Journal of Mathematical Biology* **25**: 73–88.

Lomi, Alessandro, and John Freeman. 1990. "An Ecological Study of Founding of Cooperative Organizations in Italy From 1963 to

1987: Some Preliminary Results." Working Paper 90–06. Johnson Graduate School of Management, Cornell University.

MacArthur, Robert H. 1972. *Geographical Ecology.* New York: Harper & Row.

May, Robert M. 1974. *Stability and Complexity in Model Ecosystems.* 2nd ed. Princeton, N.J.: Princeton University Press.

Mayer, Kurt B., and Sidney Goldstein. 1961. *The First Two Years: Problems of Small Firm Growth and Survival.* Washington D.C.: U. S. Government Printing Office.

McAdam, Doug, John D. McCarthy, and Mayer N. Zald. 1988. "Social Movements." Pp. 695–737 in *Handbook of Sociology,* edited by Neil J. Smelser. Newbury Park, Calif.: Sage.

McCarthy, John D., Mark Wolfson, David P. Baker, and Elaine Mosakowski. 1988. "The Founding of Social Movement Organizations: Local Citizens' Groups Opposing Drunken Driving." Pp. 71–84 in *Ecological Models of Organizations,* edited by Glenn R. Carroll. Cambridge, Mass.: Ballinger.

McCullagh, P. 1983. "Quasi-Likelihood Functions." *Annals of Statistics* 11: 59–67.

McCullagh, P., and J. Nelder. 1989. *Generalized Linear Models.* 2nd ed. London: Chapman & Hall.

McGee, John, and Howard Thomas. 1986. "Strategic Groups: Theory, Research, and Taxonomy." *Strategic Management Journal* 7: 141–150.

McLaughlin, Paul. 1991. "The Organizational Ecology of Cooperative Purchasing Associations in Saskatchewan, Canada." Ph.D. dissertation, Cornell University.

McPherson, J. Miller. 1983. "An Ecology of Affiliation," *American Sociological Review* 48: 519–535.

Meyer, John W. 1983. "Institutionalization and the Rationality of Formal Organizational Structure." Pp. 261–282 in *Organizational Environments: Ritual and Rationality,* edited by John W. Meyer and W. Richard Scott. Beverly Hills, Calif.: Sage.

Meyer, John W., and Brian Rowan. 1977. "Institutionalized Organizations: Formal Structure as Myth and Ceremony." *American Journal of Sociology* 83: 340–363.

Meyer, John W., and W. Richard Scott. 1983. *Organizational Environments: Ritual and Rationality.* Beverly Hills, Calif.: Sage.

Mezias, Stephen J. 1990. "An Institutional Model of Organizational Practice: Financial Reporting at the Fortune 200." *Administrative Science Quarterly* **35**: 431–457.

Mitchell, Will. 1987. "Dynamic Tension: Theoretical and Empirical Analyses of Entry into Emerging Industries." Paper presented at the Stanford Asilomar Conference on Organizations.

Modern Brewery Age. Various years. *Modern Brewery Age Bluebook.* Norwalk, Conn.: Modern Brewery Age.

Moody's Investor Services. Various years. *Moody's Bank and Finance Manual.* New York: Moody's Investor Services.

Mott, Frank Luther. 1962. *American Journalism.* 3rd ed. New York: Macmillan.

National Industrial Conference Board. 1956. *Sources of Union Government Structures and Procedures.* New York: NICB.

New Jersey Bureau of Labor Statistics. 1898. *Annual Report.*

New York Superintendent of Insurance. 1860–1971. *Annual Report of the Superintendent of the Insurance Department of New York.* Albany: State Printer.

Nielsen, François and Michael T. Hannan. 1977. "The Expansion of National Educational Systems: Tests of a Population Ecology Model." *American Sociological Review* **42**: 479–490.

North, Douglass. 1952. "Capital Accumulation in Life Insurance Between the Civil War and the Investigation of 1905." Pp. 238–253 in *Men in Business,* edited by William Miller. Cambridge, Mass.: Harvard University Press.

Olmstead, Alan L. 1976. *New York City Mutual Savings Banks, 1819–1861.* Chapel Hill: University of North Carolina Press.

Olzak, Susan. 1989. "Analysis of Events in Studies of Collective Action." *Annual Review of Sociology* **15**: 119–141.

―――― 1992. *Dynamics of Ethnic Competition and Conflict.* Stanford, Calif.: Stanford University Press, forthcoming.

Olzak, Susan, and Elizabeth West. 1991. "Ethnic Conflicts and the Rise and Fall of Ethnic Newspapers." *American Sociological Review* **56**: 458–474.

Park, Robert. 1929. *The Immigrant Press and Its Control*. New York: Harper.

Petersen, Trond. 1986. "Estimating Fully Parametric Hazard Rate Models With Time Dependent Covariates: Use of Maximum Likelihood." *Sociological Methods and Research* **14**: 219–246.

Petersen, Trond, and Kenneth W. Koput. 1991a. "Legitimacy or Unobserved Heterogeneity: On the Source of Density Dependence in Organizational Death Rates." *American Sociological Review* **56**: 399–409.

——— 1991b. "Unobserved Heterogeneity or Legitimacy in Density Dependence: A Rejoinder to Hannan, Barron, and Carroll." *American Sociological Review* **56**: 416.

Peterson, Florence. 1944. *Handbook of Labor Unions*. Washington, D.C.: American Council of Public Affairs.

Pfeffer, Jeffrey, and Gerald Salancik. 1978. *The External Control of Organizations: A Resource Dependence Perspective*. New York: Harper & Row.

Pinney, Thomas. 1989. *A History of Wine in America*. Berkeley and Los Angeles: University of California Press.

Pitcher, B. L., R. L. Hamblin, and J. L. L. Miller. 1978. "The Diffusion of Collective Violence." *American Sociological Review* **43**: 23–35.

Pritchett, B. Michael. 1977. *A Study of Capital Mobilization: The Life Insurance Industry of the 19th Century*. New York: Arno.

——— 1985. *Financing Growth: A Financial History of American Life Insurance Through 1900*. Philadelphia: S. S. Huebner Foundation Monograph Series. University of Pennsylvania.

Rand McNally. 1989. *The Rand McNally Bankers Directory*. Skokie Ill.: Rand McNally.

Ranger-Moore, James. 1990. "Ecological Dynamics and Size Distributions in the Life Insurance Industry." Ph.D. dissertation, Cornell University.

Ranger-Moore, James, Jane Banaszak-Holl, and Michael T. Hannan. 1989. "Effects of Density and Environmental Conditions on Founding Rates of Financial Institutions." Technical Report 89-3, Department of Sociology, Cornell University.

_____ 1991. "Density Dependence in Regulated Industries: Founding Rates of Banks and Life Insurance Companies." *Administrative Science Quarterly* **36**: 36–65.

Rose, Peter S. 1987. *The Changing Structure of American Banking.* New York: Columbia University Press.

Rosse, James N. 1978. "The Evolution of One-Newspaper Cities." Technical Report in Studies in Industry Economics, Stanford University.

_____ 1980. "The Decline of Direct Newspaper Competition." *Journal of Communication* **30**: 65–71.

Rosse, James N., Bruce M. Owen, and James Dertouzos. 1975. "Trends in the Daily Newspaper Industry, 1923–73." Report 57 in Studies in Industry Economics, Stanford University.

Rowell, George P. and Company. Various years. *Rowell's American Newspaper Directory.* New York: George P. Rowell.

Rumelt, Richard P. 1989. "How Much Does Industry Matter?" Unpublished manuscript. Graduate School of Management, University of California at Los Angeles.

Salem, Frederick W. 1880. *Beer, Its History and Its Economic Value As a National Beverage.* Hartford, Conn.: F. W. Salem.

SAS Institute Inc. 1984. *SAS/ETS User's Guide, Version 5 Edition.* Cary, N.C.: SAS Institute.

_____ 1985. *SAS Users' Guide: Statistics, Version 5 Edition.* Cary, N.C.: SAS Institute.

Schudson, Michael. 1978. *Discovering the News.* New York: Basic Books.

Scott, W. Richard. 1987a. "The Adolescence of Institutional Theory." *Administrative Science Quarterly* **31**: 493–511.

_____ 1987b. *Organizations: Rational, Natural, and Open Systems.* 2nd ed. Englewood Cliffs, N.J.: Prentice–Hall.

Selznick, Philip. 1948. "Foundations of the Theory of Organization," *American Sociological Review* **13**: 25–35.

Shapiro, Carl. 1989. "The Theory of Business Strategy." *RAND Journal of Economics* **20**: 125–137.

Šiljak, D. D. 1975. "When Is a Complex Ecosystem Stable? " *Mathematical Bioscience* **25**: 25–50.

Simmel, Georg. 1908/1955. *Conflict and the Web of Group Affiliations.* Translated by Kurt H. Wolff. Glencoe, Ill.: Free Press.

Singh, Jitendra V., Robert J. House, and David J. Tucker. 1986. "Organizational Change and Organizational Mortality." *Administrative Science Quarterly* **31**: 587–611.

Singh, Jitendra V., and Charles J. Lumsden. 1990. "Theory and Research in Organizational Ecology." *Annual Review of Sociology* **16**: 161–195.

Singh, Jitendra V., David J. Tucker, and Robert J. House. 1986. "Organizational Legitimacy and the Liability of Newness." *Administrative Science Quarterly* **31**: 171–193.

Staber, Udo. 1989. "Age Dependence and Historical Effects on the Failure Rates of Worker Cooperatives." *Economic and Industrial Democracy* **10**: 59–80.

Stalson, J. Owen. 1942. *Marketing Life Insurance: Its History in America.* Cambridge, Mass.: Harvard University Press.

Stewart, Estelle. 1936. *Handbook of American Trade Unions.* Washington, D.C.: U. S. Bureau of Labor Statistics.

Stinchcombe, Arthur L. 1965. "Social Structure and Organizations." Pp. 142–193 in *Handbook of Organizations,* edited by James G. March. Chicago: Rand McNally.

Strang, David, and Tanya Uden-Holman. 1990. "We Have Met the Enemy: Founding Rates of Health Maintenance Organizations, 1971–1982." Unpublished manuscript, University of Iowa.

Superintendent of Banks of the State of New York. 1820–1988. *Annual Report.* Albany: State Printer.

Swaminathan, Anand, and Glenn R. Carroll. 1990. "Density, Mass and Size: An Empirical Study of Selection at Founding in the American Brewing Industry." Unpublished manuscript. University of California at Berkeley.

Swaminathan, Anand, and Gabriele Wiedenmayer. 1991. "Does the Pattern of Density Dependence in Organizational Mortality Rates Vary Across Levels of Analysis? Evidence from the German Brewing Industry." *Social Science Research* **20**: 45–73.

Swedberg, Richard. 1990. *Economics and Sociology: Redefining Their Boundaries: Conversations With Economists and Sociologists.* Princeton, N.J.: Princeton University Press.

Thompson, James D. 1967. *Organizations in Action*. New York: McGraw-Hill.

Tilly, Charles. 1978. *From Mobilization to Revolution*. Reading, Mass.: Addison–Wesley.

Tirole, Jean. 1988. *The Theory of Industrial Organization*. Cambridge, Mass.: MIT Press.

Tremblay, Victor J., and Carol Horton Tremblay. 1988. "The Development of Acquisition: Evidence from the U. S. Brewing Industry." *Journal of Industrial Economics* **37**: 21–46.

Troy, Leo. 1965. *Trade Union Membership, 1887–1962*. New York: National Bureau of Economic Research.

Tucker, David J., Jitendra V. Singh, and Agnes G. Meinhard. 1990. "Organizational Form, Population Dynamics, and Institutional Change: A Study of Founding Patterns of Voluntary Associations." *Academy of Management Journal* **33**: 151–178.

Tucker, David J., Jitendra V. Singh, Agnes G. Meinard, and Robert J. House. 1988. "Ecological and Institutional Sources of Change in Organizational Populations." Pp. 127–152 in *Ecological Models of Organizations*, edited by Glenn R. Carroll. Cambridge, Mass.: Ballinger.

Tuljapurkar, Shripad. 1987. "Cycles in Nonlinear Age-structured Models I: Renewal Equations." *Theoretical Population Biology* **32**: 26–41.

Tuma, Nancy Brandon. 1980. "Invoking RATE." Menlo Park, Calif.: SRI International.

Tuma, Nancy Brandon, and Michael T. Hannan. 1984. *Social Dynamics: Models and Methods*. New York: Academic Press.

Ulman, Lloyd. 1955. *The Rise of the National Trade Union*. Cambridge, Mass.: Harvard University Press.

United States Bureau of Labor Statistics. 1926. *Handbook of American Trade Unions*. Washington, D.C.: U. S. Government Printing Office.

Utterback, James M., and Fernando F. Suárez. 1991. "Innovation, Competition and Industry Structure." *Research Policy*, in press.

Wachter, Kenneth W. 1988. "Elusive Cycles: Are There Dynamically Possible Lee–Easterlin Models for U.S. Births?" Sloan–Berkeley

Working Paper in Population Studies Second Series Number 9, Institute of International Studies, University of California at Berkeley.

Wedderburn, R. W. M. 1974. "Quasilikelihood functions, generalized linear models and the Gauss–Newton method." *Biometrika* **61**: 439–447.

Wheeler, Jean French. 1973. "Historical Directory of Santa Clara County Newspapers 1850–1972." Occasional Paper 1, Sourriseau Academy for California State and Local History. San Jose State University.

Wholey, Douglas R., Jon B. Christianson, and Susan M. Sanchez. 1990. "The Diffusion of Health Maintenance Organizations: Density, Competitive, and Institutional Determinants of Entry." Unpublished manuscript, University of Arizona.

Wiedenmayer, Gabriele, and Rolf Ziegler. 1990. "Interdependence in the West German Brewing Industry: An Ecological Perspective." Unpublished manuscript, Institut für Soziologie, Ludwig–Maxmilians–Universität, Munich.

Wilensky, Harold L. 1964. "The Professionalization of Everyone?" *American Journal of Sociology* **70**: 137–158.

Williamson, Oliver E. 1975. *Markets and Hierarchies: Analysis and Antitrust Implications.* New York: Free Press.

——— 1985. *The Economic Institutions of Capitalism.* New York: Free Press.

Wilson, Edward O., and William H. Bossert. 1971. *A Primer of Population Biology.* Stamford, Conn.: Sineaur.

Winter, Sidney. 1990. "Survival, Selection, and Inheritance in Evolutionary Theories of Organizations." Pp. 269–297 in *Organizational Evolution: New Directions,* edited by Jitendra V. Singh. Newbury Park, Calif.: Sage.

Yule, G. Udny. 1924. "A Mathematical Theory of Evolution, Based on the Conclusions of Dr. J. C. Willis, F.R.S." *Philosophical Transactions of the Royal Society, London Series B* **213**: 21–87.

Zeger, Scott L. 1988. "A Regression Model for Time Series of Counts." *Biometrika* **75**: 621–629.

Zucker, Lynne. 1989. "No Legitimacy, No History (Comment on Carroll and Hannan)." *American Sociological Review* **54**: 542–545.

Name Index

Subject Index